Thinkers and Teachers of Modern JUDAISM

Edited by Raphael Patai and Emanuel S. Goldsmith

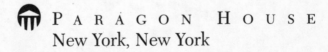

PARAGON HOUSE
New York, New York

First Edition, 1994

Published in the United States by

Paragon House
370 Lexington Avenue
New York, NY 10017

Copyright © 1994 by Paragon House

Library of Congress Cataloging-in-Publication Data

Thinkers and teachers of modern Judaism / edited by Raphael Patai and Emanuel S. Goldsmith.—1st ed.
p.   cm.
Includes index.
ISBN 1-55778-701-8
1. Judaism—20th century—Congresses.   2. Jewish scholars—Congresses.
3. Jews—Intellectual life—Congresses.   I. Patai, Raphael, 1910–.
II. Goldsmith, Emanuel S., 1935–.
BM30.T47 1994
296'.09'04—dc20   94-16063
CIP

Manufactured in the United States of America

Contents

Preface

At the initiative and under the aegis of the Council for the World's Religions, two conferences took place, one in Stansstad, Switzerland, on September 1–5, 1988, the other in Toledo, Spain, on November 9–13, 1989, devoted to the overall subject of "Influences in the Reconfiguration of Modern Judaism." Frank Kaufmann, Executive Director of the Conference, asked Raphael Patai to serve as convener and chairman of the conferences, and Patai, in turn, invited a number of scholars from Australia, England, France, Israel and the United States, and discussed with them the subjects of the papers they were to contribute. Twenty-seven scholars participated, some of them in both conferences, others in one of them. Their papers were prepared in advance, and distributed among the participants. At the conferences themselves the papers were not read, but their authors presented the gist of them in a very brief summation, and the rest of the time was devoted to their discussion.

For technical reasons the publication of the papers was delayed, but ultimately it was decided to publish them in two volumes, and Raphael Patai and Emanuel S. Goldsmith undertook to serve as joint editors. The editors decided to regroup the papers and to publish in one volume those which deal with modern Jewish thinkers—this is the present volume titled *Thinkers and Teachers of Modern Judaism*— and in a second volume, to come soon, the papers that deal with Jewish movements and events that were discussed at the two conferences.

On this occasion the editors wish to thank the contributors for their patience and their willingness to take into account in their papers some of the comments made at the conferences. Special thanks are due to Frank Kaufmann, whose interest, energy and active participation made the conferences possible.

RAPHAEL PATAI
EMANUEL S. GOLDSMITH
Rosh Hodesh Sivan 5754
May 11, 1994

Contributors

PAUL B. FENTON teaches at the Hebrew and Jewish Studies Department of the Université des Sciences Humaines of Strasbourg, France. He is the author of *The Treatise of the Pool: Al-Magala al Hawdiyya*. His major studies include "Shem Tob Ibn Falaquera and the Theology of Aristotle," and "Some Judeo-Arabic Fragments of Rabbi Abraham he-Ḥasid, the Jewish Sufi."

ALBERT H. FRIEDLANDER is Dean of the Leo Baeck College and Rabbi of the Westminster Synagogue in London. His published works include *Leo Baeck: Teacher of Theresiensitadt*, *Out of the Holocaust*, and *Riders Towards the Dawn: From Pessimism Towards Hope*.

DAVID J. GOLDBERG is Senior Rabbi of the Liberal Jewish Synagogue in London and co-author of *The Jewish People: Their History and Their Religion*. He has contributed articles on the history of Judaism to the *Macmillan Encyclopedia of Art*.

EMANUEL S. GOLDSMITH is Professor of Yiddish Language and Literature and Jewish Studies at Queens College of the City University of New York. He is the author of *Modern Yiddish Culture: The Story of the Yiddish Language Movement* and co-editor of *The American Judaism of Mordecai M. Kaplan* and *Dynamic Judaism: The Essential Writings of Mordecai M. Kaplan*.

RIVKA MAOZ teaches modern Hebrew literature in the Rothberg School of Overseas Students at the Hebrew University of Jerusalem. She is the author of *Israeli Reality: The Religious Consciousness* and *Modern Hebrew Literature: An Outline*.

RAPHAEL PATAI, anthropologist and folklorist, has written and edited over seventy books including *The Jewish Mind, The Hebrew Goddess*, and *Hebrew Myths* (with Robert Graves). In 1983 Fairleigh Dickinson University Press published *Fields of Offerings: Studies in Honor of Raphael Patai*, edited by Victor D. Sanua.

RICHARD L. RUBENSTEIN is the Robert D. Lawton Distinguished Professor of Religion at Florida State University. His many books include *After Aucshwitz: Radical Theology and Contemporary Judaism, Power Struggle: An Autobiographical Confession*, and *The The Age of Triage*.

NORBERT M. SAMUELSON is Professor of Jewish Philosophy at Temple University in Philadelphia. He is the author of *An Introduction to Modern Jewish Philosophy* and *Judaism and the Concept of Creation*.

AHARON M. SINGER is Director and Dean of Studies of the One Year Program, Rothberg School of Overseas Students at the Hebrew University of Jerusalem. His published essays include "The Holy Spirit in Talmud and Midrash" and "Human Responses to Suffering in Rabbinic Teaching."

BENJAMIN UFFENHEIMER is Professor Emeritus, Department of Bible, Tel-Aviv University. His publications include *The Visions of Zecharia: From Prophecy to Apocalyptic, Ancient Prophecy in Israel*, and *Prophetic Experience*.

MANFRED H. VOGEL is Professor in the Department of Religion at Northwestern University, Evanston, Illinois. He is the author of *Ludwig Feuerbach's Principles of the Philosophy of the Future* and *A Quest for a Theology of Judaism*.

EVAN M. ZUESSE is a professor in the department of history at Monash University in Clayton (Victoria), Australia. He is the author of *Ritual Cosmos* and of the article on "Ritual" in the recently published *Encyclopedia of Religion*.

Opening Remarks

Remarks made by Raphael Patai on September 1, 1988, at the opening of the first of the two conferences at which the papers contained in this volume were presented and discussed.

In the last two or three generations the physiognomy of Judaism and of the Jewish people has undergone such radical changes that were an observer of Jewish life who lived, say, in the first half of the nineteenth century, to return to this world, he would find little in the Jewish scene familiar to him. Next year the Jewish world, or at least the religiously conservative part of it, will remember the 150th anniversary of the death of R. Moses Sofer, better known as "The Hatam Sofer," the celebrated rabbi, talmudic scholar and yeshiva head of Pressburg (today Bratislava), who was perhaps the greatest rabbinical authority of his age (his dates are 1762–1839), and the most influential and implacable opponent of Jewish religious reform and of civic emancipation, both of which movements were in their beginnings during the latter part of his lifetime. That triple jubilee will have a special personal significance for me, because he was my great-great-great grandfather, and because for many years I have been fascinated by his personality, his ideas and his total commitment to the Torah of Israel, to what he believed were the immutable values of its teachings. Yet the Hatam Sofer would stand as a total stranger if faced with the manifestations of Jewish life in the late twentieth century, for the simple reason that since his death so many new developments have taken place in it that he would be taken aback and would apply to almost everything he saw the adage with which he opposed all innovation, "Ḥadash Asur Min haTorah"—What Is New Is Forbidden by the Torah.

The major differences that would strike the Hatam Sofer (or for that matter, any other observer with a similar historical perspective) fall, if considered systematically, into two categories: one comprises the changes that have taken place in Jewish religious life, the other the developments in Jewish communal existence. By stating this, we have arrived *in medias res* at the theme of our present conference, which is, as explicitly described in its title, "Influences in the Reconfiguration of Modern Judaism." While mentioning this title, let me acknowledge right here that it was Dr. Frank Kaufmann, the executive director of the Council for the World's Religions, and our host at this conference, who suggested this formulation at a preparatory meeting he, Dr. Rubenstein, Dr. Berenbaum and I had in Washington a few months ago.

As we shall see, or as we have already gathered if we were conscientious enough to read the papers distributed in advance, the epicenter of the quake that shook and transformed Jewish life since the demise of the Hatam Sofer was in fact either in the religious or else in the communal life of the Jewish people. And even though the shock waves produced by the changes often spread from religious into communal life or vice versa, nevertheless taxonomically it is expedient to consider them under the two headings of religious and communal separately.

As for religious changes, although Judaism has been spared the trauma of the sectarianism, schism and denominational fragmentation that has plagued Christianity and Islam, the century and a half that has passed since the demise of the Hatam Sofer has witnessed the emergence of several new Jewish religious trends of major significance. Reform Judaism was initiated in Germany toward the end of the Hatam Sofer's life (in fact, Abraham Geiger began his Breslau ministry in 1839, the very year of Moses Sofer's death); it was followed by Conservative and Reconstructionist Judaism, as well as by various neo-Orthodox and neo-Hasidic initiatives, each with its own ideology, congregations, schools and organizations. To them were added movements such as that of the *Havura*, and other, smaller religious groupings with their own, more or less distinct, characteristics. Some of the papers prepared for this conference deal with the emergence of these new (or relatively new) Jewish religious forms, with the religious thinkers and teachers who initiated or influenced them, and with the historical events that had an impact upon them.

Among the thinkers of whom we shall hear from one or more speakers are (I put them in alphabetic order), Leo Baeck, Martin Buber, Abraham Joshua Heschel, Mordecai Kaplan, Abraham Yitzhak Kook, Franz Rosenzweig, Joseph Soloveitchik and several other lesser known, but not less important, figures. Of the religious movements that form component elements in modern Jewish life we shall discuss Orthodoxy, Secularism, reactions to the Holocaust, Bible studies, modernization, the women's movement, and several other related subjects.

As for developments in Jewish communal life, we shall discuss several events that have totally, radically, and in part tragically and catastrophically, transformed it, to the point that, despite its unbreakable historical continuity, the Jewish condition in the second half of the twentieth century presents a picture startlingly different from its configuration up to World War II. In the center of these transformations stand, of course, the Holocaust, the establishment of Israel, and the Jewish exodus from the Muslim world. Several papers on these cataclysmic events were prepared for our conference, and we shall have a chance to discuss them. Let me say just a very few words about each of them.

The Holocaust has been the subject of many scholarly studies, from which we know a huge amount of details about this greatest of all crimes ever committed by human inhumanity. A less studied and hence less known aspect of the Holocaust is the unprecedented crisis which it brought about in Jewish identity, nay, in Jewish existence itself; that is, in the life of those segments of the Jewish people which dwelt in safety in lands not reached by the Nazi beast. Our papers dealing with this subject will certainly evoke considerable attention.

The establishment of Israel was not only the fulfillment of the millennial Jewish dream of *Shivat Tziyon* (Return to Zion), but also the trigger of a series of new problems in Jewish existence, such as Arab-Jewish relations, the relations between Israel and the Diaspora, the role of the Diaspora in the totality of the Jewish people. Due attention to these issues will be given in several papers.

One of the major historical developments, which was the joint outcome of the Holocaust and the establishment of Israel, was the exodus of Jews from the Muslim countries. This mass movement led to the reemergence of Middle Eastern Jewry as a significant factor on the world Jewish scene, primarily in Israel, but also in France (where today more than half of all the Jews are recent immigrants from North Africa), as well as in several other places. One of our papers will be devoted to this subject, but its implications evidently require more attention.

Another major development in Jewish religious as well as communal life has been the entering of women into synagogal and organizational activity. Women had always had important but restricted roles in Jewish religious life, but in recent years we have witnessed the occupation by women of rabbinical posts in all branches of Judaism except the Orthodox. One paper in its entirety, another partly, are devoted to this subject, and I expect that they will occasion lively discussion.

A perhaps even more important development in the post-World War II era was the inclusion of Jewish studies among the offerings of general American and European institutions of higher education. This has enabled both Jewish and non-Jewish students to inform themselves of Judaism in a secular university setting, and represented an entirely new challenge especially to instructors of Jewish ethics. We shall have the opportunity to hear and discuss a paper on this subject, while another somewhat related one will deal with the significance of modern Bible research and studies.

And, last but by no means least, there is the fundamental issue of the challenges modernization represents for Judaism. Modernization in general means the spread of Western culture all over the world, but it has a special meaning for Judaism inasmuch as until most recent times major segments of the Jewish community consciously and purposely excluded themselves from modern cultural developments. Such self-exclusion has become practically impossible in the second half of the twentieth century, and one of our papers discusses the problem created for Judaism by this new situation. We are looking forward to the reactions to it.

In conclusion of this part of my opening remarks, I want to point out that they were, of course, based on the papers of which I received advance copies. Of three papers I know only the titles, as listed in our program, and I am still looking forward, as I am sure all of us are, to reading them.

I would like now to devote the second half of my opening statement to brief indications of topics that belong to the general theme of "Influences in the Reconfiguration of Modern Judaism," but which are *not* discussed in our papers. The responsibility for these omissions lies to a large extent with me, since they are due to my failure to secure the participation of scholars who could have presented papers on those subjects. However, I do have what I believe is a valid excuse. The time frame for this conference called for three days of meetings, within which no more than twenty papers could be accommodated. Hence, once I had the tentative commitment of twenty scholars to deliver papers, my efforts to secure additional ones considerably slackened, to say the least, since the addition of more papers would have necessitated the elimination of a corresponding number of others already practically agreed upon. Still, let me share with you my thoughts about additional subjects that belong to the general theme of our conference, and that, I hope, we shall have an opportunity to take up on some later occasion.

As for thinkers who are not included in the present conference, but who certainly belong within its perimeter, among those who come to mind are Hermann Cohen, Gershom Scholem, Hugo Bergman and Yeshayahu Leibowitz. In addition, it seems to me that it would be instructive to hear about the thoughts and works of at least one outstanding contemporary Hasidic leader, such as the Lubavicher Rebbe, Menahem Mendel Schneersohn, and about the differences between him and his Satmarer rival.

As for movements, my list of disiderata is considerably longer. First of all, to balance the presentation of trends and developments in Orthodoxy, we should have a chance to consider also what has been happening in other branches of Judaism, to wit, the Reform, Conservative and Reconstructionist movements. The significance of Reform, I think, lies not only in the historical fact that it was the first modern Jewish religious movement to breach the walls of entrenched Orthodoxy, but also in having provided a less exacting framework for large segments of the Jewish people in the Western world, who otherwise would have been lost to Judaism. Whether we agree with this view or not, Reform Judaism requires attention in a conference such as this.

Barely a generation after Reform followed the emergence of Conservative Judaism, which, at least in the United States, was a reaction to it. Its significance, vitality and diversity are such that it certainly requires a close scrutiny on the part of a conference on the reconfiguration of Judaism.

In the second half of the nineteenth century crystallized the ideology and institutions of neo-Orthodoxy, which combine features from both traditional Orthodoxy and Reform. Its leading figures were Samson Raphael Hirsch and Azriel Hildesheimer, and it was yet another significant movement demanding discussion in our context.

Before referring to other developments in Orthodoxy, I would like to mention one general topic, which, I believe, is a must for a conference such as ours: it could best be titled Cooperation and Competition Among Jewish Organizations, both religious and communal. Under this heading could, and should, be discussed such global, international and national Jewish roof-organizations (if that is the proper term for them) as the World Zionist Congress, the Jewish

Agency for Palestine/Israel, the World Jewish Congress, the Conference of Presidents of Major American Jewish Organizations, and religious bodies in which Reform, Conservative, Reconstructionist and Orthodox organizations cooperate. Most of these are quite recent developments, with considerable impact on either religious or communal life, or on both.

To come back now to Orthodoxy, which in recent decades has proved to be one of the most dynamic branches of Judaism, I would like to see a discussion of the *Agudath Israel*, which has undergone a radical transformation in its attitude to Zionism, and is organizationally patterned, with its *Mo'atzat G'dole haTorah* (Council of Torah Sages) and *K'nesiyya G'dola* (Great Assembly), after ancient and venerable Jewish institutions of religious leadership.

The manifestations of Orthodoxy in Israel, some of them going back to pre-state days, are fascinating indeed in their variety. Of quite a venerable age by now is the *Neture Qarta* (Guardians of the City) in Jerusalem, a small but very vociferous group, whose religious extremism has been, and is still being, expressed in statements and activities that in any other country but Israel would be treated as treasonous. They are supported and sponsored by the Satmarer Hasidim in New York, whose anti-Zionist calumnies published in their advertisements in the *New York Times* and other papers I always find more grievous than any Arab verbal attack on Israel. A dispassionate analysis of the views and works of this group is long overdue.

A totally different type of Orthodoxy that has developed in recent years in Israel is that of the *Gush Emunim* (Block of the Faithful), a patriotic settlers' movement with a vaguely messianic coloration, sworn to maintaining Israel's rule over all the biblical Holy Land. In this context, mention must be made also of the much older *HaKibbutz haDati* (Religious Kibbutz) movement, which in its agricultural work had to face, and managed to solve, problems never envisaged by the authors of the historical Jewish halakhic codes. Related to it is the *B'ne 'Akiva* religious youth movement, which considers Rabbi Kook its spiritual leader, and whose slogan is *Torah Va'Avodah* (Torah and Work). It boasts today of several kibbutzim and yeshiva high schools.

Still within the Orthodox realm in Israel is the work of the Mizrahi
movement and its several subsidiaries, including the impressive religious research and publication program of its cultural arm, the
Mossad haRav Kook (Rabbi Kook Foundation).

To dwell for one more moment on an earlier period in the life of the
yishuv, let me mention that I would like to see a discussion of the
"Canaanite" movement, which was launched during World War II.
Subsequently it developed a political and cultural ideology aimed at
providing the foundation for a new "Hebrew" nation, which it saw as
consisting of native-born Palestinians (and later Israelis), including
also Muslims and Christians, as well as immigrants willing to join. As I
still remember from my own days in Jerusalem, it advocated a return
to biblical, and even pre-biblical, roots of Judaism, and as such had a
definitely religious aspect.

I can refer only very briefly to a few more phenomena not touched
upon so far. One is the emergence of civic religion in Judaism,
primarily in Israel, but also in America and elsewhere. Under this
heading come quite a large number of quasi-religious phenomena,
which more than deserve discussion. Among them is the gradual
veering towards religious-ceremonial manifestations in kibbutzim,
whose founders were not only irreligious, but explicitly anti-religious.
As early as in the 1930s, many of these emphatically left-wing settlements began to search for communal rituals and celebrations to
recapture what they considered the ancient Hebrew agricultural character of the Jewish holidays. One of the first rites to be revived and
reinterpreted was the Passover Seder, for which several new *Haggadah* texts were composed and printed. The kibbutz Seder was
followed by the *Ḥagigat haBiqqurim* (Festival of the First Fruits) at
Shavuʻot, which became a feast of homage to the Keren Kayemeth
(Jewish National Fund), the official institutional owner of the lands on
which the kibbutzim were built and which they cultivated. After
Israel's independence, these kibbutz festivals spread, and today
dozens of published kibbutz Haggadot are available, forming a verita-
ble new national-religious liturgy. An investigation of the religious
significance of these developments would certainly enrich a conference like ours.

The newly created kibutz holidays are paralleled by the new national religious celebrations that have been officially introduced in Israel, such as Independence Day (5th of Iyyar), declared a public holiday by law in 1949, and celebrated by public displays and festive prayers in synagogues, the latter formulated by the Chief Rabbinate, and the blowing of the shofar, the recitation of the Hallel, etc. The day preceding it (4th of Iyyar) is *Yom haZikkaron* (Memorial Day), also established by Knesset legislation, with its special prayers in memory of those who fell in Israel's War of Independence. Yet another memorial day in Israel is the *Holocaust Remembrance Day* (27th of Nissan), observed, in accordance with duly passed legislation, with special prayers.

These memorial days, while they have their origin in modern Jewish history, closely parallel *Tish'a b'Av* (The Ninth of Av), Hanukkah and other traditional Jewish holidays, which, too, commemorate historical events, partly post-biblical, and have become integral elements in the Jewish religious calendar. They are a manifestation of the vitality of the Jewish religious spirit, which continues to this day to create new feasts and forms, deserving the attention of a conference such as the present one.

We do have a paper on the reemergence of Middle Eastern Jewry on the global Jewish scene, but in addition, our kind of conference should include a discussion of the influence exerted by Jews from Muslim lands on religious life in Israel. Foremost among the Jewish festivals developed in an Arab environment and made popular in Israel is the *Maimuna*, introduced by Moroccan Jews, and celebrated after the close of the Passover. I would love to hear an informed discussion of the circumstances that have brought it about that precisely a Moroccan Jewish folk festival should have achieved such wide general acceptance in Israel. We would also like to have an analysis of such spontaneous and unorganized religious manifestations as the bar mitzvah celebrations at the Western Wall, the wearing of the yarmulke (skullcap) both in Israel and in America, etc. Likewise, to hear a discussion of the intertwining of modern political movements in Israel with the biblical roots of Jewish religion, as one can see it, e.g., in the ideology of the Likkud Party.

And lastly, a conference on new developments in Judaism should not omit a discussion of the great theme that the reemergence of Israel as the Jewish state has proved to be in the reconfiguration of modern Judaism.

As these few, and rather rapidly jotted down remarks show, the papers of the present conference fulfill only part of the program indicated in its title. However, I am sure that we all shall learn a lot from the papers we shall discuss, and from the discussions themselves. So—welcome again, and good work!

I. Ahad Ha-Am and Zionism

David J. Goldberg

Isaac Babel, the short story writer from Odessa who rode with the cossacks and was to perish in one of the Stalinist purges, memorably described himself as having "spectacles on his nose and autumn in his heart."

Such a description also aptly fitted Ahad Ha-Am (1856–1927), the ghetto aristocrat and melancholy observer, whose temperament inclined him towards contemplation rather than action; a Marcus Aurelius transported to the Pale of Settlement.

From the beginning, Ahad Ha-Am was critical of the Zionist aims advocated by Herzl and his followers. The regeneration of the Jewish spirit which Ahad Ha-Am postulated was a process which in his view would take one, even two hundred years. It is significant that the influential journal he edited—*HaShiloah*—took its name from the spring in Jerusalem whose waters, according to the Torah, "flow slowly." The revival of Hebrew culture could not be rushed. It depended, first of all, upon the spread and growth of Hebrew as the language of *Eretz Israel*. As he put it in a letter to his *Hibbat Zion* colleague Menaḥem Ussishkin, Jews could not hope to create a spiritual center in Palestine until Hebrew speakers became "a majority of the population, own most of the land, and control the institutions shaping the culture of the country."[1] It would be absurd to raise the prospect of a Jewish state before 100,000 Hebrew-speaking Jews lived in Palestine, people whose roots were in the land, whose claims were the claims of use, and whose goals would appear "practical" to the European powers and potential Jewish settlers alike. A Jewish nation might eventually flow from Palestinian roots acre by acre and cow shed by cow shed, but it was only daily work on the ancient soil of their homeland, with Hebrew as the vehicle of communication, which would enable Jews to aspire to that "higher" Jerusalem which Aḥad Ha-Am saw as the main goal and purpose of the Zionist enterprise.

It was inevitable, therefore, that Aḥad Ha-Am would regard Herzl's efforts at state-building with a disdain reminiscent of the Viennese critic Karl Kraus for Freud's psychoanalysis as "the disease that presumes itself the cure." But whether returning from the first Zionist Congress in Basel like "a mourner at a wedding feast," or writing a scathing review of *Altneuland* in which he derided Herzl for his vision of a Jewish utopia without Hebrew, Aḥad Ha-Am's disagreements with the political Zionists were, at this stage, of a theoretical, doctrinaire kind. It was the exhilarating clash of conflicting theories, barely tainted by practical considerations and fought out in the journalistic columns and Zionist caucuses of Eastern Europe.

Save for one issue, with implications even more relevant today than eighty years ago. And that was what Yitzḥak Epstein, a First Aliyah intellectual and teacher, in 1907 called "the hidden question"; namely, the attitude of Zionism to the indigenous Arab population of Palestine.

Now it could be argued that Aḥad Ha-Am's fastidious vision of a morally regenerated Jewish people bore little relation to reality; that it owed more to the isolation of the study than the bustle of the market place; that it relied excessively on the influence of barely remembered positivist philosophers like Herbert Spencer; that Herzl, adored by the Jewish masses, was infinitely more plausible as a spokesman for Zionism than his precise, aloof critic.

All of this may be true. But what cannot be gainsaid is that Aḥad Ha-Am, the skeptical observer rather than the elated man of action, recognized more succinctly than any of his contemporaries that the Zionist response to the native population would determine crucially whether or not Jewish settlement in Palestine could succeed. It is said—one hopes apocryphally—that when Max Nordau first heard that there were Arabs in Palestine, he rushed excitedly to Herzl crying, "I didn't know that! If that is the case, then we are doing an injustice."

Aḥad Ha-Am suffered from no such naïveté. As early as 1891, in his famous article, *Emet meEretz Yisrael* (Truth from Palestine)[2] he cautioned that the notions harbored by Zionists abroad about the Palestinian Arabs were not commensurate with the facts. Contrary to popular prejudice, the Arabs were *not* "all desert savages, asses, who neither perceive nor understand what goes on around them." On the contrary, they were "like people everywhere, of sharp intellect and full of cunning," and the growth of Jewish settlement would inevitably breed opposition, because "they will not yield their place lightly."

Aḥad Ha-Am developed his theme with great acuity, warning the settlers to learn the lessons of history and not provoke Arab wrath by their behavior. He understood the emotional urges driving them, the feelings of a liberated people "who were slaves in their country of exile, and suddenly find themselves with untramelled freedom, a wild freedom which can only be felt in a country such as Turkey." This "slave becoming master" syndrome had already resulted in objectionable acts by settlers "who treat the Arabs with hostility and cruelty and trespass unjustly, beat them shamefully without good reason, and even boast of having done so, and nobody stands in the breach to check this contemptible and dangerous tendency."

Being the product of his time and European background, Aḥad Ha-Am conceded that the Arab only respected strength, and that the Jewish settlers, therefore, had to be forceful in their dealings with the natives. But unless it was a use of force based on justice, it would prove detrimental both to the developing Jewish society and to its relations with the Arabs in the present and the future.

Few Zionists, needless to say, were willing to recognize Aḥad Ha-Am's description, and two contemporary travelers in Palestine, Hayyim Hisin,[3] and Menahem Ussishkin,[4] came to directly opposite conclusions. Let us assume, therefore, that reality lay somewhere between the two extremes, but note, nevertheless, that in his brief essay Aḥad Ha-Am says more, and more pertinently, about the Arab problem that Herzl managed in the 300 pages of *Altneuland*, only seven of which deal, in typically paternalistic fashion, with the potential collision between Jewish and Arab cultures. Herzl's assumption that the Arabs would recognize, and be grateful for, the technological and economic development brought about by Jewish immigration, was the standard argument adduced by all Zionist theoreticians, from the most conservative to the most socialist. As the most eloquent of them, Max Nordau, expressed it in his address to the eighth Zionist Congress of 1907, "We intend to come to Palestine as the emissaries of culture and to expand the moral boundaries of Europe to the Euphrates."

Aḥad Ha-Am was dismissive of such benign assumptions of superiority. When, in 1908, Ussishkin suggested that the Zionist Organization should produce an Arabic newspaper, he retorted, "What shall we say to the Arabs? That we want to settle in Palestine? And what will they answer? 'Good! Let us work and live together?' . . . How long shall we delude ourselves with empty phrases?"[5]

Committed as he was to the gradual expansion of the Jewish hold on Palestine, Aḥad Ha-Am gingerly avoided carrying his argument to its inexorable conclusion, viz. that there was an irreconcilable gulf between Zionist and Arab aspirations. He did, though, refer obliquely to such a pessimistic fear. When, in 1913, the liberal Moshe Smilansky complained in a letter of the Zionist Organization's hostile and contemptuous attitude towards the Arabs, Aḥad Ha-Am replied, "When I realize that our brethren may be morally capable of treating another people in this fashion and of crudely abusing what is sacred to them, then I cannot but reflect: If such is the situation now, how shall we treat others if one day we actually become the rulers of Palestine? If this is the Messiah, then I do not wish to see his coming."[6]

One can only guess with what ironic pain Aḥad Ha-Am would have regarded, in his latter years, as the revered intellectual doyen of an expanding *yishuv*, the Tel Aviv street in which he lived cleared of all traffic and activity so that he could enjoy his afternoon siesta. Whatever pleasure he took in Zionist achievements was clouded by his perennial conviction that there was another nation in Palestine, long settled and with no intention of leaving. As he wrote to Smilansky in December 1914, "In future . . . they [the Zionist leaders] will certainly understand the magnitude and importance of this question and how much we shall have to work in order to come as close as possible to a solution."[7]

Much has happened since Aḥad Ha-Am's death in 1927, and his preoccupations concerning the nature and development of the Jewish community in Palestine have been overtaken by the enormity of our history in the second half of the twentieth century. It is beyond the scope of this paper to analyze how successive generations of Zionist leaders have attempted—and failed—to cope with the central dilemma of Jewish-Arab claims to the same piece of land, and one can justifiably assert that had squeamishness of Aḥad Ha-Am's variety ever become a plank of official Zionist policy, then the *yishuv* would have been speedily liquidated, and no state of Israel come into existence. Nevertheless, his insistence on the necessity of moral *excellence* in the Jewish homeland poses a problem at least as acute for the modern state of Israel in its relationship with the Diaspora, as in its dealings with its Arab neighbors. A state which claims to be the spiritual center for *all* Jews can only substantiate that claim by striving to embody the ethical and moral teachings of our Jewish heritage. Once it seeks to justify itself by saying it is no better and no worse than a hundred other countries in the United Nations, it may have gone a long way towards normalization, but at the cost of forfeiting its unique hold on the loyalty of Jewry worldwide. That is why Aḥad Ha-Am's forebodings about the course on which Zionism had set itself were prophetic in their prescience, long before the War of Independence, the Six Day War, or the current uprising in the Occupied Territories. As a moral philosopher he knew that the manner in which a single

Jewish settler treated a single Arab peasant had a significance far beyond its individual content, and so he warned repeatedly in his writings about Jewish-Arab relations. One must hope that his warnings were not in vain, but the hour is getting late.

NOTES

1. "Zionism and Jewish Culture," in *Philosophia Judaica*, ed. Leon Simon, Oxford, 1946, p. 282.
2. *Complete Works of Ahad Ha-Am* (Hebrew), Jerusalem, 1947, p. 24.
3. Ḥayyim Ḥisin. *Massa' ba'Aretz haMuvtaḥat* (Journey in the Promised Land), Tel Aviv, 1982, p. 125.
4. *"Bli Mara Sheḥora* (Without Bitterness)," in *Sefer Ussishkin*, Jerusalem, 1934, p. 20.
5. Ahad Ha-Am, *Iggerot* (Letters), 6 vols., Tel Aviv, 1956–60, Vol. 4, p. 27.
6. Ahad Ha-Am, *ibid.*, vol. 5, p. 113.
7. *Ibid.*, p. 161.

2. Rav Kook and the Return to Zion

Paul B. Fenton

Introduction

In his introduction to the English edition of Julius Guttman's *Philosophies of Judaism*, R. J. Zwi Werblowsky interrogatively points out that while the foremost historian of Jewish philosophy included in the gallery of great contemporary thinkers Franz Rosenzweig, he surprisingly omitted the figure of Rabbi Abraham Isaac Kook. This omission is all the more startling when one considers that while the sway of modern thinkers, including Rosenzweig, have often proved as ephemeral as changing, intellectual trends, Rav Kook's philosophy has had what is probably the most influential and enduring impact on modern Jewish thought, especially in the area of religious Zionism. This preponderance is not merely of a static nature but has expressed itself as a dynamic, political ideology which has, in various forms, inspired thousands of followers in the modern world, who continue to look upon Rav Kook as their spiritual mentor and source of inspiration. With the expansion of religious Zionism in Israel today, one could even go so far as to say that far from decreasing in vitality, the popularity of Kook's thought goes from strength to strength with every passing year.

Rav Kook—A Brief Biography

Born in Grieva, a small town in Latvia in 1865, Rav Kook received a traditional education in Rabbinics and proved himself to be such an outstanding student that he became known as an *illuy*, or child prodigy at the age of nine. He continued his studies at the famous Volozhin yeshiva under the guidance of the celebrated Naftali Zvi Berlin, whose favorite pupil he had become. At the same time he was decisively influenced by Hasidic writings, especially those of the Radzin school. This influence is especially manifest in Kook's treatment of the dynamics of the holy and profane, the absence of evil and the problem of secularism. These issues had been timidly addressed within the Polish school of Hasidism, albeit in a thoroughly traditional garb. Kook was to express them in modern terms. Early on he showed an independence of mind, for in addition to his talmudic studies he cultivated an interest in Jewish and general philosophy and mysticism, the Bible and the Hebrew language, disciplines which were not encouraged in traditional circles.

A turning point came in Rav Kook's life in 1904, when, out of a passionate love for Zion, he emigrated to the Holy Land, responding to the call to become Rabbi of Jaffa. Returning to Eretz Israel after a forced stay in London, where he spent the First World War as the spiritual leader of the *Mahziqe haDat* congregation, he was appointed in 1921 as the first incumbent of the newly established Chief Rabbinate of Palestine. Not only did his erudition and piety earn him the respect of the religious establishment, but his deep sensitivity for the socialist and nationalistic ideals of the young Zionist pioneers also won him the respect of the secular population. Associating with all shades of opinion and belief, he soon became a controversial figure, especially in Orthodox and ultra-Orthodox circles, where his identification with the Zionist movement was resented. A great educator, he elaborated a new program of higher Jewish education which was implemented in the curriculum of the yeshiva which he founded and which functions to this day as the *Merkaz haRav*.

The Sacred and Profane

Rav Kook was deeply concerned with the conflictual dialectics of religion and modernism and was among the few religious Jewish thinkers who outwardly addressed contemporary problems of a social and political nature. The profound mystical tendency in his thought did not however render him oblivious to the needs of the physical world and he took an active interest in social and political affairs. Indeed, he strove to unite the physical and the spiritual and saw the Jewish national revival, the rebirth of Eretz Israel as a land, and *Am Israel* as a nation, as a providential opportunity for attaining such harmony. Kook was fascinated by the dialectical opposition of religious decline, corrosive assimilation, social reform and elated nationalism. "Ours is a wonderful generation," he writes. "It consists of opposites, darkness and light exist in confusion."

In keeping with this harmonistic concept of man and the physical world, Kook denied that there was any divorce between the sacred and profane. "The sacred and profane," he says, "together influence the spirit of man and he becomes enriched by absorbing from each whatever is suitable."

The natural position of holiness, he argued, was to be in continuous synthesis with the profane. Holiness as a state of pure spirituality was an incomplete phenomenon and one which was peculiar to the state of exile, where the Jewish people had been estranged from a normal existence. Now, however, their reestablishment in a national homeland was to bring about a return to the ideal of natural holiness.

The Doctrine of *Teshuvah*

This is in fact the kernel of Rav Kook's doctrine of the "return," or *teshuvah* in Hebrew. This theme imbued his whole life and work. Though the term was not a new one in Jewish theology, in Kook's system it took on a novel meaning. From talmudic times *teshuvah*, derived from the root *shuv* ("to return") had been the technical term to designate "return to God" or "repentance." To be sure, there was hardly a work on theology or ethics that did not have a chapter on this important theme. In the Middle Ages, the word had also been used to describe the Neoplatonic concept of the soul's "conversion" and its return to its pristine, spiritual source. Kabbalistic thought had combined these two doctrines and taught that the real meaning of repentance was the soul's reintegration of its primordial form in the *sefirah binah* through a process of *tiqqun* or "repair." Furthermore, through the cognate root, the term was also related to the traditional concept of *shivah* or the "return to Zion," a relationship which was allusively underscored in Kook's own writings on the notion of *teshuvah*.

Though he was a prolific writer, Kook never endeavored to develop a comprehensive system. His style is characterized by a chain of successive reflections emerging in spiral progression around a conceptual core which embodies his mystical insights and intellectual outpourings.

The Lights of Return

The quintessence of his thought on the subject of *teshuvah* is contained in a booklet called *Orot haTeshuvah*, "the Lights of Return." Though small in size, this work occupies an important place within Kook's literary legacy. He himself held the composition in great esteem and would meditate on it at certain solemn moments (e.g., during the Ten Days of Penitence). Though partly written systematically, it was mainly arranged by the author's son Zvi Yehudah Kook.

Since the first edition was published in Jerusalem in 1925, there have been several reprints, and numerous commentaries on various aspects have appeared. Today it has become one of the most popular and widespread of Kook's writings. The original edition carried seventeen chapters dealing with various aspects of "conversion," in the light of Kook's two-fold conception of the theme. Indeed, in Kook's view there are two dimensions to *teshuvah*, individual and collective, particular and universal. He construes "conversion" simultaneously as both a cosmic force underlying the progressive, spiritual improvement of the universe, and as the "repentance" of the individual who is in search of his own moral perfection. These two movements form one organic unity and are interconnected, for the "return" of every individual affects the whole world. Of particular significance is his fourth chapter entitled "The individual and particular return and the universal and collective return of the world and of the congregation of Israel." There we read:

> Collective conversion, which involves the elevation and improvement of the world, alongside individual conversion, which concerns each and every private individual in the finest details of his particular repentance (which are perceived only by the divine), are one and the same. Also, all cultural reforms through which the world emerges from its chaos, social and economic structures which progressively improve, together with the repair of sin from the most heinous transgressions to the slightest breach of piety, are all one inseparable unity.

The conversion of all components of the universe to their divine source is the realization of the cosmic evolutionary process. Far from regarding the scientific theory of evolution as incompatible and antagonistic to religion, Kook taught that it came closer to Jewish mystical thought than any other concept produced by modern science. Indeed, he reconciled the evolutionary concept with the kabbalistic notion of *teshuvah*, which views the cosmos as continuously striving towards the *sefirah* of *binah*, which embodies its ultimate source of perfection. To his mind, evolution was not just a lawless struggle for survival, governed only by the triumph of the strongest, but a Providential movement which supposed a meaningful existence. Unlike Darwin or Bergson, who considered evolution a product of spontaneous, natural selection or one of a blind and unguided élan vital, Kook believed that evolution was a purposeful, cosmic process directed by God, whereby each particle of reality was drawn closer to godliness as the final goal of individual and universal history.

Universalism and Particularism

Although the whole of creation is one all-embracing unit, man, standing at the center of the universe, plays a special role. He is not left unaided on the path to perfection and is guided by the example and inspiration of rare individuals, whose "merit preserves wisdom for mankind and transforms it into a living beneficial force which enhances and enriches mankind until it will ultimately reach perfection." Kook also held this goal to be of a universal dimension. The march forward towards universalism had of necessity to pass through the concept of nationality. Each nation had its particular role to play in the evolutionary process and to make its own contribution through its own specific genius: "The highest peak of the national soul is embodied in the universalistic leaning towards which that nation aspires through its very being. This impinges upon universal existence and the concept of supreme *teshuvah* is imbedded in this ultimate mystery."

Kook is saying here that through its specific contribution of a universalistic nature, each nation participates in the cosmic process of *teshuvah*. Within this scheme, the specificity of the Jewish people occupies a special place. Just as mankind is aided in its struggle for *teshuvah* by the inspiration of individual men of genius, so also is it assisted by the collective strength of an entire nation. It is the task of Israel, whose name signifies "warrior of God," to spread the divine in the universe. Jewish national identity differs from that of other nations in that its purpose is not social, economic or cultural but essentially divine and profoundly imbued with the sense of justice, which it was the first to bring to the world:

> The particularity of Israel is the pursuit of absolute justice whose realization actively embraces the whole of ethical good. Therefore every moral breach committed by an individual Jew weakens his bond with the nation's soul. Consequently, the primary and fundamental "return" is to attach oneself to the national soul and to strive with it in order to improve all means and actions in accordance with the essential content of the national soul.

Israel's chosenness is one of the central categories of Kook's thought to which he repeatedly returns. Israel's special genius within the cosmic evolutionary process is the pursuit of holiness: "Other nations have developed other talents: intelligence, morality, aesthetics. Israel, however, received that gift through which alone the humanity of all nations can become completed, the capacity for discovering the divine light in every aspect of reality."

Zionism

In keeping with his boundless love for Zion, Kook also ascribed a singular role to the Land of Israel. It is there that Israel's spiritual destiny was first forged and divine grace manifested. Since the Holy Land had been chosen by God to reveal the universal message of sanctity, it is a land possessed of extraordinary spiritual virtues. As we have stated, Kook believed Israel's sacred vocation to be the propagation of holiness. However, as a result of their homelessness and wanderings in the Diaspora, Jews had become estranged from their goal. Kook was nonetheless certain that the return to the land of Israel would renew and regenerate the holiness peculiar to the Jewish people. He was deeply convinced that the return to Zion marked the beginning of divine redemption and that the growth of the Jewish population of Palestine in his days had ushered in a new era in the rebirth of the Jewish people. He believed, as had Yehudah ha-Levi before him, that the Jew could only attain full spiritual maturity in the Land of Israel where he could assimilate the wisdom of the past and work towards the future restoration of divine harmony.

The sacred bond between the nation of Israel and the land of Israel is not one which has resulted merely from historical ties and can therefore not be understood in terms of the natural connections which bind other nations to their countries. Just as Israel had been chosen because of its inherent holiness, so had the land of Israel been set aside by reason of its spiritual virtues. The return to God passes necessarily through a "return to God's land" and national redemption will ultimately bring about the universal redemption. Kook taught that this intermediate state was fraught with countless dangers. He felt that it was a great historical tragedy that the Zionist movement had been born at a time of religious decline and that it was mainly supported by those that had shaken off the yoke of religious observance. He understood this rebellious element while emphasizing that Zionism would be incomplete as long as its spiritual dimensions were not manifested. He warned in particular against the ills of secular nationalism:

> It is proper to nurture national honor and to seek to enhance it; but national honor is not an end in itself. It can only be the by-product of the realization of our important task: to testify and be witness in the world to the name and glory of God. Man is weak. Preoccupied with the means—the increase of Israel's honor and status, he may easily forget the end—the glorification and sanctification of the One God of Israel and the world. He may forget that the all-embracing mission of Israel must reveal itself through the people of Israel, created by Him for His glory.

Kook was not perturbed by the dichotomy he perceived between the ultimate goal of *teshuvah* and the spiritual mediocrity of the intermediate stages, characterized by religious defection and the glorification of materialistic values. Spiritual shortcomings were inevitable.

Indeed the concern with material welfare would ultimately reveal itself as the means of preservation of the deepest spiritual values. He firmly believed in the fundamentally spiritual essence of the Jewish soul. He estimated that the irreligion of the secular Zionists would be a transitory phenomenon caused by the abnormalities of Jewish existence in the Diaspora. Since Israel was intrinsically righteous, the Jewish people in the Holy Land would ultimately free themselves from the servitude of alien ideologies, recover their national specificity and return to the Torah of Israel. Paradoxically, at least on the surface of things, it was this return to its own particularity that was to foster an unexpected consequence, the realization of *teshuvah* and the attaining of universalism. He saw the seeds of this process in the founding of the Hebrew University in Jerusalem in 1924, on which occasion he delivered a memorable address.

This conviction found its most forceful expression in his unbending defense of the *halutzim*, or Zionist pioneers, who had entered the country after the First World War. These "godless" elements, many of whom were animated by socialist and revolutionary ideals, aroused the bitter opposition of the extremely orthodox population for whom Israel was the Holy Land and its soil a haven of prayer and spirituality. Kook however replied that these were the artisans of the redemption. Like his close friend Rabbi Isaiah Shapira, one of the founders of ha-Poel haMizrahi, the religious workers movement, he preached that what the observant Jews accomplished by their prayers and the performance of the religious precepts, the *halutzim* accomplished by laying bricks and building the Jewish state. Since as Jews they too contained the profound spark of holiness, their real intentions were "for the sake of Heaven." If outwardly they were non-observant, this was because they had been seduced by erroneous ideologies prior to the "Messianic era." Their continued association with the Holy Land would finally restore their intrinsic holiness. Is it not written in Ezekiel 36:24–25: "For I will take you from among the nations, and gather you out of all the countries, and will bring you into your own land. And I will sprinkle clean water upon you, and ye shall be clean from all your uncleannesses and from all your idols will I cleanse you."

According to Rav Kook's interpretation, it is only after the "return to Zion" that the "return to God" and the cleansing of vices contracted in the exile will take place. Of the words he used to express this conviction the following taken from the final chapter of the "Lights of Return," are probably the most typical of his optimistic and lyrical style:

> From the profane will the holy be revealed. So also from unleashed liberty will come a yoke of love. Golden branches will spring forth from secular song and the brilliance of *teshuvah* will shine forth from materialistic writings. This will be the supreme marvel of redemption's vision. The bud will swell, the blossom flower, the fruit mature and the whole world will know that the Holy Spirit is expressed in every motion of Israel's spirit and that the ultimate goal is *teshuvah*, which will bring healing and redemption to the world.

BIBLIOGRAPHY

S. H. BERGMAN, *Faith and Reason*, New York, 1961, 121–141.

I. EPSTEIN, *Abraham Yitzhak Kook: His Life and Times*, London, 1951.

A. I. KOOK, *Orot haTeshuvah*, translated into English as *Rabbi Kook's Philosophy of Repentance*, New York, 1968.

3. Asher Zelig Margaliot —An Ultra-Orthodox Fundamentalist

Paul B. Fenton

I have chosen to speak about the life and thought of Rabbi Isaiah Asher Zelig Margaliot, who is considered one of the foremost ideologists of the fundamentalist, Jerusalem-based, ultra-Orthodox sect known as *Neture Qarta*, "Guardians of the City." Despite its claims to be the only form of traditional Judaism, Orthodox fundamentalism in the form presently described, is a relative newcomer to the religious scene. Though fanaticism, including its Judaic varieties, is as old as religion itself, the particular brand which finds expression in Margaliot's writings developed only recently in reaction to the modernist and reformist tendencies which emerged in Judaism in the secular age. As such, the inclusion of this topic in a conference on the reconfiguration of Judaism in the modern age, needs no justification.

My presentation of Rabbi Margaliot is largely indebted to the detailed study, to my knowledge the first ever devoted to this thinker,

17

written by Yehudah Liebes of the Hebrew University and published in the third volume of *Jerusalem Studies in Jewish Thought*. It is interesting, though to my mind uncalled for, that Liebes consistently compares Margaliot's doctrines to those propounded two thousand years ago by the adepts of the Dead Sea scrolls' sect.

Rabbi Isaiah Asher Zelig Margaliot was born in Poland at the turn of the century. At an early age he decided to devote himself to a life of prayer and meditation, and decided to settle in the holy city of Jerusalem. He undertook alone the perilous journey, finally arriving after many a misadventure in Eretz Israel which he never again left until his death in 1969.

In Jerusalem, Margaliot identified with the ultra-Orthodox population of the Old *Yishuv*, who were staunchly opposed to the socialist and secular activities of the Zionist pioneers who were settling the land in large numbers. While there were some that welcomed the social reforms that resulted from the arrival of the new settlers, the rigidly traditional eyed them with suspicion and even resentment. Not only were these newcomers and their way of life disruptive to the centuries-old customs of the Jerusalemite Jews but they were looked upon by the extremist Orthodox as godless heathens who had come to defile the soil of the Holy Land.

Margaliot joined and helped to found the extremist wing of the Orthodox camp—the schismatic, anti-Zionist 'Edah Haredit ("Community of the God-fearing"). This group, which was set up in 1923 by the leaders of the Old *Yishuv*, Rabbi Isaac Diskin and Rabbi Hayyim Sonnenfeld, in opposition to the newly established Chief Rabbinate of Eretz Israel, was intent on deploying every effort to fortify the Orthodox bastion and oppose the endeavors of the Zionist movement. Though numerically small, through its loud and insistent propaganda, mainly diffused by stickers and posters, the group had a large audience amongst the more radical elements of the Agudat Israel organization. Soon it became virtually identical with the *Neture Qarta*, who refuse to recognize the State of Israel and theoretically do not use its currency, social services and amenities such as state-produced electricity. Moreover, Margaliot personally associated with extremist

Hasidic groups, and particularly those of the Munkacer and Satmarer sects, with whose spiritual leaders, Rabbi Hayyim Eliezer Shapira and Yoel Teitelbaum, he carried on an extensive correspondence. The former, who died in 1935, was notorious for his anti-Zionist stance, whereas the second denounced the State of Israel as a satanic invention. Margaliot, however, considered his personal spiritual mentor to be the great Sefardi Kabbalist, Rabbi Solomon Alfandari, who passed away in 1926, well over the age of a hundred years.

Our author made great efforts to disseminate the teachings of the Kabbalah, and wrote a pamphlet in order to encourage scholars to delve into the study of the secret doctrines of Israel, a pursuit which he thought would hasten the Redemption. He even revived and popularized certain mystical rituals, such as the "midnight lament" (*tiqqun hatzot*) and the *Lag ba'Omer* pilgrimage to Shimon bar Yohai's tomb in Meron. Indeed Margaliot displayed a particular devotion to this legendary Galilean saint, the supposed author of the classic work of Jewish mysticism, the Zohar. He contributed much to the prompting of the annual pilgrimage to Meron, and towards the end of his life he actually lived as a hermit in the neighboring shrine, becoming known to his followers as the Meroner Rebbe ("the Master of Meron").

During his lifetime he proved to be a prolific writer, composing over thirty works, mainly of a devotional and kabbalistic nature. However, several of his works, such as *Qumi Roni*, dealing with Messianism, *Qol Omer Q'ra*, encouraging the study of Kabbalah, *Ashre haIsh*, dealing with segregation from evildoers, *'Amude Arazim*, concerning the shaving of the beard, do come to grips with contemporary issues.

Margaliot was not a systematic writer, and his books rather take the form of quotations from the works of his predecessors to which he added his own observations. These would often consist of long disquisitions in which certain ideological themes recur, many of which became the axiomatic principles of the *Neture Qarta*.

Israel and the Mixed Multitude

One of the fundamental concepts reiterated in his writings and high-lighted by Liebes's presentation, is the Manichean division of the Jewish people into two categories, whom he respectively calls *Yisra'el*, the "true Israelites," and the *'erev rav*, the "mixed multitude." According to Talmudic sources, the "mixed multitude" was a band of opportunists, rallied from the ranks of the Egyptian riffraff, who, to use a vulgar expression, decided to jump on the bandwagon and leave Egypt with the Israelites while the going was good. Subsequently, rabbinical apologetics would have it that these unruly individuals were responsible for all the misfortunes incurred during the wanderings in the wilderness, such as the episode of the Golden Calf. According to Margaliot the first category is to be identified with the minute, segregated ultra-Orthodox community, (*'Edah Haredit*, the only class of Jews worthy of the name Israel, whereas the rest of the so-called Jews, "they and their supporters, derive from the mixed multitude and have no connection whatsoever with the Israelitish nation."

What is more, according to Margaliot, since they are not possessed of a Jewish soul, they do not come under the halakhic principle "though he sin, he is still a Jew," since from the very outset they are non-Jewish. Margaliot finds support for this dualistic categorization in the discussions from the Zoharic literature involving the Kabbalistic notions of *qedushah* (holiness) and *qelippah* (unholiness) in the context of transmigration of the souls. The souls of the Israelites derive from holiness whereas those of the *'erev rav* proceed from unholiness: "He whose soul-root derives from holiness will be attracted to holiness, whereas he who belongs to them [the *'erev rav*] will be attracted to them and their vanities."

Margaliot even uses this spiritual magnetics to criticize those who socialize with the wicked with the sincere intention of saving them. For the author of *Ashre haIsh* there is an unbridgeable chasm between the two factions which cannot be crossed, even by repentance. Repentance, he believes, is only of value as a virtue to those whose soul is originally rooted in holiness. On the contrary, the performance of a goodly act by a wicked person can only lead to further perversion through the strengthening of the power with which evil is imbued by this very act. The final end of the "mixed multitude" is not to be united with the "Jewish people." When the Messianic epoch is finally ushered in, the "son of David" will utterly destroy the *'erev rav.* A whole chapter of his book *Qumi Ori* is devoted to the question of how the "mixed multitude" will be expelled from the Holy Land at the end of days. When these intruders, whose identity is not difficult to unmask, will cease from the land of Israel, then the Messiah will come.

In case you have not guessed that our author is referring to secular Zionists, his remarks concerning their facial traits based on the science of physiognomy may be of assistance in recognizing them. He tells us, notably, that it is prohibited to gaze upon the face of a wicked man since this can have a pernicious effect on one's spiritual well-being.

Segregation

This being the case, it is of paramount necessity for the true Israelite to separate himself from the company of the wicked. Thus the god-fearing (the *haredim*) are not to associate with the wicked Jews either in material dealings, such as commerce, or even spiritual pursuits, such as prayer. His book *Ashre haIsh* is replete with advice and precautions as to how to avoid contact with the unholy. Segregation is to be total. The two categories must be absolutely separated. The god-fearing individual must also alienate himself from his kin and relatives if the latter fall under the sway of the "mixed multitude."

Segregation also involves the affectation of outward signs of distinction. These, outlined in his work *'Amude Arazim,* include the wearing of a beard and side locks and the donning of a special garb to which our author attributes certain spiritual virtues. He is referring of course to the traditional Jerusalem Ashkenazi costume, which although obviously part-Polish part-Turkish in origin is ascribed by our author to the Patriarchs. Those who do not conform to these vestimentary requirements are not to be honored with ritual functions, such as being called to the public reading of the Torah. Segregation is so compulsory as to prohibit the use of the spoken Hebrew language, since this is the language of the heretics. The practical alternative for the ʿEdah Haredit, whose members are overwhelmingly Ashkenazi, is Yiddish.

Segregation is not only a passive attitude. According to Margaliot the true Israelite is enjoined to exhibit active hate towards the unholy. This hate is even considered a meritorious act (*mitzvah*) inasmuch as the "mixed multitude" prolong by their wickedness the length of the exile. In view of their ontological origin it is only natural that the wicked should also hate the *haredim*. Therefore it is moot to argue with the wicked, to curse them, and pray for their destruction. Conversely, it is forbidden to greet them, to give them charity or to socialize with them.

The Orthodox Traitors

The ultra-Orthodox struggle is directed not only against the secular Jew but also against the moderately Orthodox who do not identify with their combat. Margaliot holds a severely negative opinion of the Orthodox Jew who associates with the secular. In some respects, he says, they are worse than the ungodly. He is particularly vehement in his condemnation of the state religious system of schools (*Mamlakhti-dati*), "where light and darkness mingle indiscriminately . . . these are worse and more dangerous for Judaism than the schools of outright secular Jews." Worse even than apostates. The reason being the confusion and intermingling which they cause between the two camps which should remain segregated.

The object of Margaliot's most virulent criticism are the rabbis and leaders of the moderately Orthodox. He heaps his anger especially on the *Mizrahi*, the Nationalist-Religious party. He is ireful of the support they sometimes give to the secular Jews, their attempts to attract them to Judaism and their opposition to the *haredim*, which he qualifies as treachery since it strengthens the power of the *qelippah* (unholiness). Above all, his anger is limitless towards those who are dressed and act as *haredim* but defend the secular Jews. They appear to him as idolatrous prophets, they are to be considered as being worse than apostates. In his opinion their attire is but a disguise, for in fact they are satanic demons who have come to delude the Israelites on the eve of the Messianic redemption.

One particular rabbi is especially selected as the target of his poisoned arrows. Though he never mentions him by name, it is obvious that he is referring to Rabbi Abraham Isaac Kook (died 1935), the first Chief Rabbi of Eretz Israel. According to Margaliot, this personage is the highest and most occult of the degrees of unholiness, for he is disguised in the garb of the *haredim*. It is well known that Rabbi Kook continued to wear in the Holy Land the traditional attire of the Eastern European Jew, complete with caftan and *shtraymel* (fur hat). Not only does this rabbi associate with the "mixed multitude" but he extols them, leading astray his disciples, who construe his words as spiritual mysteries. Hence, says Margaliot, he is on a par with Shabbetai Zevi, the infamous, apostate messiah who also justified the most heinous sins with the deepest secrets of the Kabbalah.

The Zionist Illusion

In Margaliot's opinion the State of Israel is a satanic delusion. This he endeavors to prove in his works *Qumi Ori* and *'Amude Arazim* by copious quotations from rabbinical and kabbalistic literature, even going as far as to utilize anti-Shabbatean writings in order to emphasize the analogy between the Zionist enterprise and Shabbateanism. He polemicizes at length against those who see in the establishment of the state "the beginnings of the Redemption." In his opinion, as later in that of the Satmarer Rebbe, the State of Israel is not a Redemption (*geullah*) but a reversal (*temurah*) (terminology based on Ruth 4, 7). Indeed, since the "mixed multitude" are not worthy of the appellation "Israel," their state should rather be named Canaan and the inhabitants of Jerusalem should continue to pray "next year in the Land of Israel."

The Zionist Antichrist

Paradoxically, Margaliot discerned within the Zionist reality the signs of an immanent Messianic redemption. According to the traditional sources, before the Divine Light can be revealed in all its bounty, darkness and evil must reach their peak on the eve of the final redemption. For Margaliot this culmination of evil is realized in the establishment of the illusory Zionist state. It is during this decisive epoch that the great selection will take place between the righteous and holy, on the one hand, and the wicked and impure, on the other. Thus it is important to choose one's camp and remain aloof from the "mixed multitude."

So strongly did Margaliot feel that Redemption was at hand, that he states in the introductions to most of his books that he wrote them in order to usher in the Messianic era. However, according to Margaliot, belief in the Messianic coming implied opposition to the Zionist activities, even though they included settling of the Land. It was precisely the latter that demonstrated the Zionist lack of faith by supplanting the Messianic ideal of a miraculous return to the Land with one obtained by human and material effort. Thus all the Zionist endeavors to rebuild the Land are not only in vain but actually impede the real redemption.

To prove this, he sets out in great detail the successive stages of redemption, in particular in his work *Qumi Ori*. Here he endeavors to demonstrate from the Zohar that the Land of Israel should still be under Muslim sovereignty at the time of the Messianic redemption and that, contrary to religious Zionistic (*Mizrahi*) claims, the rebuilding of the Temple should take place prior to the ingathering of the exiles and not thereafter.

Kabbalah and Redemption

As has been said Margaliot did much to promote the study of Kabbalah, and most of his writings were dedicated to the dissemination of its teachings. He most probably believed that the end of days would be characterized by the spread of the esoteric doctrines of Judaism, which would help accelerate the process of Redemption. He considered that those who doubted the authenticity of the teachings of the Kabbalah and criticized its study belonged to the "mixed multitude." On the other hand, he mentions that members of the evildoers will also study the esoteric doctrines of the Kabbalah but not in its true spirit. Liebes surmises that Margaliot is here referring to the academic study of Kabbalah that has become part of university courses.

Conclusion

The preceding represents an attempt to present the salient features of the ultra-Orthodox ideology as expounded by one of its major figureheads. I have tried to be objective and have refrained from any comments. If certain of the ideas here exposed are found to be repulsive, it must be borne in mind that they are the expression of a conservative faction struggling against all odds to defend what it believes to be the unadulterated truth, and as such bears a lot in common with other such groups throughout the contemporary world who are endeavoring to stay the onslaught of modernism. Finally, it should be said that the *'Edah Haredit* today represents a very small minority within the Orthodox camp with very little impact, whose bark is much worse than its bite, but which nonetheless provides an interesting example of Jewish fundamentalism in its crudest and most radical expression.

4. Franz Rosenzweig's Doctrine of Creation

Norbert M. Samuelson

This essay analyzes a single concept in the thought of Franz Rosenzweig. It is part of a larger project in constructive Jewish philosophy that attempts to interpret the doctrine of creation out of the historical sources of rabbinic Judaism in the light of contemporary mathematics, physics and astronomy. The larger study will examine different pictures of the origin and general nature of the universe in the Hebrew Scriptures, ancient Greek science, classical biblical commentaries, medieval and contemporary Jewish philosophy and modern Western science.

One motive for examining creation is that it is a focal point for current debates between Christian conservatives and modernists over the proper relationship of human science to revealed authority. A far more important motive is that creation has been a root principle " '*ikkar*"of Jewish faith from biblical times through the Middle Ages, and has once again assumed its classical importance in Jewish religious thought through the publication of Franz Rosenzweig's *Der Stern der Erlösung*.

"Cosmology" is a general picture of the entire universe. "Cosmogony" is an account of its origin. In the case of Jewish thought the two are almost always integrated. I will use the term, "creation," viz., the concept "*ma'aseh b'reshit*" as it has been used through the history of Jewish philosophy for an integrated account of the two. It encompasses all joint cosmologies and cosmogonies from descriptions of an eternal universe whose ultimate principle of organization is necessity to claims that universes are created at a definite moment in time by the design of a thinking entity.

The primary text where Rosenzweig discusses his doctrine of creation is Part II, Book One of *Der Stern der Erlösung*.[1] However, that discussion presupposes what Rosenzweig already said about the concept of *Nichts* (=*nihil*, =nothing) in Part I. I presented a more detailed paper than is appropriate here, entitled "The Concept of '*Nichts*' in Rosenzweig's *Star of Redemption*" at the Internationale Franz Rosenzweig Konferenz in Kassel, W. Germany, on December 10, 1986. This paper is based primarily upon the detailed argumentation in that earlier paper.

The Nothing of Creation

In the very opening sections of the introduction to the first part of the *Star*, Rosenzweig makes it perfectly clear that whatever else he means by *Nichts*, it is individual rather than general, it stands outside of what past philosophic reasoning can encompass even though it is real, and its opposites are *Sein*, and *Etwas*.

Again, *Nichts* relates with what is individual rather than what is general. In the case of man, individuality refers to his life and will. In the case of God, individuality expresses His freedom, and in the case of the world, individuality involves its concrete, contingent content. In contrast, the world of *Sein* is a world of natures that reason comprehends through laws and definitions that express what is both universal and necessary. In other words, reality is composed of a series of opposites—nothing and being, individuals and universals, contingency and necessity—in each case philosophic reasoning can only comprehend the latter, and only by understanding both can we come to terms with all of reality. Being is the subject matter of the form of reasoning appropriate to philosophy. Beyond philosophy is metaphilosophy, whose subject matter is *Nichts*.

Rosenzweig's so-called "new philosophy"[2] moves from the Hegelian rational sciences of theology, cosmology and psychology and their corresponding elements God, world and man, by way of negation to Rosenzweig's meta-rational sciences. As Hegel's sciences posit something (an *Etwas*), their negation yields three distinct instances of nothing (*Nichts*) that are the starting point of Rosenzweig's analysis. Rosenzweig calls them "irrational objects,"[3] but "irrational" should not be understood to mean incomprehensible. They are no more and no less intelligible than are irrational numbers in mathematics. Rather, just as a new math was required to encompass irrational as well as rational numbers, so Rosenzweig begins a new philosophy to encompass the irrational as well as the rational elements of reality.

The Creator God

Rosenzweig's goal in Part I of the *Star* is to start with something concrete, through analysis to negate it as known, and then to posit or affirm it as something that otherwise is unknown. In each case meta-scientists begin with something concrete that is subsequently negated. They are not just nothing; they are the nothing of what was negated.

Rosenzweig introduces in Book One his model meta-scientific sentence and describes its logical mode.[4] Its form is "y=x." The left hand term is the grammatical subject, the semantic subject and a negative supposition (*Setzung*). Conversely, the right hand term is the grammatical predicate, the semantic content, and an affirmative determination of the subject (*Bestimmung*). In Rosenzweig's logic, a sentence of this form expresses a universal conditional (If anything is a *y* then it is a *x*) and not an identity claim.

Rosenzweig's metaphysics affirms in his symbolic language, "A=A."[5] The "A" of the left-hand place[6] is the point of departure. It is the *Nichts* of any knowledge of God from the conclusion of Maimonides's theology. God and God alone is nothing of which anyone can think. The left-hand "A" is an act of affirmation of a negated essence. In classical terms, it is the act of negating of God everything that is finite. Conversely, the "=A" is an act of negating an infinite number of somethings any of which would limit God if they could be affirmed of Him, precisely because they are something (*Etwas*).[7] In other words, God is free because nothing can be affirmed of Him. He is free from every limitation. He is infinitely free, because there are an infinite number of things that He is not; and He is eternally free, because nothing that will ever come to be will be God. Consequently, God as God is continuously not what He creates.

The right-hand "A" is called divine essence (*Wesen*).[8] It is an asymptopic movement of divine freedom towards the idea of divine essence. The freedom is a force with a direction, whereas the essence simply is and therefore has no direction. The freedom is a potentiality, whereas an essence is an actuality. It is this movement that "A=A" expresses. Through the endless passage of time in which an unceasing number of somethings are created, the more divine freedom (God as subject) becomes his essence (God as content). As such "A=A" is a statement that can only be understood in terms of Hermann Cohen's calculus. The sentence expresses an equation for the activity of creation which, when diagrammed, has a particular nothing as its starting point and constantly approximates but never reaches an end point or limit that is 1.

In this context, "*creatio ex nihilo*" expresses that the relative nothing of the knowledge of God (the "*ex nihilo*") is the origin from which God acts to become God (the "*creatio*"). The *nihil* is divine freedom. It is a negative supposition that whatever is or will be is not God. The *creatio* is the equal sign of the equation "A=A." The equation expresses a function in infinitesimal calculus.

The Created World

The somethings that are not God that God creates are the content of the world. Creation expresses a relation between God and world. In God's case, creation is the function expressed in the equation (A=A) that is God. In the world's case, creation is the function expressed in the equation (B=A) that is the world becoming God.[9] B is a total distinctiveness that constitutes the complete, absolute individuality of everything that becomes real in the world. It is the act of negation (*das Nein*) of the *Nichts* of the world which, when conjoined to God's act of affirmation (*das Ja*), gives rise to each "individual (*einzelnes*) something (*Etwas*).[10] God's Physis is expressed in the equation of the world as "A." In this logical syntax, the nature of God becomes the universal (*das Allgemeine*). The equal sign expresses their conjunction (*das Und*). The individuals of the world are produced by an endless process of interaction between the particular (B) and the universal (A). Each side of the equation is incomplete without the other. The universal is passive. It simply is, and as such it needs application. This need generates a force of attraction (*eine anziehende Kraft*) upon the particular, which, because it is aimless, is drawn to the universal.

In the process that is the world, whose equation is "B=A," the B becomes conscious that it is being attracted towards the A, and thereby is transformed from a mere particular (*Besondere*) into an individual (*Individuum*).[11] An individual is a meaningless, totally unique creature who becomes conscious that it no longer is aimless and increasingly becomes dominated by a universal. To the extent, but only to the extent, that the individual is dominated by its universal, it becomes its species (*Gattung*).[12] As the particular is not the same as the individual, so the species is not the same as the universal. Species is not just a universal. It is a particular or individuated universal or universality. Its individuality is its freedom, and its universality is its essence. In this conjunction the individual is related to God, whose nature gives it direction and meaning.

"B=A" also expresses the process of life. "B" is the *Besondere*. It is the content of the world that includes every particular as particular. "A" is the *Allgemeine*. It is the passive form of the world that includes every form and order of the world as form and order. The equal sign expresses a non-reversible relation between A and B in which B is continuously attracted to A. "B=A" states that B penetrates and fills A.

The All or the universal is the pole of being; the distinctive or the particular is the pole of nothing. Rosenzweig's nothing is a relative, concrete nothing that actively becomes Rosenzweig's something. That something ultimately is expressed as the limit of an equation in Cohen's version of the infinitesimal calculus. Being is the limit of that equation. It is Rosenzweig's absolute, universal something that passively attracts Rosenzweig's nothing. In other words, nothing is the opposite of something and functions as the point of departure in an equation whose end or limit is absolutely something. That equation expresses the world of individuals through all time in terms of a life process that Rosenzweig identifies with creation.

Beyond Philosophy

In summary, creation itself is a non-temporal relation that holds between God and world. It is a relation that is expressed in logical symbolism as a function whose equation is modeled on calculus. That equation is geometrically mapped in two-dimensional space. One dimension is God, and the other is the world. The function is an asymptote, whose starting point in Cartesian coordinates is $(0,0)$, and whose end point is $(1,1)$. The "1" in both cases is their essence, which, as an ultimate limit, is simultaneously God's oneness, God's power, the world's unity, and the world's content. The "0" in each case is the *Nichts*. Like an infinitesimal, it is a relative nothing out of which everything positive arises. Together with the *Sein* of philosophy, *Nichts* is the fundamental principle of Rosenzweig's new thinking. In contrast to *Sein*, it is particular rather than passive. If it were not for

The Algebra of the Elements
God: A=A
Man: B=B
World: B=A

The Geometry of the Elements

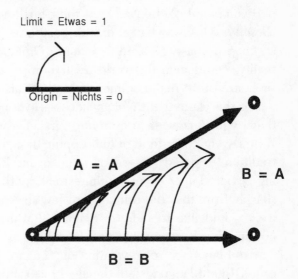

nothing there would only be static, eternal concepts. With nothing there is a vital world of concrete living entities that change and have options, move and are free.

Rosenzweig tells us that Part One reaches the outer limits of what can be known through philosophy, and it merely deals with possibilities for knowledge, not certainties, because we have not as yet moved beyond the actuality (*Tatsachlichkeit*) of the isolated, hypothetical elements of reality to their structure in relationship. To know their relationship, which is the only way that these mere hypotheticals can be real, requires a different mode of thinking that lies beyond the capability of logical thought.

The elements emerged and developed in the process of a movement of thought from the *Nichts* of knowledge (*Wissen*) to the *Etwas* of knowledge prior to any visible reality. Part of understanding visible reality will be understanding the relationship of creation that holds between the elements, God and world. That relationship will connect the *Etwas* of God as unlimited power, that emerged out of the *Nichts* of God as infinite freedom, with the *Etwas* of the world as *Gattung*, that functions as the limit of the directional motion of man and other particulars out of the *Nichts* of their birth as what is utterly unique (*Besonders*). Knowledge of the relational movement of creation (*Schöpfung*), as well as of revelation (*Offenbarung*), is knowledge of reality.[13] God, man and world are in themselves only elements, and, as such, are proto-real, i.e., mere hypotheticals.

It is this claim that theology necessarily must transcend philosophy that I will now want to examine. First, I want to note that whereas Rosenzweig's paradigm of philosophic thought is Hegelian, in Jewish tradition the paradigm was Aristotelian, and Rosenzweig's "new thinking," rooted in Cohen's infinitesimal method, does not break as sharply from the "old thinking" of Jewish Aristotelianism as Rosenzweig would like to believe. Second, I want to argue that there is nothing that Rosenzweig wants to express as theology in his so-called "spoken language" of revelation that cannot be expressed in the so-called "silent language" of the algebraic symbolism of creation.

I

For Aristotle, as for Rosenzweig, the real world is composed of two radically different principles—matter (*hyle*), and form (*morphe*). The former is what accounts for the individual, contingent, concrete content, while the latter expresses general natures. Similarly, being (*ousia*) belongs to the world of forms that constitute the subject matter that philosophy expresses through necessary definitions and universal laws, while privation stands on the edge of intelligibility in Aristotle's science pointing to a reality of concrete chance happenings that lie beyond philosophical reason's grasp. In contrast, any attempt to apply what Rosenzweig says about God in this case to Aristotle's theology is more problematic. However, here the difficulty has nothing to do with their respective use of the term, nothing. Rather, the issue is their understanding of God, for Rosenzweig's deity is subject to negation while Aristotle's is not.[14]

Furthermore, the initial *Nichts* in all three meta-sciences are definite nothings. They are not just nothing; they are the nothing of what was negated. In other words, Rosenzweig's *Nichts* in the new philosophy occupies a place similar to if not identical with Aristotle's understanding of privation, in clear opposition to what otherwise might be called absolute nothing.[15]

At the conclusion of the introduction to Book One[16] Rosenzweig makes explicit his ontology of something and nothing. Rosenzweig claims that Hermann Cohen's philosophical application of the infinitesimal calculus provided him with a model for constructing reality from what is practically (but not absolutely) nothing. As the old philosophy began with pure form (à la Aristotle), so the new philosophy begins with pure matter (again, à la Aristotle).

Furthermore, the terms *Gattung*, *Besondere* and *Individuum* function in Rosenzweig's metalogic in the same way that the corresponding terms form (*morphe*), matter (*hyle*) and individual substance (*ousia*) function in Aristotle's physics. Rosenzweig's *Nichts*, like Aristotle's *hyle*, is not absolutely nothing. Both terms name a principle of individuality, contingency and potentiality that reason needs and points to but cannot as reason encompass. Rosenzweig's *Nichts*, like Aristotle's *hyle*, is a fundamental principle by which the concrete world of material entities is comprehended. That intelligibility is expressed through a relationship in which Being (*Sein*) constitutes the opposite pole.

Yet, it must also be acknowledged that whatever the similarities between Aristotle's and Rosenzweig's ontologies, Rosenzweig's philosophy really is new. It is by no means simply Aristotle in existential clothing. The something that follows from Rosenzweig's negation of nothing is not something positive. It is not an Aristotelian form or being; rather, what follows is something that is still negative. However, what it is is the negation of what is negative, and as such that is not a mode of thought beyond philosophy. Rather, it is something that falls under what Kant called an "infinite judgment."

||

While the new thinking is not as new as Rosenzweig thought it was, from the perspective of the world of early twentieth century Germany that saw all of philosophy in Hegelian terms, Rosenzweig's *Star* shines bright as a radical departure in human knowledge. It turns philosophy and science away from the static abstract logic of *Sein* to the dynamic, concrete meta-logic of *Nichts*. However, it is precisely this historically understandable, continued dependence of Rosenzweig's thought on an inadequate model of Hegel's dialectic that lies at the heart of his need to posit a mode of audible over symbolic language, which in turn was his motive for advocating a form of theology that is independent of philosophy.

Rosenzweig describes his algebra as a language of logic that is prior to real speech. It is an unspoken language of inaudible, elemental words, viz., "A", "B", "A=", "=A", "B=", "=B", "A=A," "A=B", "B=A" and "B=B". That the language can be made totally explicit reveals its poverty in comparison with the spoken language of prophecy whose grammar expresses the structure of reality.[17] Whereas the scientific language of algebra can only express the elements of reality, the prophetic language of grammar can speak of the relations in reality—creation, revelation and redemption—between the isolated elements. In other words, Rosenzweig (like Buber) posited an ontology of relations in which elements have distinct existence only in conceptual abstraction, in marked contrast to a Cartesian ontology of substances in which relations, if they can be justified at all, have only derivative reality.

To express the relational nature of reality, Rosenzweig constructs out of his three source words a new, now audible, language of root-words (*Stammworte*) whose grammatical categories presuppose the order of lived reality.[18] The formal parts of the grammar include nouns, verbs and predicates. The source predicate term "Thus" arises from the source word "Yes"; pronouns and indefinite articles express the positive "something" (*Etwas*) of the audible sentence (*Satz*) as an individual thing whose particularity is fixed when the term, in association with the definite article, is placed in the object position. However, it is the verb rather than the noun that expresses the relational nature of reality. Nouns are subordinate to their verbs as the things that they express have reality only as terms of a relation.

The fundamental philosophic thrust behind Rosenzweig's discussion of symbolic logic and linguistic grammar is a critique of Descartes's mathematical method of doing philosophy. Rosenzweig, like his peer Martin Buber, (in fact building on Spinoza's critique of Descartes's *cogito* that substance is a hidden, undemonstrated assumption) urges that philosophy reexamine its original supposition that ontology begins with substances, and instead rethink its conceptualization of reality on a model that makes relations rather than substances fundamental. Rosenzweig believed that Descartes's substance-oriented ontology, his commitment to the use of algebra, and his attempt to place philosophy on a scientific basis mutually entail each other, so that in order to reject Cartesian ontology, Rosenzweig also casts aside the use of mathematics and even scientific thinking in general. It is on this uncritical, practically unstated jump in Rosenzweig's thought that I want to focus attention.

Rosenzweig made this intellectual leap clearest in his discussion of the advantages of theology's doctrine of creation out of nothing in contrast to Idealism's purported contrary commitment to some notion of the generation of the universe along the lines of a Neoplatonic doctrine of emanation.[19]

Rosenzweig's argument can be summarized as follows: To express something symbolically and to think scientifically solely out of the sources of human reason is the same thing. The model for all such thinking is the algebraic form "$y=x$." Now this form is adequate to express a two-term relation, viz., the relation between the variables y and x, but it is limited in that it cannot express any relation that is more complex. For every algebraic expression there is a comparable geometric figure mappable in Cartesian coordinates, and the dimensions of that figure correspond to the number of variables in the algebraic expression. Hence, two variable equations are represented in two-dimensional space, three variable equations in three-dimensional space, etc. However, scientific thinking is limited to two variable expressions which, as such, cannot adequately express three-dimensional reality. That reality is three-dimensional is expressed in Rosenzweig's symbolism by designating the number of elements precisely as three. That he judges scientific reasoning to be inadequate is represented by the fact that well-formed propositions in his formal logic can only admit two variables.

In this form the fallacy of Rosenzweig's argumentation should be apparent. There is no such thing as logic. Rather, there are logics, i.e., multiple sets of rules to structure formal ways of speech. Rosenzweig's elemental logic is only *a* logic which is inadequate for the very reasons that Rosenzweig himself states. The reality that he wants to express is three-dimensional, and as such requires a three-dimensional rather than a two-dimensional calculus.

It is of interest to note that while Rosenzweig restricts the use of algebra to thinking about elements, he does not so restrict geometry, since his ultimate picture of reality is a solid Star of David constructed out of two pyramids—one joined at points representing the elements (God, man, world), and the other joined at points representing their interrelationships (creation [between God and world], revelation [between God and man], and redemption [between man and world]). This device in itself illustrates that something is wrong with Rosenzweig's argument, since, without doubt, this geometric shape in principle has an algebraic counterpart.

My central point is that Rosenzweig made a radical separation between logic and language that has no justification either in Rosenzweig's arguments or in fact. To take but one small example, the standard equation in Newtonian mechanics that a quantity of kinetic energy equals one half the mass of an object multiplied by the square of its velocity ($E = \frac{1}{2}mv[2]$) is an algebraic equation whose geometric counterpart looks like a pyramid.[20]

In fact algebraic expression can be well formed with any number of variables/dimensions, and three is no more reasonable for expressing reality than two (Einstein used four). Rosenzweig's error was to equate Hegel's philosophy with philosophy and Hegelian logic with logic.[21] In fact logic(s) is a kind of language and the grammar(s) of ordinary spoken language is a kind of logic. Hence, Rosenzweig's radical separation between the kind of thinking involved in picturing elements and describing relations, founded on his radical separation between silent and spoken language, is without justification.

NOTES

1. *The Star of Redemption*, henceforth to be referred to as *The Star*. All page references will be to Julius Beltz's German edition (Heidelberg, Lambert Schneider, 1954) and William Hallo's English translation (Boston: Beacon Press, 1972) in such a way that "n/m" means page n of the German edition and page m of the English translation.
2. *The Star*, pp. 12ff/7ff.
3. *The Star*, pp. 28/19.
4. *The Star*, pp. 38–39/27–28.
5. *The Star*, pp. 39–46/28–33.
6. *The Star*, pp. 39/28.
7. *The Star*, pp. 42–43/30–31.
8. *The Star*, pp. 42–43/30–31.
9. Compare *The Star*, p. 66/50 with *The Star*, p. 86/65.
10. *The Star*, pp. 62–66/46–50.
11. *The Star*, pp. 64/47–48.
12. *The Star*, pp. 64/48.
13. *The Star*, pp. 118/90. It is important to note that at this stage of Rosenzweig's thinking no reference is made to redemption (Erlösung).
14. I do not mean to suggest that Rosenzweig adopted Aristotle's ontology. On the contrary, from what he says in several passages in *The Star* (e.g., *The Star*, pp. 71–72/53–54), it seems clear to me that Rosenzweig rejected what he thought was Aristotle's ontology, but he misunderstood Aristotle. Furthermore, in spite of his error, he adopted an Aristotelian ontology that he did not realize was Aristotelian.

15. No claim is made that Rosenzweig understood what he was doing in these Aristotelian terms.
16. *The Star*, pp. 29–32/20–22.
17. *The Star*, Zweiter Teil, Einleitung, Grammatik und Wort—Der Augenblick, pp. 120–123/108–111.
18. *The Star*, pp. 138–145/124–131.
19. *The Star*, pp. 153–155/138–140.

20.

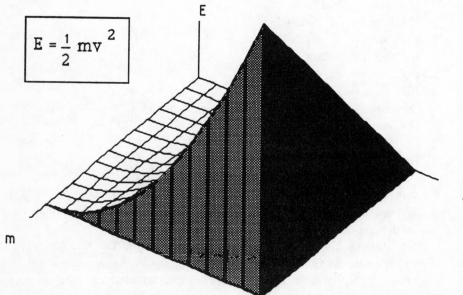

21. The ordinary language philosophy of Wittgenstein is but one example of an alternative approach to philosophy that Rosenzweig's critique ignores. In this connection it is of interest to note that Rosenzweig exhibited some slight uneasiness with his critique of Hegelian philosophy as philosophy when he observed in passing the confidence of English philosophy in language. (*The Star*, p. 162/146.)

5. Buber and the Arab-Jewish Conflict

Manfred Vogel

We propose in this paper to undertake a critical examination of Buber's views regarding the Jewish-Arab conflict with respect to the small piece of land which the Jews call "Land of Israel" and the Arabs call "Palestine." We propose to raise this critical evaluation of Buber not from a vantage point located outside the sphere of his thoughts and concerns, but rather from a viewpoint that should be very congenial to him and which indeed he himself has articulated very eloquently on other occasions. That is, our critique will be raised from, so to speak, the inside rather than the outside. We shall attempt to present considerations which, we believe, Buber in terms of his own basic philosophical-political-religious position should find congenial and telling, but which at the same time contradict and undermine his views on the specific question of the Arab-Jewish conflict. Essentially, the thrust of our critique would be that when it came to this specific issue Buber somehow forgot the "down to earth" realism which is so characteristic of his thought in general, and fell into an idealistic utopianism which he at other times criticized so harshly and poignantly. To put the matter in the Thou-It terminology of the Buberian dialogue, the very heart of our critique will lie in the contention that when it came to the specific issue of the Jewish-Arab conflict Buber somehow neglected the exhortation which he himself has made on many other occasions: That if one is to deal realistically and therefore legitimately with any issue that falls within the sphere of human affairs one must always balance the criteria emanating from the Thou-sphere with the criteria emanating from the It-sphere. In other words, in dealing with the human domain one cannot apply exclusively the Thou-sphere; rather one must inevitably deal with both the It and the Thou spheres. For the human domain does not belong to the realm of the pure Thou (this being a realm belonging to the divine or to the angelic but not to the human); it belongs to the realm of the inextricable It-Thou sphere. And it is precisely when we forget this, when we forget to take account of the considerations emanating from the It-sphere (thus wishing to apply the criteria generated by the Thou-sphere in their pure form without mitigating, i.e., "refracting," them through the It-sphere), that Utopianism is perpetrated. It is one of Buber's most insightful contributions (a contribution which, by the way, very authentically reflects the viewpoint of Judaism, thus making Buber's position in this respect very "Jewish") to insist that in all matters pertaining to the human sphere the criteria and considerations emanating from the pure Thou-sphere must be "refracted" through the It-sphere. Yet with respect to the Jewish-Arab conflict Buber does not seem to practice what he preaches, thus violating one of the most fundamental and important tenets of his position. In this sense, if our proposed critique is substantiated, we would have succeeded in raising a critique that is internal rather than external to Buber's own viewpoint.[1]

One more word before plunging into the substance of our critique. I think it is fair to say that most of the people working in the area of modern Jewish thought and, indeed, in the area of religious thought generally, would agree that Buber was a very important figure in these areas and that his thought has made important contributions to the field. As such, it would seem to me, that any attempt to engage Buber critically could only be viewed as an undertaking that is worthwhile and laudable. And this, of course, would encompass the critical examination of Buber's political thought, and here specifically his thoughts on the Jewish-Arab conflict.

In the past one could have argued that such an examination of Buber's views on the Jewish-Arab conflict could only be taken as an abstract, intellectual, academic exercise—an exercise which could have some interest in the closed circle of Buberian scholarship but which could not possibly have any pragmatic bearing on practical events. For it is a very well-known fact that as regards his views on the Jewish-Arab conflict, Buber had very little impact on the attitudes and views of world Jewry and even less on those of Israeli Jewry. Even at the height of his fame when Buber was celebrated in the Western world as one of the great religious thinkers, and his thought in its many facets was widely discussed not only by the scholars but also by the masses, Buber's views on the Jewish-Arab conflict were almost completely ignored (the exception to this being some of his disciples like Professor Ernst Simon, and Hans Kohn, and some academicians from the Hebrew University who constituted the small party of *Brit Shalom* founded by Judah L. Magnes). But in recent times, with the growing frustration at not finding a solution to the conflict, one can detect an openness to views and sentiments that approach Buber's position (I have in mind in particular the increased discussion indicating a growing receptivity to the "cantonization plan"). In such a context Buber's views assume the potential of becoming rather influential, and hence examining them in a critical spirit is not only an interesting though idle theoretical exercise, but an undertaking that may well assume some concrete, practical significance. For whatever the final decision may be, whether one is persuaded by Buber and adopts his stance or whether one is led to reject his position, the decision should not be made merely on the basis of visceral feelings or emotional inclinations. It should be made only after a careful and thorough intellectual examination of the pros and cons involved in Buber's position. I hope that my critical evaluation of Buber's views may contribute a little to this necessary intellectual airing of the problematic.

We come now to the very substance of the task at hand, namely, the critical evaluation of Buber's position with respect to the Jewish-Arab conflict. Of course, before one can undertake such a critical evaluation one must know what Buber's position with respect to the issue at hand is. Normally, therefore, one would start such an undertaking with a descriptive presentation of Buber's views. Fortunately, however, we can in this case dispense with such an introduction, for in the last few years two excellent descriptive presentations of Buber's views of the Jewish-Arab conflict have appeared in press. We refer to Paul Mendes-Flohr's A Land of Two Peoples and to Maurice Friedman's biography of Buber (especially Volume 3). We will, therefore, limit ourselves to merely enumerating those points in Buber's position on which we wish to comment. These points are: 1) Politics should be subject to ethical standards. 2) The Jews must recognize that the Arabs have also rights to the land. 3) The Jewish right to the land cannot be based either on Biblical revelation or on an historical claim. 4) A solution can be achieved only on the basis of trust. 5) The best solution in these circumstances, i.e., the solution that is ethically the most justified, is the creation of a bi-national state.

As regards the first point, I would agree that the dictum that politics should be subject to ethics must apply in the case of Judaism. This is so because Judaism is a unique phenomenon where the religious is inextricably bound to the ethnic-national, and where indeed ultimately the latter is subjected to the former (namely, it is the religious dimension which requires the ethnic-national dimension, and the ethnic-national dimension enters the picture for the sake of the religious dimension, rather than the religious dimension being merely an expression of the cultural creativity of the ethnic-national dimension). The religious dimension in Judaism is by its very essence ethically oriented—the predicament it addresses and commensurate to it the redemption it yearns for are by their very essence ethical in nature, the predicament being the perpetration of social injustice and the redemption being the yearning to establish the righteous community. Hence the ethnic-national dimension in Judaism cannot but subject itself to the requirements of the ethical. The conduct, the behavior, of the ethnic-national collectivity must be guided by the standards and values of the ethical-religious worldview that is Judaism, by the standards and values of the ethics and religion of social justice. Still, in most other ethnic-national collectivities where the ethnic-national dimension is not inextricably bound to the religious or where, furthermore, the religious dimension is by no means, as far as its essence is concerned, constituted by the ethical concern, the dictum of subjecting politics to ethics may not apply.[2] True, Judaism expresses in its universalistic aspect the hope and prayer that eventually all the other ethnic-national collectivities would come to follow the model of Judaism and subject politics to the ethics of righteousness. But in their own terms, i.e., in terms of their own structure, in terms of their relation to the religious dimension, and in terms of the way in which the religious dimension is structure to them, there is no such prescription, such necessity. Judaism, however, for better or for worse, does have this prescription, and so one must accept Buber's stricture when dealing with Judaism—one must submit the claims and the policies of the Jewish community, i.e., in this specific case, of its Zionist expression, to the scrutiny of ethics.[3]

Similarly, we must also accept Buber's claim that it is incumbent upon the Jews to recognize the rights of the Arabs to the land. Indeed, it would seem to us that this point was accepted by most Zionists. Of course, there were a few (as there will always be) who would not concede this point, and some who, although conceding the point, felt either that the claims of the Jews were so overpowering as to cancel the claims of the Arabs, or that as Jewish spokesmen and leaders it was incumbent upon them to look after and espouse the rights and interests of the Jews and not be overly concerned with the rights and interests of other parties, e.g., the Arabs. As regards this last group, it should be noted, however, that although, in view of what we said above with regard to the first point, such a position should not be tenable from the Jewish vantage point, it is nonetheless a position which, with a few notable exceptions, is practiced widely by most other ethnic-national groups. Most ethnic-national groups instinctively look after their own interests exclusively and don't care very much about the problems, interests or rights of other ethnic-national groups. I have not seen any Arabs rush to the defense of the rights of the Jews, though there were many occasions when such a defense was sorely needed—and not only in the remote historical past but in the recent persecution of Jews in Syria, Iraq and Yemen, for example. Thus, those Zionists who wanted to look only after Jewish interests and rights were merely acting as most members of other ethnic-national groups would have acted. Still, from the Jewish point of view their position, in the last analysis, is not tenable. Thus, there is really no quarrel with Buber's claim that the Arabs also have a right to the land. The question is what to do with these rights, particularly if one also grants that the Jews too have a right to the land (and we still have to establish this!). The intractable ethical dilemma is what to do when you have a clash of two opposing rights, as we shall see below.[4]

In moving now to the third point, which attempts to delineate the ground in which the Jewish right to the land can be based, we start to depart from Buber's position. We would still be in complete agreement with Buber that biblical revelation, i.e., the account in Hebrew Scripture whereby God promises the land to Abraham and his descendants, is not a valid ground on which one can base the Jewish right to the land. True, for those who accept Hebrew Scripture verbatim as the precise record of the divine revelation this would indeed constitute the best imaginable ground—what ground can be more valid than the divine word? Still, the fact remains that for all those who do not accept Hebrew Scripture verbatim as the precise record of divine revelation such ground must remain without validity. What is even worse in this situation is that there is no underlying common context or discourse in which one can attempt to persuade, prove or convince the other of the validity of one's claim. We are therefore completely at one with Buber in rejecting the validity of quoting scriptural verses as a legitimate ground in which to base the Jewish right to the land.

But when Buber proceeds to dismiss also the historical claim of the Jews to the land, we must in no uncertain terms part company with him. For it would seem to us that Buber is throwing away much too lightly and too readily what we would consider to be, in the last analysis, the most valid ground for the claim of the Jews to the land.[5] True, the historical claim takes us to events that have occurred a long time ago, i.e., to the time when the Jews were first in possession of the land and then were deprived of it and driven away into exile. But in the context of ethics there should be no statute of limitations. If we are to evaluate claims in terms of rightness and wrongness, time should not be a consideration. A wrong that is an ancient wrong is no less a wrong because of the fact that it has been around for a long time. And this is even more so when, as is the case here, consequences of that wrong continue to affect its victims and, indeed, affect them in such a tragic way. No, from the Jewish side one cannot give up the historical claim, for without it there is not much of a case for the Jewish side.

Indeed, if we stop to examine a little bit more carefully the grounds which Buber advances for the Jewish claim, we would have to conclude that they are rather dubious and weak. For Buber seems to ground his claim on behalf of the Jews' right to the land on two considerations. One is that the Jews too care for the land and see and feel themselves connected to it; the other is the need of the Jews for a place either as refuge from persecution or for the preservation and maintenance of their cultural heritage. But I don't think that these considerations can really grant the Jews an ethically justified right to the land. For the first consideration is very subjective and can in no way provide ethical justification for the claim. It is similar to the claim that grounds itself in biblical revelation. Just because I like something or care for it or see myself attached to it does not give me a right to that thing. Take the analogy of a stranger who in every respect would make an ideal father for a child and who indeed cares very much for the child and wants to be the child's father. Still, it would not be ethically justified to say that this person has a rightful claim to be the child's father, not even if the real rather of the child has been most cruel and neglectful of the child.

And as to the second consideration, it would seem only too clear that the second rationale which it advances would certainly not be able to provide ground for ethical justification. For while it is well and, indeed, most laudable to want to preserve and sustain one's culture and heritage, surely this could not provide the ethical justification for an intrusion into someone else's "home." No matter how significant and precious this heritage may be in my eyes or, for that matter, even in the eyes of the world at large, it clearly cannot provide an ethical justification for imposing on another innocent party, particularly when the imposition is of such a grievous nature as the intrusion into the living space of that party. This leaves the first rationale and here admittedly the foregoing difficulty may not apply. For a case can indeed be made that in order to save one's life, be it the life of an individual or the life of a collectivity, one is ethically justified in doing everything short of killing other innocent parties. Thus, for example, if the only way to save my life is for me to break into someone else's apartment and seek refuge there, indeed, seek perpetual refuge there, then it seems to me that such an act might be ethically justified. It would seem to me that in circumstances where an attacker is pursuing me and the only way in which I can escape his murderous intention is by taking refuge in someone's apartment, I would be ethically justified in breaking into that person's apartment, and as long as the attacker continues to lurk outside the apartment (even if it be indefinitely), in staying inside the apartment. So, it would appear that on this ground one could indeed make a case for the Jewish intrusion into Palestine.

But here another difficulty arises. Granted that in such circumstances intrusion may be ethically justified, the further question of "Why specifically Palestine—why intrude into this land and not into another land?" must inevitably arise. For surely, the same case that was just made for the intrusion into Palestine could be made for an intrusion into any other land. Indeed, in this context the Arab's complaint of "why me?" carries a lot of force. Thus, it seems to us that Buber's attempt to justify the Jewish claim to the Land of Israel on non-historical grounds would be most unsatisfactory. Indeed, this only reinforces the position we stated above, namely, that without the historical claim there is really no ethical ground for the Jewish claim.

If, however, one turns to the historical perspective one could, it would seem to us, establish a very persuasive ground for the Jewish claim to the Land of Israel. For after all, the Jews did not only reside in, but actually possessed, the land prior to the Arabs' residency in it.[6] This possession was taken away from the Jews by force and as such, although the loss of the possession of the land became a fact of reality, it can have no standing in any ethical consideration or evaluation. For surely, such a dispossession and expulsion which has been attained by the resort to brute force can have no sanction in ethics.[7] Thus, from the vantage point of ethical consideration it cannot be granted that the Jews have lost possession of the land. From the vantage point of ethical consideration they still must be viewed as the rightful possessors of the land. And this conclusion is greatly reinforced by the further consideration that the Jews for their part have indeed never accepted the dispossession and expulsion as the last word, and have never given up the hope and expectation to be restored to their homeland. Indeed, far from giving up their connection to the land they have reasserted it on a daily basis in word and deed.[8]

Thus, we must conclude that the Arabs who settled in Palestine had the misfortune of settling in a land that was not, ethically speaking, free to be possessed by someone else. The situation, it seems to us, is analogous to the case where a person comes to possess property that is stolen. Even if the person himself was in no way involved in the stealing and came to possess the property in all innocence, if the original owner is around and lays claim to the property, the person is out of luck. So, the right to the land which the Arabs claim is not at all that secure; indeed, it is quite shaky. Add to this the further consideration that, on the one hand, the position of the Jew in Diaspora-existence has become totally untenable to the point of threatening the very possibility of his existence (is this not the clear message of the Holocaust?) and that, on the other hand, the Arabs are in possession of vast tracts of land, far beyond their need, and the ethical equation by which one tries to reconcile the two claims tilts, it would seem to us, in favor of the Jewish claim. For on the one hand, as we have argued above, a good case can be made that an individual or a collectivity whose very life is threatened has every moral right to do everything it can to save its life except depriving another innocent party of its life.[9] And, on the other hand, a case may be made that, as with respect to individuals, our conscience would not allow us to let an individual die of starvation while other individuals wallow in unnecessary luxuries, so also with respect to collectivities our conscience should not allow us to let one nation perish for lack of space or food while other nations have so much of it that they do not know what to do with it.[10]

Still, we are willing to accede to the proposition that notwithstanding the foregoing considerations the Arabs do have an ethically justified claim to the land by virtue of their residency in it for so many years. We thus have here a clear clash between two rightful claims.[11] This brings us to the last two points, the first of which (i.e., point 4) deals with the method by which a solution is to be achieved and the last (i.e., point 5) with the very nature of the solution.

As regards the fourth point, it is quite clear that for Buber the crux of the approach to overcoming the conflict centers on the fostering of trust between the two parties. For him, if a solution is to be achieved, it can be achieved only on the basis of trust. Thus, he rejects the considerations and calculations of *Realpolitik* in favor of building and fostering trust between the parties. And although he appreciates the fact that for trust to work it cannot be a one-way street but must be practiced by both sides, he nonetheless places the onus for its introduction and pursuance on the Jewish side inasmuch as he sees the Jews as the "interlopers" or the "intruders" who thus bring about the problematic. It is, therefore, according to him, up to the Jews to persuade the Arabs that they do not want to displace them or deprive them of all their lands. It is this pursuance of a policy which bases itself on trust rather than on self-interest and power, the policy which he calls "prophetic politics" or the politics of "biblical humanism," that he sets as the alternative to *Realpolitik*. For while policies pursued on the basis of *Realpolitik* are in his view clearly doomed to failure, a ray of hope and promise can be detected in policies based on "prophetic politics." He is, therefore, tireless in continuously criticizing the Jewish side for not doing more to assuage the fears of the Arabs and foster their trust.

What is one to say to this? Our fundamental criticism is that Buber's approach is unrealistic. First, it would seem to us that Buber misapprehends the real ground for the Arabs' opposition to the Jews. He seems to think that the Arabs' opposition is primarily motivated by their fear of being dispossessed, namely, by the fear of individual Arabs of losing their property. Now, if this were really so, then the other side could indeed do something to alleviate such fear. But this is not where the problem really lies. Individual Arabs, by and large, are not really afraid of losing their property and if, per chance, they were, it could easily be overcome. No, the real problem lies not on the individual but on the level of the collectivity. And here we have the intractable problem of the clash between collectivites—the natural refusal of any collectivity to share power with another and, indeed, the tendency of any collectivity to eject another from its midst. Thus, the real problem lies in the fact that the Arabs *qua* collectivity just cannot tolerate the presence of the Jewish collectivity in what they consider their land. And if this be the case, then there is really nothing that the other side can do to assuage the opposition, except commit suicide, i.e., give up its claim and remove itself altogether from the fray. Buber's call on the Jew, therefore, to foster trust in the Arab is not only unjust in placing the onus for the fostering of such trust primarily on the Jewish side, but it is also unfair in placing on the Jewish side a task that is not feasible. In calling on the Jew to perform a "mission impossible" Buber certainly assures himself of plenty of opportunity to criticize the Jewish side of failure but in truth it is he who should be criticized.

It seems to us that Buber's basic shortcoming in this whole matter lies precisely in his displacing realism with an illusory utopianism—a shortcoming which he so vigorously and devastatingly criticized when he encountered it in others. Essentially, Buber's mistake lies in his resorting to a mode of relating that is feasible in the context of the pure Thou-dimension (indeed in this dimension it is the only mode of relating that is feasible) and demanding that it be applied in a domain where the Thou-dimension is not the only dimension but is joined by the It-dimension. Namely, trust is indeed the only feasible mode of relating between beings who are constituted exclusively as Thou-beings. Thus, among angels trust is not only a feasible mode of relating but the necessary, inescapable mode of relating. And if indeed men were angels then Buber's advocacy of trust would be very much to the point and quite legitimate. But man is not an angel; he is not constituted exclusively as a pure Thou-being. Rather he is constituted as an It-Thou being and because of the presence of the It-dimension it is illusory and indeed dangerous to build exclusively on the basis of trust. Now, it is certainly in order and indeed legitimate to call for some degree of trust (after all, man is also constituted as a Thou-being); but in the last analysis one must build on the basis of the calculations of the It-dimension. And just because the prospects of settling the Israeli-Arab conflict when viewed in the context of *Realpolitik* are not too encouraging it is not a sufficient reason to advocate what Buber calls "prophetic politics."[12]

At the risk of sounding waggish, we may suggest that Buber's recommendation to pursue politics on the basis of trust rather than on the basis of achieving a balance of power or of interests (as *Realpolitik* would dictate) is, indeed, but a reflection of his belief that politics is not "the art of the possible" but rather that it is the "art of the impossible." Buber of course took this definition of politics seriously. It went hand in hand with his belief that "before moral necessity there is nothing impossible," for to the extent that politics were to be based on morality and seeing that before morality there is nothing impossible (this being so by virtue of the fact that in morality "you can because you will it") it follows that in politics too there is nothing impossible—hence the definition of politics as the art of the impossible. We would suggest, however, that Buber can build this syllogism and hence move from morality to politics only because he overlooks one important difference between morality and politics. Namely, while morality is built on intentions and as such is constituted in terms of the inner world of man, politics is built on overt actions and as such is constituted in terms of the outer world of the collectivity and the state. This difference should block a simple, mechanical, unquestioning transfer of characterizations from the domain of morality to the domain of politics: characterizations that may be valid in the domain of morality may be quite invalid in the domain of politics. Thus, for example, concerning the issue before us one could well argue that with respect to intentions, it is perfectly sensible to say that "you can because you will it," but that with respect to overt actions such a statement is nonsense—with respect to an overt action, I may well will something and, indeed, will it with inordinate strength and yet not be able to execute it. But if I cannot say that "you can because you will it" then I can also not claim that politics is the art of the impossible. No, politics is not the art of the impossible, though pursuing it on the basis of trust makes it an art that is impossible.

Finally, as regards the fifth and last point, i.e., the point concerning the nature of the solution to the conflict proposed by Buber, it would seem to us that Buber's favored solution of establishing a bi-national state is patently not a viable solution. For, first of all, speaking generally, a bi-national state is a recipe for trouble—it has always been so and it will always be so. It is a concoction that simply does not work. Indeed, we have any number of instances in which history has created what might be validly construed as a bi-national state, and in all these instances the result has been sheer trouble. Thus, take, for example, Cyprus (Greeks and Turks), Northern Ireland (Irish and Scots) or Canada (English and French). We should learn our lesson from the tragedies of these instances where today one is at a loss as to how to undo the harm and the suffering that such fait-accompli instances of bi-national entities present. Certainly, it would be not only the height of folly but morally reprehensible to go ahead after these experiences and create *de novum* a bi-national entity. It would be tantamount, to use the Yiddish adage, to ordering a healthy person into a sick bed.

But aside from such general considerations, the notion of a bi-national state is totally unviable from the specifically Jewish perspective because it fails to meet the pressing needs of either Judaism or of the Jews in the modern world. What do we mean? Well, let us keep in mind that with the proposal to create a bi-national state Buber also abdicates the need for the Jewish people to regain sovereignty in a clear-cut, exclusive manner; indeed he even rejects the need for it to attain a majority in the land. Now, logically, these abdications are quite consistent with each other and, indeed, they even entail one another. The basic abdication which, in turn, implicates the other is the abdication of the need for sovereignty. Thus, we would suggest that Buber could propose a bi-national state only because he already has abdicated or at least greatly minimized the need for sovereignty. Had he kept the need for sovereignty clearly before his eyes the bi-national state would not have been an acceptable solution. For in the same way that two persons cannot share the crown at the same time so two nations cannot share sovereignty at the same time. Whatever exact arrangement he might have had in mind when proposing the bi-national state (and it is not at all clear to me what indeed he did have in mind), it is crystal clear that in this type of arrangement the Jewish people could not possibly have the full range of the power of sovereignty at its disposal and this is, in our view, as will be made clear presently, the crux of the problematic in Buber's position. Likewise, Buber could reject the need for a majority only because he has already abdicated the need for sovereignty. For otherwise, had he been a proponent of sovereignty, he would have had to uphold the need for a majority in the land (for surely as a child of the modern world he readily recognized that in our day, democracy must be taken as non-negotiable, which means that sovereignty can be legitimately established only on the basis of a majority).[13]

These positions, by the way, are not espoused by Buber accidentally or haphazardly. Rather, they clearly reflect, and are very consistent with, the fact that Buber in his Zionist views and activity was very much influenced by the orientation of Ahad Ha-Am. Indeed, Buber's readiness to abdicate sovereignty and to reject the need for a majority are quite consistent with Ahad Ha-Am's view of what constituted the Jewish predicament in the modern world for which Zionism was to be the answer. For if, as Ahad Ha-Am maintained, the predicament is diagnosed to lie in the disintegration of the cultural heritage of Judaism, i.e. in the inability to sustain and foster it in the circumstances of the modern world, due to the wide-spread assimilation of the Jews in consequence of the Emancipation, then indeed the solution by which to overcome this predicament does not have to entail the need for sovereignty or for a majority. Basically what is called for by the inner logic of this position is just for a sufficient concentration of Jews in one place so as to counteract the pull to assimilation. There is a need for a "critical mass" but not necessarily for a majority and certainly not for sovereignty. Thus, Buber's readiness to abdicate or, at least, mitigate the requirement for sovereignty and for a majority should not be all that surprising or outrageous if one keeps in mind that his Zionism was greatly influenced by the "cultural Zionism" of Aḥad Ha-Am.[14]

But this, of course, would not necessarily change the fact that from the Jewish viewpoint (indeed, both from the perspective of Judaism and from the perspective of the Jewish people) such an abdication of sovereignty is really untenable. It may well only underlie the conclusion that not only Buber but also Aḥad Ha-Am has failed to fully grasp the Jewish predicament on this point, and this notwithstanding their undisputed perceptiveness into many other facets of the phenomenon of Judaism. Thus, it would seem that not only Buber but also Aḥad Ha-Am failed to really appreciate the problematic when it was precipitated in terms of the very physical survivability of the Jews in Diaspora-existence in view of the rise of modern nationalism and its concomitant modern anti-Semitism. Buber does not seem to have devoted much thinking in this direction.[15] He seems to have been much more occupied with the problematic as it precipitated itself in terms of Judaism rather than of the Jews. And likewise with Aḥad Ha-Am although he seems to have been also concerned to some extent with the question of the survival of the Jews (but here too, his concern with the problematic centers predominantly on its aspect of assimilation rather than on its aspect of physical rejection or annihilation as a result of modern anti-Semitism). But the aspect of physical rejection or annihilation is a real and most pressing problem for Jewry in the modern world (is this not the real lesson of the Holocaust?). It is a problem that clearly goes to the very heart, to the very essence, of the Jewish phenomenon and that as such must take precedence over any other and cannot be ignored or tolerated by the Jewish people or by anyone who is concerned with the viability of this phenomenon. Now, this problem, given the way the world is, can be overcome only if sovereignty can be regained by the Jewish people. In the context of the circumstances of the modern world (i.e., in the context of the rise of modern nationalism and anti-Semitism on the one hand, and the emancipation of the Jews on the other) the prospects for Jewish survival in a mode of existence that is exclusively Diaspora-existence and does not include sovereignty are threatened in a most serious way. For the Jews to survive in this new set of circumstances, which constitutes the modern world, they must regain sovereignty and as such this must indeed become for them an essential task that is simply not negotiable.[16] Thus, when Buber's proposed solution to the conflict abdicates on the part of the Jewish side this claim to exclusive sovereignty, it cannot possibly be embraced by the Jewish side.

And not only this. Buber's proposed solution of a bi-national state runs foul not only of the question of the possibility of Jewish survival in the modern world but also of the further question of what the full and authentic expression of Judaism requires. Namely, even if one were to disagree with our analysis above and so not accept our contention that Jewish survival in the modern world requires the regaining of sovereignty by the Jews, one would still be faced with our further contention that Buber's proposed solution would not allow the full and authentic expression of that structure-of-faith, of that of *Weltanschauung*, whose concrete, historical expression we know as mainstream Judaism.[17] For in this structure-of-faith the vocation which is assigned to the community is to ultimately establish itself as a righteous community on this earth (in the religious language this was articulated as the establishment of the "kingdom of heaven" upon this earth). And this being the case, the fundamental requirement *sine qua non* for the community must be for it to possess sovereignty. For without possessing sovereignty the community cannot even begin to carry out its vocation to establish itself as a righteous community;

indeed, how can it if it does not possess the power to regulate its life (and sovereignty is nothing else but the possession of such power)?[18] Thus, if the return to the land is to have meaning not only in terms of the needs and interests of the Jews but also in terms of the needs and interests of Judaism, the regaining of sovereignty becomes doubly essential, thus making its abdication by the Jewish side even less feasible.

Indeed, it is very surprising that Buber failed to see the need for the regaining of sovereignty. That he failed to see it in terms of the needs and requirements of the Jewish people may be perhaps understandable. Maybe he lived too close to the Holocaust and so, although he lived through it, he was not in a position to be affected by the full force of its implications (it takes time for such matters to sink in) and thus remained, in the last analysis, a child of the sanguine spirit of the pre-Holocaust era. And in any event Buber's thoughts in this matter were really centered on the analysis of the predicament and needs of the Jewish people—he was never really a political Zionist of the ilk of Herzl or Nordau. But that he failed to see it in terms of the needs and requirements of Judaism is a puzzle. For after all, Buber's Zionism was very much generated by his concern for the renewal of Judaism. One could not argue that Buber's thought was not involved and, indeed, heavily involved (practically throughout his life) with the needs and requirements of Judaism. And to deepen the puzzle even more, there can be no denying that it is Buber who, perhaps more than anyone else, perceived and persistently and eloquently expressed the fact that the fundamental religious vocation of Judaism is to establish the righteous community. But if this is so, if Buber was deeply aware of the need for the renewal of Judaism and also fully cognizant of the fact that the vocation of Judaism lies in the establishment of the righteous community, how could he have possibly failed to see that the attainment of sovereignty must be a non-negotiable item for the Jewish side of the conflict? This is the puzzle. It only goes to show that even a "giant" may falter on occasion.

NOTES

1. This, by the way, would not only give the proposed critique much more force and poignancy (seeing that a critique which can be raised on the same assumptions and presuppositions as those which underlie the object of the criticism is so much more telling and powerful in its thrust than a critique which bases itself on altogether different assumptions and presuppositions), but it would also be aesthetically and even ethically more fitting with respect to Buber's position on the Jewish-Arab conflict. For such a critique would parallel Buber's own critique of Zionism, namely, his critique of the Jewish claim which precipitates the Jewish-Arab conflict. This is so, seeing that Buber's views on the Jewish-Arab conflict always constituted a critique of the position of Zionism, and indeed, a critique that claimed to be internal and not external to the very values and presuppositions on which Zionism is built. Buber was a lifelong Zionist joining the movement in its inception when he was a young adult, and remained a Zionist until his last day. Yet, at the same time, from the beginning and continuing to his last day, there was also always a tension between his position and that of the movement—he was always occupying the position which he himself described as that of the "loyal opposition," i.e., the position of the critic (to wit, the "opposition"), but always the critic who pursues his criticism from the inside (to wit, "loyal"). Thus, our critique of Buber's position, if successful, would emulate Buber's critique of the position of Zionism; hopefully we can challenge Buber in the same way that he challenged Zionism.

2. Thus, while Buber's position is clearly valid for Judaism, the diametrically opposite position, espoused by a number of the leading intellectual figures in post-World War I Germany, e.g., Max Weber and H. Meinecke, whereby politics is to be distinguished and separated from ethics (the former being an aspect pertaining exclusively to the collectivity while the latter is an aspect pertaining exclusively to the individual), may well be valid with respect to the "nations of the world."

3. In this connection it is interesting to note that in point of fact Jewry is the only ethnic-national entity which has been called upon to submit its most elemental right, the right of existence, to moral scrutiny. No other ethnic-national entity has had to justify its claim to its homeland, i.e., its claim to its very existence, on ethical grounds. For all other ethnic-national enti-

ties such a claim is, in the last analysis, grounded exclusively in power. As such, we do encounter here a clear instance of the uniqueness of the Jewish ethnic-national entity.

4. Before leaving this point it should be noted that the Arabs' right to the land is grounded exclusively in the act of possession. But the possession was initially effected exclusively by force. There can be no denying that when the Arab-Muslim waves were gushing forth from the Arabian peninsula in the seventh century and sweeping through the whole of the Middle East and North Africa, the Arabs established their rights exclusively by brute force. It was the sword or Islam—a grounding that would hardly pass the scrutiny of ethics. True, this was the way of the world at the time, and the vast majority of all other ethnic-national groups did exactly the same. Still, it does not change the fact that the Arabs' rights are based on an act of possession which, in turn, is ultimately grounded exclusively in sheer force. But even more, this act of possession was lost by the Arabs to the Turks in the fifteenth century—the Turks, by the same resort to force, prevailed upon the Arabs and established their right of possession. Thus, for the last four centuries the Arabs' right to the land is not, strictly speaking, grounded in the act of possession but merely in the act of residency. And even as far as the act of residency is concerned, they never constituted the sole, exclusive residents of the land. There were always a handful of Jews residing beside them. Thus, strictly speaking, the Arabs' right to the land is grounded in the fact that they constituted the preponderant majority of the residents of the land. Still, we would not want to have all these qualifications and reservations be construed as if they deprived the Arabs of a right to the land; all we have tried to do is to sort things out and to establish this right as precisely as we can. And what we come up with is that the right is grounded in the fact that the Arabs constituted the preponderant majority of the residents of the land. This does not deprive the Arabs of the right to the land but it certainly throws a different light on the counter-claim of rights on the part of the Jews. For now it is not a question any more of possession and dispossession but rather a question of safeguarding the status and privileges of a majority against the intrusion of a previous minority which is trying to become a majority. The ethical judgment of this latter situation must be radically different from the ethical judgment of the former situation. So the various qualifications and reservations that were introduced above

were not mere quibblings or pedantry. Indeed, this clarification is needed, seeing that Buber and, for that matter, most other people who readily grant the Arabs' right to the land, do not spell out precisely on what grounds that right is established. They seem to take it for granted as if it were self-evident. But evidently this is not necessarily the case.

5. Unfortunately, it would seem that this tendency to minimize or disregard or readily concede points and considerations that are supportive of the Jewish side in the conflict is characteristic of Buber's handling of the matter throughout, and we will have occasion to encounter it again below.

6. The fact that the Arabs too, in turn, have come to possess the land through force, i.e., through the conquest of the land from some other people, would not, it seems to us, affect the ethical consideration of the case. Namely, the argument that the Jewish possession of the land should have no standing in any ethical consideration of the issue because the Jews initially came into possession of the land by means that are not ethical, i.e., the use of force, is not legitimate. For if this were the case then the issue of a right to a land or of a possession of a land would simply not lend itself to ethical evaluation, seeing that there would not be a single concrete case where a valid claim from the ethical perspective for possession of a land could be made, inasmuch as in every case before us today possession has been attained and established by the resort to force. But just because something was originally established by resorting to means that are not acceptable to the ethical perspective does not mean that the ethical perspective cannot be involved, i.e., may not be applied, with respect to problems which may arise subsequently. Where the resort to force may enter the ethical calculus and vitiate the ethical justification of a claim to the possession of a land is only in the case where the victims of such a resort to power are still around, and this is clearly not the case with respect to the Jewish claim to the Land of Israel. The Canaanites and Amorites and the Jebusites and all the other people who originally lived on the land are not around today; if they were, the picture would be quite different.

7. And since the victim of this resort to brute force *is* around today, the act should have a bearing on our ethical considerations and evaluations.

8. This is an important point to stress. For otherwise it could have been argued that had the Jews forgotten the land, this could have been taken as signifying their abdication. And if this were the case, then the land would

have been after all freed for its next possessor even though the original act of dispossession remains invalid and unacceptable from the ethical vantage point. But this clearly has not been the case.

9. Of course, what would constitute innocence may be a very hard point to decide in some instances, and in such instances we may well have legitimate differences of opinion. But we need not enter into a discussion of this issue at this point.

10. By the way, it is interesting to note that while in recent years one has come to hear more and more about the demand for the redistribution of wealth among nations (especially with respect to the discrepancy between the first and the third world), this demand, as far as we know, has not been in any way applied to the discrepancy between the fortunes of the Jewish nation and that of the Arab nations, even though the discrepancy here is so much more distressing and offensive—a discrepancy not merely in terms of wealth, i.e., in terms of the standard of living, of the material comfort available, but in terms of life and death, i.e., in terms where one side is threatened by demise for lack of space while the other possesses unbelievable opulence and excess both in space and wealth.

11. On this point we agree with Buber, though we differ with him on the relative "weight" to be assigned to each side. While Buber is much more appreciative of the Arab claim, we are much more appreciative of the Jewish claim. Also, while Buber thinks in terms of finding the "best" solution in these circumstances we are much less sanguine and would attempt to find the least evil alternative. In these circumstances there cannot be a good solution, only an evil one, and so the aim must be to find the least evil solution possible. The difference between the two approaches may be only one of emphasis, yet it is important in revealing the state of mind and the "coloring" through which the issues before us are perceived.

12. Indeed the name "prophetic politics" in this context is doing the prophets an injustice. True, the prophets did preach in terms of trust but the trust they were speaking of was clearly a trust in God, a being constituted exclusively as a Thou, and not a trust in fellow man. Indeed, the prophets explicitly warned the Israelis against trusting the nations that surround them.

13. Buber, however, did not only reject the need for a majority; he actually expected that not too many Jews would reside in the land, and, what is even more significant, he accepted this anticipation quite willingly.

14. Still, it would seem that Buber even goes beyond Ahad Ha-Am in moderating his requirements. Thus, while the inner logic of Ahad Ha-Am's position at least requires that there should be a concentration of many Jews in the land, Buber opts not to insist on this requirement. I think the reason for this divergency lies in the fact that while in the thought of Ahad Ha-Am the stress is on the viability or the preservation of the cultural heritage (and as such the attainment of a "critical mass" of Jews in one place is clearly indicated), Buber's thought is not so much concerned with the preservation as with the renewal of the cultural heritage of Judaism, and this does not necessarily require the concentration of a large number of Jews in one place. And what is perhaps even more relevant to the rationale we are trying to offer is the fact that Buber views such renewal as very much connected to the establishment of an intimate linkage with the land. In other words, Buber is not only sympathetic to the position of Ahad Ha-Am but he is also very sympathetic to the cosmological-mystical position of A. D. Gordon. For while for the preservation of a cultural heritage, the presence of a viable community is required, and consequently a certain "critical mass" of its members being concentrated in a specific place is called for, the renewal of a cultural heritage in terms of establishing an intimate link to a specific land really requires only individuals (it is the work of individuals and not of a collectivity), and as such, there is no pressing need to attain the concentration of a "critical mass" in a specific place.

15. This is particularly strange if one keeps in mind the times through which Buber lived; but the fact remains. True, in a way Buber was very much involved with the problematic but this, of course, was inevitable. Much more significantly (and this is really the ground for our observation), his involvement was by and large with the question of securing refuge for victims of the problematic. And this cannot be taken as grappling with the problematic in an effort to overcome it: rather it is tantamount to accepting it and merely attempting to accommodate to its effects.

16. We should be clear, however, that this does not mean that all Jews must live under Jewish sovereignty, i.e., in a Jewish state. Our analysis does not at all lead to this radical Zionist demand. It is more minimalist. It requires only that a Jewish state be in existence, while allowing the possibility of there being at the same time Jews living outside such a state. Similarly, while it requires that there be a state with exclusive

Jewish sovereignty, in principle it does not require any particular extent for the borders of such a state. Thus, whether borders should be in conformity with one of the biblical delineations, or with the delineation of the League of Nations, or the British Mandate, or the U.N. resolution of 1947, or the Armistice of 1949, or the war of 1967, or whatever is really not essential. Any borders would in principle do. The extent of the borders enters the picture only secondarily in terms of such questions as the security or the viability of the state.

17. We have in mind the prophetic expression in the biblical period and the non-mystical halakhic expression in the rabbinic period.
18. The rabbis must have known this albeit instinctively and subconsciously for they viewed Diaspora-existence not only as a punishment for the Jews, but as a state of affairs in which the religious expression of Judaism must per force remain truncated.

6. Buber's Socialist and Political Views: A Critique

Benjamin Uffenheimer

Martin Buber is one of the most controversial, paradoxical and fascinating figures in the Jewish world of the twentieth century. He has had a deep impact on Jewish thinking and research, on Zionism and on the Christian world alike. It is paradoxical that while Christians all over the world admire him as the most authentic representative of Judaism, he remains a bone of contention in Jewish circles. Nevertheless, his work and his personality undoubtedly reflect the deep, revolutionary changes undergone by the Jewish people in this century. Indeed, when he published his volume of essays, *Ein Kampf um Israel* (*Reden und Aufsaetze*, 1921–1932), in the early thirties, he could not yet guess the apocalyptic and messianic dimensions this struggle for Israel would assume in the decades which followed; his involvement in these events left a deep imprint on his role as a Jewish philosopher and teacher.

In reviewing the life and work of Martin Buber, we shall focus our attention on three issues which are closely interrelated: 1) Buber's impact on Jewish thinking and Jewish studies in this century; 2)

Buber's socialism and its sources; 3) the influence of Buber's socialist views on his approach to the political problems of Zionism. In conclusion, we shall offer some critical remarks on Buber's Zionism in the light of modern Jewish history.

Let me begin with a short description of Buber's impact on modern Jewish thinking and research. His paradoxical uniqueness lies in the fact that he was a Jewish religious thinker who rejected the Halakha, the very core of traditional Judaism, as petrified and irrelevant. He believed in revelation, but explained it in general terms of inspiration, with no concrete content whatsoever. He was brought up in the spirit of Jewish tradition until the age of fourteen in the home of his grandfather, Shlomo Buber. After graduation from the Polish high school in Lemberg, however, he plunged into the depths of Western, and especially German, culture, and wandered aimlessly for some years as a student of philosophy, psychology and art at the universities of Vienna and Berlin. He returned to his Jewish identity in 1898, at the age of twenty, when he joined the Zionist movement. Owing to his Jewish background, his Zionism was quite different from that of post-assimilatory Jews like Herzl and Nordau, who aimed at changing the political situation of the Jewish people mainly by diplomatic and organizational efforts. Unlike their so-called political Zionism, which was engendered by growing anti-Semitism, Buber was motivated by his vision of the revival of Jewish culture, which had taken shape already in modern Hebrew literature, and the establishment of an ideal society of justice, human equality and creativity in Eretz Israel. The new Jew, the Halutz, the pioneer of the Land of Israel, was destined to bring about these changes by his creative spontaneity, aroused by his daily work on the soil of Eretz Israel.

Buber's personal involvement in the Jewish renaissance movement resulted in two epoch-making oeuvres, his studies on Hasidism and the bible. The common trait of both these scholarly contributions to Jewish studies is their inherent quest for relevancy to our present situation, which he explained in terms of his existential philosophy of dialogue. Much has been written on the greatness and weakness of both works, and on their close ties with his philosophical and social convictions. But even his critics admit that his new understanding of the Hasidic sources and the bible contains challenging repercussions which reach far beyond the arbitrament of factual scholarship. In his Hasidic writings,[1] he introduces the Western and Western-Jewish world to a movement which was despised by the rationalistically minded nineteenth-century *Wissenschaft des Judentums*, thus paving the way to a positive approach to the irrationalistic trends which have contributed to the spirit of Judaism over the ages. This sympathizing hermeneutics of Hasidism ushered in a new era in Jewish studies which recognized the centrality of Jewish mysticism for the understanding of Judaism, as exemplified by G. Scholem and his school. In his biblical studies,[2] Buber emphasized the peculiar traits of the biblical mode of expression, focusing his attention on what he called "Leitwort" or "Leitmotif" for the understanding of biblical prose, poetry and prophetic discourse. He contended that the biblical writers used this literary device in order to allude to their moral tendencies, which in turn had a deep impact on Buber's social and political philosophy.

Buber's approach to the problem of "man and society" was grounded in his general disappointment with the militant nature of modern nationalism, which kindled World War I and gave rise to the various socialist movements with their inherent universalistic tendencies. His social thinking was influenced by religious socialism on the one hand,[3] and by the work of Ferdinand Toennies and his friend, Gustav Landauer (murdered in 1919), on the other.

A central problem tackled by Buber time and again in his social and political writings over six decades was the relationship between morality and politics. This also influenced his interpretation of Zionism and his assessment of the Jewish-Arab conflict which has haunted the Zionist enterprise in the Land of Israel since its beginnings one hundred years ago.

In this context, Buber rejected the basic approach of two outstanding German scholars, the sociologist Max Weber[4] and the historian Friedrich Meinecke,[5] who contended that the realm of politics should be separated from ethics. In their view, politics was the art of promoting collective interests according to the principles of utility and raison d'état, whereas ethical values were valid exclusively in the relations between individuals. Weber forged two basic conceptions: *Verant-wortungsethik* or morality based on accountability, being the principle of the politician, and *Intentionsmoral* or morality based on intentions and absolute values valid only in interpersonal relationships. Buber argued that man is an indivisible unity, a living entity whose actions are determined by his character, his views, his principles and the situation in which he finds himself. In this respect, religious and moral values are bound to influence his political decisions; otherwise he would be "devoured by the political principle"[6] in which human values are no longer valid. Roughly speaking, the political principle implies that public regimes are the "legitimate determinants of human existence" (op. cit.). Here truth is no longer dealt with in religious or metaphysical terms as something absolute. It is not defined in terms of individual relativity, i.e., "right is what is advantageous to me," but in terms of collective relativity, i.e., "right is what is advantageous to the people," which actually means "advantageous to the brutal power interests of the ruler or the ruling clique." During this century, in two terrible world wars and in numerous acts of genocide, including the Holocaust, this separation of morality from politics was bound to open a demonic abyss. Practically speaking, this separation is based on a misuse of ideologies like socialism and nationalism. Today it is Muslim fundamentalism which operates in the same way, misusing religious slogans for the benefit of ruthless power politics.

The positive starting point of Buber's social and political philosophy is the basic relationship between man and his neighbor—what Buber calls the Dialogue, which also involves a social principle with political implications.

In his early writings, Buber based his distinction between what he later called the social and political principles on two concepts taken from the work of the German sociologist Ferdinand Toennies (1887) *Gemeinschaft und Gesellschaft*—society and community. Toennies differentiates between an artificial-mechanical and an organic formation. "Society" denotes the mechanical order of self-seeking individuals held together by force, compromise, convention and common interests. Each member is occupied with his own private business, which often degenerates into mutual hostility. Marxism, the dominant form of modern socialism, seeks to overcome this atomization of present-day life by absorbing everything into the power of the state, thus completing the modern process from community to society and choking spontaneous, genuine relationships between man and man. Unlike Marx, who explains the deformation of modern capitalist society by economic factors exclusively, Buber contends that the basic factor is the degeneration of fundamental human relationships outside the economic sphere. "Community," on the other hand, is a natural group bound together by kinship, religion, common ideals, the development of close personal friendship and brotherhood. It goes without saying that Buber's socialism aims at the restructuring of community, of close, direct relationships between men and groups, based on common possession and human openness.

The anarchistic socialism of Buber's friend Gustav Landauer was also a source of inspiration. In his treatise *Aufruf zum Sozialismus* ("Call to Socialism"), Landauer proclaimed that the ultimate aim was the transformation of humanity into a "community of communities." Buber associated himself wholeheartedly with this kind of socialism, which he conceived would be established outside the state in a decentralized social-organic setting. Far from being part of a "political program," the emergence of community would rather involve immediate and direct action by people who would undertake to live their lives according to an ideal. Buber's concept of realization is crucial in this context, bearing witness to the universalist, messianic expectations which motivated both Landauer and himself. The social utopia envisaged here is based on the antithesis of mechanical-organical, word-deed, intellectual synthesis-actual living. Substantially, these ideas, which had already been propounded by Proudhon and Kropotkin (see Buber's *Paths in Utopia*, chap. 5, pp. 38–45), were born of a deep mistrust of the state and its institutions. Both Landauer and Buber were aware that an organic community had never been fully realized except on a small scale and on virgin soil. The exception alluded to by Buber was the collective and communal settlements of

Eretz Israel, the *moshavim* and *kibbutzim*, which he characterized in *Paths in Utopia* as a "paradigmatic non-failure." It was his deep conviction that the new community developing in Eretz Israel should be structured in line with the organic principles of socialism. These village communes were based on local needs rather than on abstract ideas and theories, but, at the same time, they successfully integrated ideal motives inspired by socialist and biblical teachings on social justice. In 1952, Buber said: "The coming state of humanity in the great crisis depends very much on whether another type of socialism can be set up against Moscow, and I venture even today to call it Jerusalem" (from an address on Israel at the Jewish Theological Seminary in New York City, 1/4/1952).

Buber was aware that the "community of communities" was a utopia which must wait until all men are endowed with the spirit of mutual openness, love, and the ability to maintain direct, genuine relationships with others. But in this unredeemed world, where the forces of evil still threaten the lives of individuals and groups, and where man is expected to be loyal whenever the vital interests of his group are at stake, violence remains unavoidable. The question which haunted Buber in this context is the dilemma of personal morality versus the needs of the group, man's distress when confronted with the collision of duties arising from his existential situation. How to act in a given situation?

Buber has no clear-cut answer at his disposal. He is hesitant, contending that there are no rigid dogmatic laws and no abstract rules for political behavior. In every concrete situation, man must make his decision taking into account the vital needs of his group, its power interests, and his duties to the absolute. Buber calls this narrow ridge between conflicting duties the "demarcation line." One cannot do more than make an honest effort to realize the good in the deformity of public life, where group interests demand one's loyalty. Buber speaks about *quantum satis*. I quote:

> *Quantum satis* means in the language of lived truth not "either-or" but
> "as much as one can". . . . Here there is no "once-for-all," for each

situation demands decision. The demarcation line between service and service must be drawn anew—not necessarily with fear, but necessarily with that trembling of the soul that precedes any genuine decision. ("Validity and Limitation of the Political Principle," *Pointing the Way*, 1953, p. 217.)

This is the general ethical and sociological setting of Buber's personal involvement in Zionist politics. When faced with Arab hostility to Zionism and the State of Israel, however, his personal romantic convictions and the necessities of the harsh, sometimes cruel reality, were bound to clash. To use his own terminology, he often placed the "demarcation line" very far from that of general Zionist consensus. Or, to quote Scholem's vivid, lapidary statement upon taking leave of Buber at his open grave: "He was a great thinker—without a system, a great teacher—without disciples, a man of advice—whom no one took heed of."

Indeed, Buber would have willingly endorsed the first two lines. He was not interested in abstract dogmatic philosophical systems; nor did he seek disciples in the classical sense. All he wanted was to teach people to approach reality open-mindedly and without prejudice. Buber's possible consent to the third line seems to be implied in one of his last talks with Ernst Simon. "What will people think of me after my passing away?" he was heard asking himself. "Perhaps he was one of the last utopians," came the reply.

Before entering into a detailed analysis of Buber's political approach let me briefly enumerate the main points of his position:[7] 1) Politics should be subject to ethical standards; 2) The Jews must also recognize the Arab rights to the land; 3) Jewish rights to the land cannot be based either on biblical revelation or on historical claim; 4) A solution can only be achieved on the basis of trust; 5) The best solution under the circumstances, i.e., the solution which is ethically most justified, is the creation of a bi-national state.

As a matter of fact, these were more or less the guidelines of *Brit Shalom*, an elitist group of professors and prominent personalities who were deeply involved in the Zionist work in Eretz Israel. This group was established by the founder and president of the Hebrew University, Dr. Judah Leib Magnes. Owing to the high standing and merits of these men, their influence on public opinion and in particular on the mandatory government was disproportionate to the actual size of the group. In a certain sense, the "Peace Now" movement in Israel, whose influence on the Labor movement should not be underestimated, took over the political heritage of this group. It would seem that a painstaking analysis of Buber's political Zionist views in light of the present situation is therefore worthwhile.

The first point, that politics should be subject to ethical standards, has been the traditional dictum in the war of defense waged by the Zionists ever since the days of the Hashomer group. That the Israel Defense Forces continue to uphold the self-contradicting concept of "purity of arms" (*tohar hanesheq*) is further witness of this. In Judaism the ethnic-national dimension is in its very essence subject to the religious dimension, and the religious dimension is to a large extent ethically oriented. As we have seen in the foregoing discussion, Western social philosophers would not have subscribed to this approach. In fact, much of the ruthless aggressiveness of our Arab enemies springs from their religiously oriented politics. They explain their religion in nationalistic terms, a fact which is very important for an understanding of the behavior of the Arab countries towards each other, towards Israel, and towards the rest of the world. Contemporary Judaism, for better or worse, is far from sanctioning a militant mentality of this type. Ever since the establishment of the State of Israel, we have agreed to submit the claims and political tactics of the Jewish war of defense to the scrutiny of ethics. Hundreds of statements by Weizmann, Ben-Gurion, Berl Katzenelson, Jabotinsky, etc., the behavior of our forces in battle, as well as the general trend of our educational system bear witness to this humane mentality.

As for the second point, that it is incumbent upon the Jews to recognize the Arab rights to the land, we ask: what kind of rights? Buber did not spell out precisely on what grounds that right is established. He took it for granted, as if it were self-evident. We must make it clear, however, that the Arabs' claim to the land was founded exclusively on the act of possession. This possession was initially effected by brutal force, as waves of Muslim Arabs from the Arabian peninsula gushed forth in the seventh century, conquering the whole of the Middle East and North Africa. Nevertheless, the Arabs never constituted the sole inhabitants of the land; there was always a Jewish minority living beside them. So, strictly speaking, if the Arabs have any claim, it is that they were the preponderant majority. This does not deprive the Arabs of their rights, but it throws a different light on the counter-claim of rights on the part of the Jews. For now it is not a question of possession and dispossession but rather of safeguarding the status and privileges of a majority faced with the intrusion of a former minority which claims to have been the original possessor of the land. Ethically, this situation must be judged very differently.

In moving to the third point, which refers to our right to the Land of Israel, Buber raises three arguments applying to the past, the present and the future (cf. "The National Home and the National Policy of Palestine" in Mendes-Flohr, 81–91). He starts by refuting what we generally call historic rights. His contention is that every chapter in world history which is used for justifying a certain claim was preceded by another chapter which in turn may support a quite different, even conflicting claim. Consequently, it is impossible to define a right in terms of time. On the other hand, he underscored that there exists an ancient *link* between Israel and its land which resulted in "a perpetual good for all of humankind" (op. cit., 84). Thus he seems to be alluding to what the bible called Israel's election.

In attempting to render this idea in secular terms he cites the unique link between Israel and its land, insisting that this resulted in the moral consciousness of bearing a special message of universal dimensions, or "a perpetual good for all of humankind." This reasoning is in line with exegesis of the prophecies of Amos (cf. Buber, *The Prophetic Faith* [New York, 1949], pp. 96–110). Amos maintained that the core of this idea is Israel's unique moral accountability (Amos 3:1–8). Buber's contention as to the repercussions of Israel's ancient link with its land is his first argument in this context. The second relates to the creative pioneering work which is going on in the present, transforming a wasteland into a settled country through years of hard manual labor. This enterprise also takes into consideration the needs of the Arab inhabitants. The third argument applies to the future: the new settlements in Eretz Israel being grasped as the beginning of a worldwide social revolution, a concrete social transformation of interpersonal relations amounting to a restructuring of human society. Indeed, this position of Buber, which had a certain affinity with the romantic, cosmological approach of A. D. Gordon, had a deep impact on the pioneers during the first decades of this century. Its weakness, however, became evident when the other side, the Arabs, refused to acknowledge this link between Israel and Palestine, being completely disinterested in the "permanent good for humankind" inherent in it. Thus, it was obvious that the subjectivist argumentation and Buber's abdication of the objective-historical right was haphazard. Moreover, our historical claim, far from being founded on a single arbitrary chapter or event, as Buber contends, is rather the outcome of 3,000 years of Jewish history, including 2,000 years of life in the Diaspora, during which the Jews repeated three times a day the supplication to return to Zion, and never ceased to live in Eretz Israel as a minority. Again, when the Arabs refused to recognize the legitimacy of the Zionist return, rejecting also the benefits it now bestowed upon them, the Zionist argumentation had to take recourse to the basic objective fact of the homelessness of the Jewish people and its need for a homeland on this earth. In this context, the claim of historical rights amounts to redressing a wrong which has already lasted for 2,000 years.

If one adds to this the fact that the position of the Jews in the Diaspora had become totally untenable, to the point of their existence being threatened, while the Arabs owned vast tracts of land far beyond their need, the ethical equation tilts even further in favor of the Jewish claim. We acknowledge the moral right of any individual or collectivity whose life is in danger to do all it can to save itself with the exception of depriving another innocent party of its life. On the other hand, our conscience would not allow us to let an individual die of starvation while others wallow in needless luxury. The same holds true for collectivities. How can we allow one nation to perish for lack of space or food, when other nations have more than they know what to do with?

Now let us consider the last two points, which deal with the method of achieving a solution of the conflict and the very nature of its solution. It is quite clear that for Buber, the crux of the problem is fostering trust between the parties. He rejects calculations of *Realpolitik* in favor of building good faith. In practice, he places the onus on the Jews, inasmuch as he sees them as the "intruders" and the source of the problem. It is the Jews who should pursue a policy based on trust rather than self-interest and power in order to persuade the Arabs that they do not want to displace them or deprive them of all their lands. This is what Buber calls "prophetic politics" or the "politics of biblical humanism."

Let us demonstrate the practical consequences Buber drew from his basic position. Even in the beginning, when the Allied powers met in Paris in January 1919 and were still sympathetic toward the Zionist cause, Buber warned his fellow Zionists about leaning too much on the imperialist powers instead of searching for ways to come to terms with the Arab peoples (Mendes-Flohr 39–41, taken from *Der Jude*), in particular with the exploited working class, the fellahin. In an essay written in 1920, he argues that Arab hostility to Zionism was but a cunning contrivance of the effendis, the wealthy Arab landowners (Mendes-Flohr 44–46). Therefore he calls upon the Zionist leadership to eschew Britain's patronage, and to forge an alliance with the Arab masses. Before the twelfth Zionist congress which convened in Karlsbad (Czechoslovakia) on September 1–4, 1921, in the gloomy atmosphere of the Arab disturbances with their acts of atrocity, he delivered a lengthy academic address, reminding the congress to avoid the posture of self-righteous egocentric nationalism. These reprimanding allusions annoyed Berl Katzenelson, the representative of the pioneering workers. Impassionately he contended:

> The quest for peaceful co-existence with the Arabs is not new. The Jewish worker has [always] sought to foster humane relations between Jews and Arabs . . . For the time being, however, there is still a great distance between us. Before we can draw the Arab [masses] close to us

in peace [we must acknowledge] that our life is in danger. Moreover, we must secure life and property; only then will we be able to negotiate an understanding with the Arabs. To those who preach morality [to the *Yishuv*] we have only one thing to say: Come to Eretz Israel and prove that you could establish more amicable relations with the Arabs than we have . . . It is clear to us that the movement's important political work in the present is: renewal of Jewish immigration to Palestine, the fostering of Halutziut, that is the pioneering spirit, the strengthening of our self-defense and the consolidation of our position in Palestine. (Mendes-Flohr 7–8).

Here the self-realizing Zionism of the working pioneers challenged Buber's patronizing, reprimanding posture, demanding that he join this great enterprise and become personally involved in it instead of preaching. Katzenelson insisted that Zionist priorities could not be compromised and their realization could not be made contingent on the chimerical hope of Arab consent to the Zionist enterprise. Buber denounced this approach as *Realpolitik* stemming from self-righteous egocentric nationalism. For Katznelson and the pioneers in Eretz Israel who faced the day-to-day dangers, this was the only way to survive and to take a stand against Arab violence.

The gap between Buber and the *Ihud* on the one hand, and the Labor movement, *Mapai*, on the other, deepened during and after World War II. The bone of contention was the so-called Biltmore Program (May 1942), in which the Zionist movement declared the establishment of a Jewish state in Eretz Israel to be its immediate aim after the war. The urgency of this decision was broadly accepted by public opinion after the war when the diabolic dimensions of the Holocaust shocked the Jewish people and close to two million survivors lingering in the refugee camps of Europe were desperately knocking at the locked doors of Eretz Israel. But Buber and the *Ihud* together with the leftist *Hashomer Hatzair* movement fervently opposed this program. In 1947, Buber still wrote:

The cleansing of the Jewish-Arab atmosphere is much more difficult today than it was only a few years ago. Above all, this is the result of an entirely fictitious program, which does not comprise any possibility of realization, and which relinquishes the realistic Zionism of toil and reconstruction—the Biltmore Program. This program interpreted as admitting the aim of a minority to "conquer" the country by means of international maneuvers has . . . aroused Arab anger against Zionism . . ." ("The Bi-National Approach to Zionism" in Mendes-Flohr.)

During those days when the *Yishuv* was fighting for free immigration in order to save the survivors of the Holocaust and in order to consolidate its own demographic situation, representatives of the *Ihud* proposed a compromise solution to "moderate" Arab leaders, the Nashashibi family, to assent to a yearly immigration quota of 30,000 Jews—a proposal which was immediately turned down.

These examples may suffice in order to demonstrate that Buber's "line of demarcation" was far away from that of the Zionist movement. It seems that he misapprehended the real grounds for Arab opposition. If it were primarily motivated by the fear of dispossession of certain individuals, something could be done to alleviate and assuage this fear. But no, this is not where the real problem lies. We are not dealing with the individual but the collectivity. The Arabs as a group cannot tolerate the presence of a Jewish collectivity on what they consider their land, "their holy Arab soil," to put it in Sadat's language. This position has come to the fore time and again in our generation: in the Arab disturbances in 1921, 1929, 1936; in 1941 when the Jerusalem Mufti joined Hitler's massacre; in 1947 when seven Arab armies attempted to throw the Jews into the sea; in 1967 when Nasser again tried to annihilate Israel; and in 1973, during the Yom Kippur War. The most recent manifestations are the so-called Palestinian National Covenant of the PLO and the military preparations of Syria, Iraq, Saudi Arabia, Egypt and Libya, which include the establishment of a poison gas industry (see Michael Ledee, *Commentary*, July 1989).

Chaim Weizmann, in a letter dated January 17, 1930, was to the point in saying:

All the Arab objections to what we have done in Palestine during the last few years, ultimately boil down to one single thing: that we have come, are coming and mean to come in increasing numbers. . . . [And he concluded:] I say it clearly and with a full consciousness of my responsibility: I shall not for a shibboleth give up our national hopes . . . We have to look to the end; and we have no right to commit national suicide . . . We must not sin against the right nor betray the future of our people (quoted from Mendes-Flohr 11–12).

To follow Buber's advice in the above cases would amount to committing suicide, to giving up our claims to Eretz Israel. His one-sided call on the Jews to foster Arab trust is not only unrealistic but also unfair in that all the responsibility for Arab hostility is placed on the Jews. All in all, Buber's urging us to pursue the politics of trust rather than what he calls the politics of power interests or *Realpolitik*—in other words, his urging us to pursue a messianic policy in this unredeemed world, is inconsistent with his own basic position that the community of communities will have to wait until the transformation of man. It was Max Weber (*Politik als Beruf*) who defined the difference between the moralist and the politician: the moralist is characterized by his intentions, the politician—by the outcome of his deeds. Indeed, Buber speaks in the voice of the moralist who has never borne the burden of responsibility.

In conclusion, some remarks on Buber's proposed solution, the creation of a bi-national state. I understand that after the establishment of the State of Israel and the War of Independence, Buber and his colleagues, as well as *Hashomer Hatzair*, stopped promoting this idea. In private, even Ernst Simon admitted that the whole idea of a bi-national state was inappropriate. Everyone knows from modern history that a bi-national state is a recipe for disaster. What we must keep in mind is that Buber and his friends from *Brit Shalom* were in effect dismissing the Jewish need to regain sovereignty in a clear-cut, exclusive manner. It follows that he even rejected the need for a Jewish majority in the land. What is really surprising is how Buber failed to see that without sovereignty, a Jewish majority and unlimited immigration, the pressing needs of the Jewish people, of Judaism, and of the Zionist endeavor, could not be met.

In fact, Buber was trying to persuade us to live as a minority in an

Arab state without taking into consideration the nationalist-fundamentalist trends which have been forging Arab public opinion since the 1930s. His recommendations amounted to risking the destruction of the Jewish presence in Eretz Israel. It is also a riddle to me how Buber could have envisaged the creation of an ideal socialist society with the Jews living as a minority in a backward feudal environment.

Summing up our analysis, I would like to point out that Buber's socialism and his views on morality and politics are based on the anthropological error that man's nature is substantially good. His refusal to admit the ontological reality of the forces of evil in society prevented him from assessing the seriousness of the dangers facing the Zionist enterprise and the urgency of Zionist dynamics for the rescue and deliverance of the Jewish remnants after the Holocaust. Therefore he did not admit the revolutionary character of these events, playing instead with the idea of overcoming the forces of evil by dialogue. I contend that the great thinker Martin Buber made outstanding contributions to the revival of modern Jewish culture and to social philosophy. His political position, however, was built on abstract principles without an awareness of the nationalist mentality of the Arab world. It is to the credit of the Jewish people that his spiritual contributions are appreciated and discussed to the present day, while his political theses were rejected from the very beginning.

NOTES

1. Rivkah Schatz-Uffenheimer, "Man's Relation to God and World in Buber's Rendering of the Hassidic Teaching," in P. A. Schilp and M. Friedman (eds.), *The Philosophy of Martin Buber, The Library of Living Philosophers*, London-Cambridge, 1967, pp. 403–434.
2. B. Uffenheimer, "Buber and Modern Biblical Scholarship" in H. Gordon and J. Bloch (eds.), *Martin Buber, A Centenary Volume*, Ben Gurion University of the Negev, New York, 1984, pp. 163–214.
3. Renate Breispohl (ed.), *Dokumente zum Religioesen Sozialismus in Deutschland*, Müchen: 1972.

4. Max Weber, *Politik als Beruf*, München: 1919, pp. 58–67.
5. Friedrich Meinecke, *Die Idee der Staatsrason*, München: 1924.
6. Buber, "Geltung und Grenzen des Politischen Prinzips," 1913, in Hinweise, pp. 345–346, "The Validity and Limitation of the Political Principle," in *Pointing the Way*, (ed. M. Friedman), London: 1953, p. 213.
7. Cf. Maurice S. Friedman, *Martin Buber—The Life of a Dialogue*, New York, 1955, 1960; Paul R. Mendes-Flohr, *A Land of Two Peoples*, New York: 1983.

7. Leo Baeck: New Dimensions and Explorations

Albert H. Friedlander

The life and work of Leo Baeck, one of the founders of contemporary Jewish thought, is part of the common domain of the study of religion. Research on Leo Baeck has continued, and a new interest in Baeck has prompted both American and German publishers to prepare a paperback edition of the one full length study on Baeck's teachings available in German and English. Regular seminars on Leo Baeck appear as part of the curriculum of universities in Great Britain, the United States and Germany. Frequently, in scholarly and in popular journals, contemporary questions are related to Baeck's teachings, with Baeck viewed as a representative figure of Jewish life whose insights can clarify issues particularly related to the new dialogue between Judaism and Christianity. In this paper, I would like to add to the growing literature in the field by reexamining Baeck's view on suffering; his response to Germany after his release from the concentration camp after the war; and the response to Baeck from friends who survived to build on his teachings.

|

An earlier work of mine (*Leo Baeck and the Concept of Suffering: The Claude Montefiore Memorial Lecture*, London, 1973) began with one of his rare statements dealing with the darkness through which European Jewry had just passed, and was given in 1946. However, there is an earlier text dealing with his own experiences in Theresienstadt, written on the 1st of August 1945, barely three months after his return from that camp. (The *Jewish Forum*, London, published an English translation "Life in a Concentration Camp" in March 1946; and the *Leo Baeck Institute Bulletin 18/19* reprinted the German text from the manuscript in the possession of S. Adler-Rudel. Here, I will use the German text, in my translation.)

Baeck was a very private person. In his sermons, and in this text, the word "I" does not appear. He describes one of the deepest experiences of suffering known to a people or, indeed, to a person. He does not dwell upon the horror, and does not show it graphically by taking an individual experience, or a person caught in a web of evil and responding to it. Instead, his vision of the *individuum ineffabile*—the human being touched by God—emerges in a quiet discussion of the qualities residing in humanity when encountering the darkest experience of suffering—the Maimonidean category of evil inflicted by humans upon humans:

> One of the individual traits of Jewish existence and of the Jewish Genius is the connection between phantasy and patience. Many possess phantasy and everywhere there are people with patience, but the living interconnection between the two, the mutual interpenetration of creative tension and vision is a particularity of the Jewish soul. Here is one of the reasons why this people survived and why it can continue to survive. Whether or not survival took place in one of the concentration camps and in Theresienstadt depended upon outer circumstances: sickness, torture, annihilation could pass by or exterminate. But inner survival in its essence needed the continuance of both phantasy and

patience. Patience—the tensile strength to resist which did not permit inner vitality to cease: perhaps a man does not die until he no longer wants anything; and phantasy—this imagination which always and despite everything keeps showing a future: perhaps a person only ceases to be when he can only see the past and the present moment. Both phantasy and patience must be there. Patience comes to stand erect through phantasy; without it it could sink into simple slavery. And phantasy has its connection to everyday life through patience; without it, it would be a dream, lost in a world of slumber within the day.

This is so *typically* Baeck: the erection of polarities in which the dynamic tension of human experience is depicted; the establishing of a foundation for survival which can be applied to almost any situation; the setting up of essence vs. existence. But then, so rare for Baeck, he brings a graphic picture of the experience of moving through the gate into the camp, asking himself: "What was the first thing experienced by one who entered?" The gate of the camp becomes the gate of fate. The experience of imprisonment, of being massed together, 45,000 pushed into a space too small for 3,000; dust; mud; and

the vermin, from every place and any corner, the great army of the crawling, jumping, flying against that army of sufferers walking, sitting, lying; the voracious ones against the starving: a daily battle by day and by night. This was the world; month after month, year after year. And the mass swallowed up the individual. He was enclosed in it, just as he was surrounded by lack of space, by dust and dirt, by the swarming insects . . . by unending hunger—in the camp of the concentrated, never alone for a moment.

In theory, Theresienstadt was a "model" concentration camp for the "prominent." At times, Red Cross delegates would be seen, taken on tours where they could not see. And it was not an extermination camp. But then, it did not have to be one. Death came on its own. The daily fight against death, in the midst of suffering, is here internalized by Baeck: vision and patience, the outreach of imagination necessary to endure suffering, comes to be stated with great clarity.

How does one escape this suffering? Baeck lists various stations. There was the daily caravan of death. He describes the deep dark corridor of the fortress, where the long row of coffins appeared each day—often, over a hundred on the day. Heaped on top of one another, the dead listened to the Psalms—up to the final "I will let them see my help"—and then the coffins gained their freedom. The officiant was permitted fifty steps out of the darkness; then he returned. The coffins continued to their place of burning, free at last.

There was the other way of "escape" from the camp: the transports to the East. Month after month; often day after day. The question of what was known and what was guessed arises again here. In this text, three months after leaving Theresienstadt, Baeck again stresses the terrible suspicion set against the principle of hope, of a phantasy needed to survive each day and the next day:

> No one knew for certain (where the transports would go). One only knew: they went to the East. A cloud of sorrow, of fear and of horror kept enveloping the camp. That, of course, was the password of the master-jailers: keep the Jews uncertain. Give them no rest.

Baeck describes how those assigned to the transports were given new numbers, were isolated. "As the lot came upon them," he says. But he had removed himself from the areas of power where the lots were determined. Others describe in great detail how Baeck came to be the pastor, rabbi and teacher of the community in the midst of their extreme suffering. Baeck does not mention himself. In the text which follows, Baeck clearly describes his own work, but without mentioning himself. The conceptual structure of vision and patience as a bulwark against surrendering to the darkness turns into a description of the way in which the darkness was held back: again, the ideational structure and the experience of existence come to join together:

> The battle between the "mass" and the "community" continued unabatingly. Humans who had not known one another tried to help one another physically and spiritually. They gave one another from their

possessions, from their spirit. Humans found one another, here and there. In the early morning hours and late at night they came together for divine worship, wherever a room was available. Out of windows, out of the hallways of the houses, the voices of those at prayer, the sounds of the Torah reading entered the streets. Or, they came together in the darkness of a long evening in the loft of a barracks, immediately under the roof. Pressed tightly together, they stood there to listen to a lecture on Plato, Aristotle, Maimonides, Descartes and Spinoza. They listened to talks on Lock, Hume and Kant, or on the eras and issues of history, on music and the creative arts and poetry; on Palestine then and now, on commandments, prophecy and messianic ideas. These were hours, hours belonging to all, where a community rose up out of the mass, where narrowness became wide. They were hours of freedom.

It was Baeck's prescription against the ultimate surrender to the suffering they were enduring. Here, he saw phantasy and patience reasserting themselves as individuals and a community realized their inner capacities. The fact that it was Baeck who gave the lectures was not considered important by him, not worth mentioning. But it mattered to the group, who saw their faith vindicated by their rabbi and teacher. They might still recite their prayers "for our sins are we punished," might still be aware of a tradition equating suffering with punishment for all who have done evil. But, perhaps, Baeck's teachings about the Jewish response to suffering could realize themselves in the way Baeck envisaged in the closing peroration in which he summarizes his own belief in the confrontation with the darkness he had left behind so short a time ago:

(These hours of freedom) nourished phantasy and the creative tension of patience. Many were given the strength to walk upright through the uncertainties and into the uncertain. All had to learn that they could carry an ultimate certainty within themselves, the certainty of truth, justice, and peace. Something of this deep conviction, something from this patience and this vision is now presented as a gift through this picture of these people and of those days.

At the very moment of giving his testimony of suffering—and Baeck did not become this personal again in his public utterances—the "teacher of Theresienstadt" already began to instruct the next generation. He did not want to stress the details of the suffering, but rather the Jewish response. He did not want to stress the evil and acts of persecution, but rather the response of the persecuted, the nobility of the human soul, the essence and existence of the Jewish people. While in Theresienstadt, he continued to write the book which in some ways became his testament: *This People Israel: The Meaning of Jewish Existence*. But at that point, one has to recognize that the very experience of suffering for Israel and for the individual Jew had to become part of his Judaism. The Baeck who had emerged out of the camp was no longer the irenic, neo-Kantian, distant and unemotional person (outwardly; the inner fires were always there) who had entered the camp.

II

We must come back to the basic concept of suffering as seen in Baeck's early writings (much of it, as indicated is available in the Montefiore Lecture of 1973) (op. cit.). Yet it is intriguing to see that he does, in some ways, come to the confrontation with those who had been responsible for the untold suffering which branded and effectually destroyed Europe during the dark decade. What is most notable here is that it is not a wild tirade against the Nazi leaders and their henchmen who had actually committed the murders and unspeakable acts of brutality. Baeck's sensitive vision reaches out to include the silent bystanders, the passive participants—and not only in Germany itself. In his presidential address to the World Union for Progressive Judaism, July 28, London 1946, "The Task of Progressive Judaism in the Post War World," Baeck apparently speaks to the victors more than to the defeated criminals. He is not concerned with evoking repentance within the German community now facing the wrath of the nations. He is more concerned with the establishing of a world in which there will be less suffering, in which compliance with evil will be less likely. Addressing the leaders of Progressive Judaism in the world, and noting the presence of the non-Jewish community, Baeck says:

> Since the last Conference . . . a terrible ordeal has swept over the Jewish people and over humanity. It has once again proved that the Jewish people and humanity are inseparable from one another. This ordeal has been so terrible, it has become such a torment . . . because men who were responsible for parts of the world, for the leadership of great communities, remained silent when they should have spoken, and stood by and looked on when they should have stepped forward to act and to help. Once again, there came to the present generation Jeremiah's word of indictment: "They mean to heal the hurt of my people slightly, saying: peace, peace, when there is no peace." The sin of silence and of looking on lay upon the world. This disaster has come upon humanity because the moral enthusiasm and the moral passion were lacking . . . Everything and all of the manifest forms of Jewish life has been hit by the severity of the loss and of the suffering. We must never forget what we have lost or whom we have lost.

Again, we are introduced to the sufferers, the silent witnesses who can only speak from the grave and for whom we must say *kaddish*. Where once a traditional teacher might have invoked the merit of the fathers in a plea to God to alleviate the suffering of the children, the martyrs are brought before us to show the inner qualities of Jewish life which can help us surmount suffering. And the reasons for suffering are not placed into the lives of the dead, but into the actions of the living. Baeck's great respect and even affinity to Maimonides is here put to the test, since his approach confronts a traditional structure where good and evil, pain and pleasure are placed into the lives of individuals and groups supervised and judged by an omniscient and omnipotent God. Richard Rubenstein, in a clear presentation of the problem of good and evil, summarizes the traditional position of Maimonides admirably:

> Man has "the ability to do whatever he wills or chooses among the things concerning which he has the ability to act" and that "it is in no way possible that He (God) . . . should be unjust," Maimonides af-

firmed unconditionally that "all the calamities . . . and all the good
things that come to men, be it a single individual or a group, are all of
them determined according to the deserts of man . . . in which there is
no injustice whatsoever." (Ibid.) Maimonides went so far as to insist that
no feeling of pain or pleasure, no matter how minute, can be other than
a divinely inflicted punishment or reward. Maimonides was so insistent
upon misfortune as punitive that he quoted with approval Rabbi
Ammi's dictum that "there is no death without sin, and no suffering
without transgression." (BT Shab. 55a) (Richard Rubenstein, "Evil," in
Contemporary Jewish Thought, eds., Arthur A. Cohen and Paul R.
Mendes-Flohr, NY: 1987, pp. 204–5).

The positive thinking of the "early" Baeck had already distanced itself
from Maimonides in terms of the reasons for human suffering and in
the way of coping with the tribulations of the Jewish people. And yet,
bound to the notions of Covenant and the task of the martyr in the
world, accepting the God who "tests" His people and permits them to
see virtue in their pain, Baeck had not broken with the traditional
approach. It was more that his emphases had shifted: one did not ask
for the reasons, but simply tried to cope with the human situation in
which suffering was a given. After the Holocaust, this was no longer a
tenable position for most thinking Jews. The death of a million children in the camps could not be a punishment for sins. It could not be a
testing or a purification. It was simply monstrous. As Rubenstein
indicates:

> Jewish religious thinkers attempted to mitigate the harsh and uncom-
> promising ethical rationalism of covenant theology . . . to reaffirm the
> abiding validity and credibility of God's relation to Israel, while reject-
> ing the punitive interpretation of the Holocaust. Thinkers such as
> Arthur A. Cohen and Eliezer Berkovits have limited God's role to that
> of a teacher of free human agents and identified the Holocaust as the
> work of human beings who have rejected the teachings. (Ibid., p. 209).

Richard Rubenstein has rejected this and various other approaches
(Maybaum, Fackenheim). For him, one may accept the Covenant—

or the non-punitive character of the Holocaust; but not both. A new, as yet unformulated metaphor may now have to restore the integrity of post-Holocaust Jewish theology. The quiet conviction of Baeck's affirmation of the Covenant despite the Holocaust might be respectable but unacceptable to him. Perhaps a far clearer picture must be achieved of the relationship between Baeck and the rabbis of the *midrash* who lived after the destruction of Jerusalem and could yet laugh with Rabbi Akiva in the face of suffering and martyrdom, and accept the teachings of Ben Zoma (read in the Haggadah by all of us on the first night of Passover):

> Rabbi Eleazar ben Azariah said: "I am now over seventy years old; but I never understood why the story of Exodus has to be recited by night until Ben Zoma expounded it thus: The Torah states (Deut. 16.3) that thou mayest remember the day when thou camest out of the land of Egypt all the days of thy life. "The days of thy life" would imply the days only; "all the days of thy life" includes the nights also.

As I have said elsewhere (Founders Day Address, HUC 1980, Cincinnati):

> We want to exclude the nights; we want to live in the sunlit day. But it is in the nights that the message of redemption matters most to us. VAY'HI EREV VAY'HI VOKER: between dusk and dawn there is the passage of the night, a middle that cannot be excluded in logic or in religion. We have to seek God in all our ways; we have to find God in all our ways. And if the God we find is not always the God we want to find, we must learn to live in that knowledge as well. (p. 9)

Personally, I would include both Richard Rubenstein and Leo Baeck into my reading of the Ben Zoma passage. Both bring the night of the Shoah into their understanding of God and humanity. Baeck moves from *erev* to *boker*, while Rubenstein still battles with the darkness. Both are authentic voices of Judaism. If I have taken Baeck and his teachings as structure of thought and pathway of action, demanding action from the living and seeing a continuance of a Covenant which demands the same from the individual and from the community, it does not render me unaccessible to the moral indignation and bitter challenge of an eloquent voice in our time. I would accept the charge of inconsistency against Baeck's position—but when is theology consistent? In that darkness, faith moved beyond reason.

III

The 1946 Address to the WUPJ was a challenge to the guilty bystanders of the Holocaust. And much of Germany is included in this. There are many—my friend and colleague Lord Jakobovits, Chief Rabbi of the U.K. and the Commonwealth, who to this day would not visit Germany. (The nearest he came to it was within a dialogue I helped organize for a Catholic Center in Aachen: they crossed the border to Maastricht, in the Netherlands, where the Chief Rabbi entered into a challenging discussion with them.) But there came a time, there *had* to come a time, when Leo Baeck returned to Germany and confronted the German community. The year was 1952. It was an important year for German-Jewish confrontation. Martin Buber had come to Frankfurt to accept the Peace Prize from the Frankfurt Book Fair. And he spoke words of reconciliation. In 1978, forty years after the Kristallnacht, the German Chancellor, Helmuth Schmidt spoke at a commemorative occasion on the theme of "Truth and Tolerance." The heart of the speech was an expression of hope for a new dialogue with the Jewish community, one which would build upon the candor expressed by Martin Buber: "Fifteen years ago, the German-Jewish philosopher Martin Buber asked in the St. Paul's church: 'Who and what am I that I could dare to express forgiveness here?'" (Martin Buber, "Acceptance Speech at Frankfurt Book Fair," 1952)

In 1939, Martin Buber had spoken of the end of the German-Jewish symbiosis, taking a position particularly espoused by Gershom Scholem in later days, although Scholem went further in his assertion that such a symbiosis had actually never existed. And it was not the

intention of Buber's Frankfurt speech to renew the previous relationship. Buber saw Germany's guilt; he spoke of Auschwitz and Treblinka. But—and here he differed from many Jewish voices of that
time—he did not demand that German opponents to Hitler should
have chosen martyrdom. He saw them in their flaws: deaf, blind,
unresponsible. And yet, unlikely as it seemed to those examining the
situation from the outside, Buber did not rule out the possibility that
there were those who simply did not know what was happening.
Buber did recognize that there were a few non-Jewish friends who
resisted, who saved lives: the *haside umot ha-'olam* ("righteous gentiles"). For their sake—as Abraham pleaded at Sodom—he saw the
possibility for a new beginning.

In October 1952, almost at the same time, Leo Baeck published an
article in the *Merkur* entitled "Israel and the German People." The
opening lines of this important presentation bring together the
themes of reproval and reconciliation:

> Only a profound, one almost wants to say a loving yearning for inner
> openness and outer clarity can permit anyone to speak about peace
> between Israel and the German people. Only this truthfulness in which
> thought and speech join together as a specific particularity, which leaves
> no room for ulterior thoughts or excuses, gives a justification here to
> confirm or to deny, to hope or to doubt . . .
>
> But now for the other pre-condition. It is, as it were, the pre-
> condition of a *Kairos*-assumption with its question which must be
> asked: Given, that this foundation of a matter-of-fact objectivity to-
> gether with a personal dimension . . . is clearly established, should this
> dialogic confrontation really commence NOW? There is an old Jewish
> saying, "If one tries to rush the hour, it flees away."
>
> Has the time come? Some say . . . that the Jews should make their
> peace with this span of time, with the goodness and monumental
> sadness contained in it. Centrally, with the good. But with the sadness?
> Sadness will come to join sadness. But was there not something else,
> something completely and utterly different in that time? Should peace
> be made with all of that otherness, with all the ways in which the image
> of God was destroyed at that time?

Quite simply, Baeck speaks here about honesty in human relationships, whether in a one-to-one confrontation or in the reencountering of Israel with Germany. The time *was* early: 1952, and Israel and Germany were moving towards a gray area of uncomfortable relationship which has not yet been fully resolved. Baeck's call for total honesty where the intellectual and moral dimensions could join together and where sentimentality could be avoided was not heard. Over the years, large reparations were given and accepted for (partly) wrong reasons; an element of guilt was present on both sides, and awkwardness and the uncomfortable skirting around issues continues. Yet it may well be argued that Baeck's call for honesty, if not heard within the political sphere or even in the field of religion (some entrenched positions—God's punishment of German Jewry's assimilation; the sins of parents transmitted to children; etc.) has been partly realized in the area of scholarship in its secularity. Yad Vashem (Israel's Institute of Holocaust Studies) presents the dimensions of horror in so far as one can look in the face of Medusa through a mirror. At the same time, the Avenue of Righteous Gentiles sponsored by that institute gives recognition to those whom Baeck already recognized as standing in the shadows of the Holocaust: the rescuers who cared and refused to go along with the multitude to do evil.

The present always wants to change the past, as it wants to dominate the future. Does Hegel's Owl of Minerva fly only at dusk—do we really gain understanding of that past darkness by letting our categories of understanding organize the incomprehensible horror into coherent patterns? "The time cannot be turned around," says Baeck with Kirkegaard. But every time, every era contains new possibilities. How and when can one reach out towards these? In 1952, too close to that darkness, as Baeck knew, he still had to ask fundamental questions of both sides. The Jews? Which ones? "Those who live today as they lived yesterday and the day before yesterday? Or those Jews who survived yesterday as through a miracle? Or those whose lives were annihilated?" Every Jew lives with those shadows—wherever he lives. Who can speak for the shadows? And from whence comes the address?

No man can set these questions and can call forward those to whom these questions are addressed. They are asked by that which was done and was done unto them. "It" asks, not "he," not a person. But it is not an "it," but a "he," a person, which must answer. Humans, individual persons, must come to terms with a happening, with a collective happening. And it remains essential that the questions must find receptivity both here and there. Sooner or later, there will come an answer, the true answer: that is the hope. (op. cit., *Der Merkur*, October 1952)

The closing word in this powerful message by Baeck then tries to place this hope within the contemporary world in which the two sides meet:

Two peoples, both of them bound into one fate, cannot permanently turn their backs towards one another and walk past each other. It can mean much to humanity if such a peace is prepared and examined honestly, that is, without forgetfulness, and, if God wills, if that peace is then established. (Ibid.)

There was, at best, a quiet and sincere appreciation for these words of Leo Baeck. They did not have the impact of Martin Buber. This is not surprising. Buber was far more in the public's eye, and had earlier accepted—in 1951—the Goethe Prize of the University of Hamburg. He had not gone to Hamburg to receive it, but defended himself against the attacks from the Jewish community through letters in the public press in which Buber had stressed the need to support the decent, humane circle within Germany in their fight against the old enemies. When asked to speak in Hamburg (January 1952) Buber declined in words which link his attitude to that of Baeck:

As much as it has been granted me in every genuine meeting with a German to accept him without reservation as a person, and to communicate with each circle made up of such persons, it has still not been possible for me up to this time to overcome the facelessness of the German public, which has persisted for me since the events of 1938 and thereafter. A public that is not made up of persons each of whom has been selected, cannot fulfil the indispensable presupposition for my speaking publicly: being able to regard every face that I turn toward as my legitimate partner. Among the burdens which the history of this age has laid on me, I experience this as one of the most difficult. (M. Buber, in a letter to Bruno Snell quoted by M. Friedman *Buber's Life and Work*, Vol. 3, New York, 1982–3, p. 111. Here, cited from E. B. Philipson's "Buber's Jewish Self-Definition," unpublished Ph.D. dissertation.)

Yet Buber did go to Hamburg in 1953, in June; and, in September, he went to the Frankfurt Book Fair to accept the Peace Prize. *Pointing the Way*, his 1957 collection of essays translated by Maurice Friedman, contains the lecture in the Paulskirche, where he begins with a statement related to the earlier Leo Baeck article—a Jewish scholar trying to come to terms with the total horror set within a humanity that was not totally depraved. And yet:

About a decade ago a considerable number of Germans . . . killed millions of my people in a systematically prepared and executed procedure whose organized cruelty cannot be compared with any previous historical event. . . . Those who took part in this have so radically removed themselves into a sphere of monstrous inhumanity . . . that not even hatred, much less an overcoming of hatred, was able to arise in me. And what am I that I could be here presume to "forgive"!

With the German people it is otherwise. I have never . . . allowed the concrete multiplicity existing at that moment within a people—the concrete inner dialectic, rising to contradiction—to be obscured by the leveling concept of a totality constituted and acting in just such a way and no other.

When I think of the German people of the days of Auschwitz and Treblinka, I behold, first of all, the great many who knew that the monstrous event was taking place and did not oppose it . . . but my heart . . . will not condemn my neighbor for not . . . becoming a martyr. Next there emerges before me the mass of those who remained ignorant . . . and who did not try to discover what reality lay behind the rumors (representing) the anxiety . . . of the human creature before a truth which he fears he cannot face. But finally there appear before me . . .

those who refused to carry out orders and suffered death . . . those [opposers] . . . put to death . . . those who could [not] stop it . . . [and] killed themselves. Reverence and love for these Germans now fill my heart. (M. Buber, *Pointing the Way*, New York, 1957, pp. 232–233)

Buber continued to express his concern for what he saw happening in the Germany after Auschwitz. He had compassion for the young people, and saw the need to open dialogue with those in Germany who were involved in the battle against evil, the *homo humanus* against the *homo contrahumanus*. He felt that the Hamburg and the Frankfurt Prizes both called to him to join in the battle carried out at the present time under the darkness still covering Germany. And he heard the call addressed to him as a Jew, who cannot leave the battlefield where the struggle takes place against all that is contrahuman. Like Baeck, Buber called for candor and directness in address and answer as the pre-condition for genuine talk: where there is no trust, there cannot be speech. "In a genuine dialogue each of the partners, even when he stands in opposition to the other, heeds, affirms and confirms his opponent as an existing other" described this specific encounter for him as well as the human situation. In demanding truth and recognition, in building upon truth, Buber arrived at the final statement of his acceptance speech:

The name Satan means in Hebrew the hinderer. That is the correct designation for the anti-human in individuals and in the human race. Let us not allow this Satanic element in men to hinder us from realizing man! Let us rather release speech from its ban! Let us dare, despite all, to trust! (Ibid., p. 239)

It is quite clear, then, that Baeck and Buber walked the same path which traveled towards a reconciliation. In 1952 and 1953, it was a dangerous path to tread. It was more difficult for Buber, living in Israel with its open wounds and its bitter memories. Buber was pilloried there. His giving of the Peace Prize money towards Arab-Israeli reconciliation was only an extra wound for the group which had also opposed him because of his political attitude in Israel. Baeck, living in London and at times Cincinnati, had less problems, since he was surrounded by a progressive Jewish community who worshipped him (unfortunately too often from the distance) and who had less scar tissue to excise from their hearts. In some ways, Baeck moved once again into the center of Jewish communal life: as president of the World Union for Progressive Judaism, lecturer at the Hebrew Union College, revered teacher of the Reform and Liberal movements in Israel where German refugee rabbis also formed a circle around him.

Baeck did not really write about his Holocaust experiences. He did not create a new theology of suffering or make radical changes in his teachings. The changes and new emphases had already been established in the text he finished basically in Theresienstadt: *This People Israel: The Meaning of Jewish Existence*. As has been demonstrated, it was the shift from essence to existence (his first major work was *The Essence of Judaism*). Yet the two works are one, a logical development of a clear, rational, ethical and pious approach to all of the Jewish tradition. All of Baeck's writings form a consistent, interlocking structure and are at the heart of Judaism—even when Rosenzweig tried to place him into the periphery. Buber, so often considered the great teacher of Judaism to the outside world, is far more at the edge of Jewish life—but, it must be stated firmly, totally Jewish and authentic as a Jew in every utterance he made. He moved much closer towards Germany in his attempt of dialogue and reconciliation; visited more often, published, spoke, taught and affirmed that dimension of a continuing dialogue carried on between Jews and Christians who had come out of the darkness maimed and dumb. Few Christians realized how much had been destroyed within Christianity and in themselves through the cancer of apathy and silent compliance—let alone acts of violent evil. All Jews knew that the wounds inflicted upon their family and upon themselves would not be healed within their lives; one could only learn to live with the pain. Yet remembrance and hatred are not automatic companions. There is the curious misconception among Christians that the Jewish insistence upon remembering the Holocaust rises out of implacable hatred (which many even consider to be justified). Few understand that the category *Zakhor* is a dominant part of Judaism in which the generations are linked together, and through which God is reminded of the Covenant. But remembrance cannot live long with hatred. Baeck and Buber, in their own ways, were messengers of this to a Germany awakening out of a nightmare which had left many of them crippled in a still poisoned land.

IV

In 1952, when Baeck's cautious approach to a resumption of discussions between Israel and Germany appeared, he lived in Cincinnati as a teacher of Reform rabbis, at the Hebrew Union College. I saw him most days, during the spring semester, and we spent much time together, partly to discuss my future. (I was about to be ordained.) Baeck felt that it was my task to transplant something of the German Jewish heritage within the fertile soil of American Jewish life. "Germany is finished," Baeck said to me on more than one occasion. He was certain that Jewish life would diminish and eventually disappear in that land, and that there was no need and indeed no call for me to return to my birthplace out of an obligation to German Judaism. My choice should probably be between South America and the United States. My Spanish would be of help if I were to join the German refugee rabbis Lemle or Pinkus; but Leo Baeck had come to love American Jewish life and looked forward to its growth and development. And his teaching at the Hebrew Union College meant that he could direct new disciples into a rabbinate that would have new dimensions and challenges.

Why, then, did he still look at Germany and reach out hesitatingly towards a dialogue? One must go back to the 1952 lecture, to Baeck's demand for truthfulness—the only pattern in which an eventual expression of repentance by Germans could eventually take place. And, as Baeck taught, there is no repentance without actions of atonement. He saw at that time that such actions had not come to the fore, and warned against rushing "time." A "forgiving," a "forgetting" would not only be a dishonest obscuring of the past, but would also deny Germany the necessary acts of atonement.

At a later time, Ernst Akiva Simon, Baeck's friend and colleague, expressed this point of view in a statement on Germany in which he still searched for acts of atonement:

> The new Germany can only "work through" or "overcome" its most recent past (whatever the term is) if it is ready for a genuine task of turning back (*teshuvah*, return). The meaning of "turning back" is that one attempts to undo the consequences of evil deeds, to the fullest extent possible. No one who died is awakened by a return, but the return can help avoid new murders and new war. An energetic peace policy which brings Israel and its neighbors closer towards an understanding would be such an act of return. Then, Israel might be able to continue the task of rebuilding in peace and with humanity. If you (Germans) really want to return, do all in your power to let all the nations on earth find the way towards God's peace, not least Jews and Arabs in the Holy Land.
>
> We Jews were God's witnesses under the greatest oppression and deepest suffering; we hope to remain God's witnesses, in our own state, under conditions of freedom. (Ernst Simon, *Das Zeugnis des Judentums*, Berlin, 1980.)

Whether or not the time has come; indeed, whether or not Ernst Simon's hopes for Israel as well as for Germany have moved closer to fruition, continues to be a question of concern to us. But the balanced hope and doubt of Leo Baeck in this area is still applicable to our own situation. Recently, looking through my files, I came across my notes of an interview I had with Ernst Simon (on December 23, 1965) when I was preparing my work on Leo Baeck. Most of the theological comments entered the book, but there were also warm, personal statements about Baeck which again bring him to life in the rereading. Simon did not always agree with Baeck, but defended him against Rosenzweig's criticism of being an apologete. "Baeck, like Schleiermacher, defended religion against its despisers," said Simon. ". . . But he did not adopt any of Schleiermacher's views, despite Leon Roth's statement . . . Baeck was a great human being . . . with a hard core of inner integrity." And Simon appreciated Baeck's traditional practices, the hour of prayer and study which opened every day of Baeck's life.

In the end, Baeck inspired his colleagues as much as his students. All of them knew: the day is short, and the work beckons.

And the *Kairos*-time may be closer than we imagine.

8. Soloveitchik's Lonely Man of Faith

Aharon Singer

O Wedding-Guest! this soul hath been
Alone on a wide wide sea:
So lonely 'twas that God himself
Scarce seemed there to be.

J. B. Soloveitchik was not only a master of Torah learning, but was conversant with Western philosophy and the world of science and technology. He was one of the rare Jewish Orthodox theologians who took seriously the challenge of modern thought and culture. The main objective in this paper is not so much a critique as an appreciation of his attempt to bring the traditional Jew into direct confrontation with the world. I will first present a faithful précis of Soloveitchik's "Lonely Man of Faith" (in his own words wherever possible). This will give a sense of the man as well as his thought. The tone and emotive power of the man, no less than the cogency of what he is saying, is critical to understanding his impact on those who take his teaching seriously. The summary will be followed by a discussion of the appeal of his

essay to one who does not share his passionate commitment to Halakha (Jewish law) and God's inscrutable will. The paper will then
conclude with some critical remarks.

> What can a man of faith like myself, living by a doctrine which has no
> technical potential, by a law which cannot be tested in the laboratory,
> steadfast in his loyalty to an eschatological vision whose fulfillment
> cannot be predicted with any degree of probability, let alone certainty,
> even by the most complex, advanced, mathematical calculations—what
> can such a man say to a functional utilitarian society which is *saeculum*-
> oriented whose practical reasons of the mind have long ago supplanted
> the sensitive reasons of the heart? (8)

Soloveitchik moves directly to the heart of the matter. Alienated and
out of step with the modern world, he attempts to understand the
dislocation and anguish he feels. As a man of faith, he is caught
between two divine mandates: one to subdue the earth, the other to
crave redemption. He will not deny the demands of one to satisfy the
other. Both have their legitimate place and are ontologically centered
in the human condition. He dramatizes the two dimensions by relating each to one of the two versions of man's creation.

Adam the first, created in the divine image, imitates God by master-
ing nature. "God, imparting the blessing to Adam the first and giving
him the mandate to subdue nature, directed attention to the functional and practical aspects of his intellect through which man is able
to gain control of nature." (11, 12) Adam is faced with an indifferent
cosmos. To affirm his humanness, he must assert his dominion. In
doing so he overcomes his helplessness and takes on dignity. "The
brute's existence is an undignified one because it is a helpless existence. Human existence is a dignified one because it is a glorious,
majestic, powerful existence." (13, 14)

Soloveitchik thus affirms the world of technology for it empowers
man to overcome his environment, endowing him with dignity and
human responsibility. "Man reaching for the distant stars is acting in
harmony with his nature created, willed and directed by his Maker. It

is a manifestation of obedience to rather than rebellion against God." (16)

Adam the second, when confronted with the same *mysterium magnum* of being, is troubled not by the functional question of how, but by the metaphysical why, what, who. Why was the world created? What is the purpose of it all? "Who is He who trails me steadily, uninvited and unwanted, like an everlasting shadow . . . Who is He whose life-giving and life-warming breath Adam feels constantly and who at the same time remains distant and remote from all?" (17) Adam the first is bold, at home in the universe of his making. Adam the second, open to the inner recesses of existence, is overcome with loneliness which "is nothing but the act of questioning one's own legitimacy, worth and reasonableness." (22) The central issue for Adam the second is what to do with his loneliness.

> "To be" is a unique in-depth experience of which only Adam the second is aware, and it is unrelated to any function or performance. "To be" means to be the only one, singular and different and consequently lonely. For what causes man to be lonely and insecure if not the awareness of his uniqueness and exclusiveness? Since loneliness reflects the very core of the "I" experience and is not an accidental modus, no accidental activity or external achievement—such as belonging to a natural work community and achieving cooperative success—can reclaim Adam the second from this state. (27)

Even as he experiences his singularity that isolates him from all creation, he yearns for redeemed existence. Tragically, the more he seeks redemption, the more he experiences loneliness. To transcend his condition he must first accept defeat. He must realize the inadequacy of his fragmented self to achieve redemption. He must establish a relationship with someone outside himself to break the self-inscribed circle of solitude. To accomplish this he must contract something of himself to make room for another, just as God withdraws within himself so that there be place for his creatures. At this stage, Adam looks for a companion as a step toward the creation of a new kind of community.

His quest is for a new kind of fellowship which one finds in the existential community. There, not only hands are joined, but experiences as well; there, one hears not only the rhythmic sound of the production line, but also the rhythmic beat of hearts starved for existential companionship and all-embracing sympathy and experiencing the grandeur of the faith commitment; there, one lonely soul finds another soul tormented by loneliness and solitude yet unqualifiedly committed. (28)

While Adam the First also seeks out a companion it is not related to loneliness, "but to aloneness, a practical surface-experience." Their relationship is a practical one related to the need for a work partner, qualitatively different than an existential co-participant. "Thus, the natural community fashioned by Adam the first is a work community, committed to the successful production, distribution and consumption of goods, material as well as cultural." (22)

Through the sacrificial gesture Adam the second and Eve the second were able to break out of their singularity. But, claims Soloveitchik, communication between them was possible only through the formation of a covenantal faith community, an allegiance to a greater discipline which requires sacrifice, retreat, defeat on the part of both Adam and Eve.

The difference between the natural community of Adam the first and the covenantal faith community of Adam the second is clear. The first is a community of interests directed to success in a material cultural sense. While this is a divine mandate it consists of only two personae, the "I" and the "Thou" who join hands to gain their common interests. The covenantial faith community is formed in distress and defeat and involves not only I and Thou but He. "Adam the second was introduced to Eve by God, who summoned Adam to join Eve in an existential community molded by sacrificial action and suffering and who Himself became a partner in this community." (28) The covenant which consists of God's commandments crystallized in Halakha, brings God into the companionship of the faith community. Adam the first in his search for God, is met with an exasperating paradox. While finding God everywhere in creation, the moment he turns to Him he experiences divine transcendence and mystery. The intimacy and immediacy of God's presence is insured by the covenantal community where the solitary "I" together with the solitary "Thou" experience that presence through Torah. The man of faith turns to the covenant where he finds God as father, brother, friend, teacher. God becomes immanent in the Torah. His will expressed in its teachings and Halakha is responsive to Adam's need for communication with others and his craving for God's nearness. It provides the content and expression to find both and to transcend his loneliness. The yearning for redemption begins in the singularity of the individual. The realization takes place within the community where the individual finds communication and communion with God and his fellow, where his existence is confirmed as "worthwhile, legitimate, and adequate, anchored in something stable and unchangeable."

Prophecy and prayer are the media through which the faith community experiences the presence of God and establishes communication with others. Soloveitchik calls these communities of prophecy and prayer covenantal communities for three reasons. 1) In both communities a relationship is established between God and man. God and man meet on Mt. Sinai in the prophetic sense. In authentic prayer man finds himself in the presence of God and is conscious of being in God's presence. 2) Both communities consist of "I", "Thou" and "He." The prophet was ever conscious that God's word was addressed to the people whom the prophet represented. Similarly, efficacious prayer always includes others expressing "human solidarity and sympathy or the covenantal awareness of existential togetherness." 3) Both communities are encounters with God that are inseparable from the normative content of Halakha. What distinguishes prophecy from mysticism is its clear teaching of a religious ethical norm. Prayer, too, is qualified by Halakha specifying not only the content and intent of prayer but the moral character of the worshipper. "If man craves to meet God in prayer, then he must purge himself of all that separates him from God." (41)

Both the prophetic and prayer colloquy engender a warmth and fellowship, a We-consciousness expressed in a common commitment to a divine call. This shared commitment makes possible the closing of the gap between singular individuals. Without the covenantal experience of the prophetic or prayerful colloquy, Adam absconditus would have persisted in his He-role and Eve abscondita in her She-role, unknown to and distant from each other.

> Only when God emerged from the transcendent darkness of the He-anonymity into the illumined spaces of community knowability and charged man with an ethico-moral mission, did Adam absconditus and Eve abscondita, while revealing themselves to God in prayer and un-qualified commitment, also reveal themselves to each other in sympathy and love on the one hand and common action on the other. Thus the final objective of the human quest for redemption was attained; the individual felt relieved from loneliness and isolation. The community of the committed became, *ipso facto*, a community of friends—not of neighbors or acquaintances. Friendship—not as a social surface-relation but as an existential in-depth relation between two individuals—is realizable only within the framework of the covenantal community where in-depth personalities relate themselves to each other ontologically and total commitment to God and fellow-man is the order of the day. (45)

Existential insecurity stems not only from loneliness and isolation. There is also the experience of being a temporal being. "The whole accidental character of his being is tied up with this frightening time-consciousness. He began to exist at a certain point—the significance of which he cannot grasp—and his existence will end at another equally arbitrary point." (46)

Here, too, the covenantal community addresses the plight of the individual faced by temporality.

> . . . all boundaries establishing "before," "now" and "after" disappear when God the Eternal speaks. Within the covenantal community not only contemporary individuals but generations are engaged in a collo-quy and each single experience of time is three-dimensional, manifest-

ing itself in memory, actuality and anticipatory tension . . . a paradoxical time awareness, which involves the individual in the historic performances of the past and makes him also participate in the dramatic action of an unknown future, can be found in the Judaic *masorah* community. . . [The individual] is not a hitch-hiker suddenly invited to get into a swiftly traveling vehicle which emerged from nowhere and from which he will be dropped into the abyss of timelessness while the vehicle will rush on into parts unknown. Covenantal man begins to find redemption from insecurity and to feel at home in the continuum of time and responsibility which is experienced by him in its endless totality. He is no longer an evanescent being. He is rooted in everlasting time. (46,47,48)

Having joined the covenantal community does not bring the redemption the man of faith seeks. Both the majestic natural community and the covenantal faith community are authorized by God. No sooner has the man of faith attained one when he is forced back into the other. "One is engaged in a continuous oscillation that makes complete redemption unattainable. The task of the convenantal man is to be engaged not in dialectical surging forward and retreating, but in uniting the two communities into one community where man is both the creative, free agent, and the obedient servant of God." (50,51)

Ultimately, Soloveitchik is committed to a monistic approach to reality. There can be no division of secular and sacred. Thus the two contrasting typologies are found in the same individual part of "the whole of an all inclusive human personality." "The perfect dialectic expresses itself in a plurality of creative gestures and at the same time, in axiological monodeism." (52) Commanded to move from one community to another, the man of faith remains rootless with no home to call his own. Soloveitchik characterizes him as "a straying Aramean was my father" (Deuteronomy 26:5).

Finally, Soloveitchik turns to a non-existential source of loneliness, namely, the social-historic situation of western man. Western civilization has abandoned the metaphysical polarity that makes him a part of the covenantal as well as the majestic community. In fact, he has the

presumption of trying to take over the covenantal community applying the methods of success and domination alien to that community.
Religion becomes a useful tool to make him happy. "The prime
purpose is the successful furtherance of the interests, not the deepen-
ing and enhancing of the commitments, of man who values religion in
terms of usefulness to him and considers the religious act a medium
through which he may increase his happiness." (57) But, contends
Soloveitchik, majestic man needs covenantal man, because he also
attempts to evaluate his creative accomplishments and legislate in the
ethico-moral and aesthetic realm which requires a transcendental
norm to gain perspective and permanence.

The frustration is that the covenantal commitment is untranslatable
in cognitive terms. Only peripheral elements can be so projected.
While prayer may act as a purifying, ennobling experience it is a far
cry from standing before God in common fellowship and at the same
time surrendering oneself to God. The man of faith must not compromise his commitment to bring his apocalyptic message to majestic
man. He must uphold his singular pristine faith no matter how incompatible with a utilitarian society.

> This unique message speaks of defeat instead of success, of accepting a
> higher will instead of commanding, of giving instead of conquering, of
> retreating instead of advancing, of acting "irrationally" instead of being
> always reasonable . . . the act of faith itself is, unchangeable, for it
> transcends the bounds of time and space. Faith is born of the intrusion
> of eternity upon temporality . . . Faith is experienced not as a product of
> some emergent evolutionary process, or as something which has been
> brought into existence by man's creative cultural gesture, but as some-
> thing which was given to man when the latter was overpowered by God.
> Its prime goal is redemption from the inadequacies of finitude and,
> mainly, from the flux of temporality. (63,64)

Soloveitchik contends that the redemptive, therapeutic qualities of
faith depend on their rootedness in the Absolute, beyond history and
the vagaries of human fallibility. The relativization of faith would be
destructive to the majestic community no less than the covenantal. In

sum, Soloveitchik believes that the divine origin of the majestic, technological community notwithstanding, it is the covenantal faith community in which a living relationship with God takes place. It is here that moments of redemption are experienced. While it is God's inscrutable will to have the man of faith live out his anguished existence between two worlds, he does share the compensation of the prophet Elisha who was "indeed lonely, but in his loneliness he met the Lonely One and discovered the singular covenantal confrontation of solitary man and God who abides in the recesses of transcendental solitude." (67)

One is immediately struck by the passionate, confessional tone of Soloveitchik's "Lonely Man of Faith." "I would like, hesitantly and haltingly," he writes, "to confide in you, and to share with you some concerns which weigh heavily on my mind and which frequently assume the proportions of an awareness of crisis." Like the Ancient Mariner he feels compelled to tell his "tale of a personal dilemma." Taking his cue from Elihu the son of Berachel he admits, "I will speak that I may find relief; for there is a redemptive quality for an agitated mind in the spoken word and a tormented soul finds peace in confessing." The terms he employs to describe his dilemma make palpable the crisis he is experiencing. "Loneliness," "torment," "agonizing solitude," "tragic," "despair," distress," "misery," "estrangement" are words that saturate his discourse. It is clear that the issues he struggles with are of ultimate concern, not an intellectual exercise or philosophic treatise to vanquish his philistine foes. He is the earnest member of R. D. Laing's analytic group who broke off an argument with another member protesting, "I can't go on. You are arguing in order to have the pleasure of triumphing over me. At best you win an argument. At worse you lose an argument. I am arguing to preserve my existence." (43)

Soloveitchik disarms us further when he speaks of the source of his anguish as stemming from different overlapping causes.

I must address myself to the obvious question: why am I beset by the feeling of loneliness and being unwanted? Is it a Kierkegaardian anguish—an ontological fear nurtured by the awareness of non-being threatening one's existence—that assails me, or is this feeling of loneliness solely due to my own personal stresses, cares and frustrations? Or is it perhaps the result of the pervasive state of mind of Western man who has become estranged from himself, a state with which all of us as Westerners are acquainted? (7)

When Soloveitchik concentrates on the ontological and cultural origins of his loneliness, the psychological dimension is ever present. His evocation of the relationship of Adam the second and Eve has unmistakable emotional overtones.

> . . . there one hears not only the rhythmic sound of the production line, but also the rhythmic beat of hearts starved for existential companionship and all-embracing sympathy and experiencing the grandeur of the faith commitment; there, one lonely soul finds another soul tormented by loneliness and solitude yet unqualifiedly committed. (28)

He often appeals to emotional relationships to illustrate the existential crisis. Thus, he evokes the relationship with a dying friend, a parent, and a rebellious child, to demonstrate the inadequacy of communication. (44)

A distinctive emotional tone is sounded when describing the intimacy with God, the third partner in the covenantal faith relationship. "Who is He to whom Adam clings in passionate, all-consuming love . . . Who is He whose life-giving and life-warming breath Adam feels constantly? . . ." (17) The man of faith is able to reach the point when everything "has to give in to an 'absurd' commitment. The man of faith is 'insanely' committed to and 'madly' in love with God." (67) But most revealing is the emotional content of Soloveitchik's personal experience of God. He painfully relates his encounter with God when he returns home from the hospital where his wife is terminally ill.

> . . . the need for prayer was great; I could not live without gratifying this need. The moment I returned home I would rush to my room, fall down on my knees and pray fervently. God, in those moments, appeared not

as an exalted, majestic King, but rather as a humble, close friend,
brother, father: in such moments of black despair, He was not far from
me; He was right there in the dark room; I felt His warm hand, in a
manner of speaking, on my shoulder, I hugged His knees, in a manner
of speaking. ("Majesty and Humility," 33)

The profound effect that his relationship with his wife has had on
Soloveitchik's teaching, is reminiscent of what some biblical scholars
have attributed to the prophet Hosea. While his faithful and loving
relationship with his wife acts as a living intimation of the communication and communion possible between Adam the second and Eve,
conversely, the disintegration of their communication with the onset
of her death serves to underscore "the ontological remoteness" between two people. ("The Community," 11)

A crescendo of pathos is evinced when Soloveitchik identifies with
God with whom he shares (in a manner of speaking) the same ontological condition. "I experience a growing awareness that . . . this
service to which I, a lonely and solitary individual, am committed is
wanted and gracefully accepted by God in His transcendental loneliness and numinous solitude." (7) Aware of the strong emotional
element, he identifies it as a component of the existential nature of
humankind. "As a *homo absconditus*, Adam the second is not capable
of telling his personal experiential story in majestic formal terms. His
emotional life is inseparable from his unique *modus existentiae* and
therefore, if communicated to the 'thou' only as a piece of surface
information, unintelligible." (44)

Having been invited into the soul of an anguished man of faith
totally committed to a dynamic relationship with God who is always
commanding, and who is now intimately present, now despairingly
absent, we are left bereft, for the moment, of our critical faculties. It is
rare indeed to find a philosopher or theologian who is witness to his
own truth.

Another captivating level of Soloveitchik's teaching is his general
approach to religion. "He leads me beside the still waters" is the end
of the process and never fully realized in an uneschatological world.

Even when redemption is experienced for a fleeting moment in the context of the covenantal faith community, one is cast back into a dialectical condition that has no room for green pastures. The demands of the religious life require the mobilization of reason and faith, will and emotion. One is to control his environment, bend it to his will, overcome his sense of helplessness, assert his sovereignty and responsibility. At the same time he must be able to surrender his will, withdraw from his moment of triumph, accept defeat, recoil from domination and the obsession to succeed. In his essay "Catharsis," Soloveitchik insists that heroism is not only conquest of external reality, but self conquest in the areas of aesthetics, emotion, intellect and morality. "Biblical heroism is not ecstatic but rather contemplative; not loud but hushed; not dramatic or spectacular but mute. The individual, instead of undertaking heroic actions sporadically, lives constantly as a hero." (42) The man of faith is caught in a complementary movement by alternatively advancing and retreating. Religion is a dialectic of warring forces that may find a synthesis in the philosophic thought of Hegel, but not in the existential nature of man. God is both immanent and transcendent; man is to be majestic and humble, cosmic and covenantal, a solitary, singular individual who defies convention, resists and protests an immoral society, and a responsive member of the community who must make the paradoxical leap over the abyss in order to share his singularity with others. In short, religious faith embraces all layers of the human being and is

> a raging, clamorous torrent of man's consciousness with all its crises, pangs, and torments . . . out of the straits of inner oppositions and incongruities, spiritual doubts and uncertainties, out of the depths of a psyche rent with antinomies and contradictions, out of the bottomless pit of a soul that struggles with its own torments I have called, I have called unto Thee, O Lord. (*Halakhic Man*, 142)

Undisciplined and unsystematic as Soloveitchik is, one can discern movement in his thinking. A comparative study of his first major philosophic study *Halakhic Man* and "The Lonely Man of Faith" reveal a major revision of focus and concern. The former was concerned with placing the 'talmid hakham' (religious scholar) in the front line of intellectual achievement. Soloveitchik was bent on demonstrating that the autonomy which Kant trumpeted was realized in the heteronomy of Halakha no less than in theoretical mathematics. The creativity, intellectual integrity, dispassionate and rigorous research wedded to a moral vision were not the exclusive possession of philosophy and science. In this work he eschewed the mystic, pietistic exercises of the *homo religiosus* who is the antithesis of cognitive man. He disparaged the *homo religiosus* for being ever suspended "between the two poles of self-negation and absolute pride, between the consciousness of his nothingness and consciousness of the infinity deep with him. *Homo religiosus* can never be free of this oscillation." (*Halakhic Man*, 69) While halakhic man was subject to the same spiritual split, he had the Halakha to stabilize and mend the split. (Ibid.) In "The Lonely Man of Faith," on the other hand, the concerns of the *homo religiosus* now become central. The emphasis is no longer on the bold, confidence and assertiveness of halakhic man, but on the loneliness and ontological insecurity of covenantal man. Kierkegaard, not Kant, is a major referent and point of departure. The existential problem of man's loneliness, singularity; the difficult but desperate need to communicate and commune with other lonely singular beings; the ontologically grounded dialectic of ruling over being and at the same time submitting to the rule of Being; and the social dislocation of a society indifferent to the transcendent commandments of the man of faith—these were the crucial issues. It is not accidental that the covenantal faith community, not Halakha, is the new formulation for the life of Torah. The concentration is on relationship, not simply on a sacred text from on high. In the new context, the oscillation between self-negation and absolute pride is not mended, but instigated and maintained by Halakha.

> When man gives himself to the covenantal community the Halakha reminds him that he is also wanted and needed in another community, the cosmic-majestic, and when it comes across man while he is involved

in the creative enterprise of the majestic community, it does not let him forget that he is a covenantal being who will never find self-fulfillment outside of the covenant and that God awaits his return to the covenantal community . . . I have the distinct impression as if the Halakha considered the steady oscillating of the man of faith between majesty and covenant not as a dialectical but rather as a complementary movement. (51)

Halakha takes on a new significance. Gone is the Archimedean point that is outside and above the turbulence of the soul, beyond the maelstrom of the affective life, a true source of peace and tranquillity. Gone is the objectification that turns the mind away from the devastation of the death of a loved one into the dispassionate study of the laws of mourning. (*Halakhic Man*, 73, 76) Apart from its other functions, Halakha now keeps awake the existential yearning that points to redemption, but forbids its realization.

There is a persuasive appeal of a living faith that leaves room for growth, for paradox, for the ebb and flow of primal forces in man whether we label them existential or otherwise. However, we would be doing Soloveitchik an injustice if we reject his invitation to engage him in serious conversation. "If my audience will feel that these interpretations are also relevant to their perceptions and emotions, I shall feel amply rewarded. However, I shall not feel hurt if my thoughts will find no response in the hearts of my listeners." I must confess to both responses. Soloveitchik's interpretations are relevant to my perceptions and emotions as I have outlined above. But there are some misgivings that must be articulated.

A first reservation relates to Soloveitchik's typology of Adam the first. While affirming the creativity and God-given mandate to control and reign supreme over the cosmos, he wages a withering condemnation of majestic (technological) man. He is self-serving, ego-centered, bent on total domination, interested only in impressing society, not in cultivating his inner worth. Soloveitchik writes of the "demonic quality laying claim to unlimited power . . . diabolically insists on being successful." (62,64) Without the restraining balance of covenantal man, the majestic man becomes a hollow man devoid of a soul. Having attributed to majestic man the dignity and majesty of a partner of God in creation and having vaunted modern technology as a divine commandment, he demonizes the whole enterprise. Hartman rightly observes that Soloveitchik indulges in a severe *ad hominem* attack for he fails to demonstrate that in fact these values are intrinsic to Western culture. (*A Living Covenant*, 104) In the end, Soloveitchik has demeaned the very people he sought to exalt. Are all non-covenantals compromisers, surface people devoid of human sensitivity and conscience? Experience teaches otherwise. People unaware or unaccepting of the covenant nurture inner lives of infinite worth neither bowing nor scrapping to the gods of power, convenience, success or self-aggrandizement. And is it true that a covenantal faith is a sine quo non of human communication? No doubt a shared language of faith, a similar world view, an appreciation of the same values, the acceptance of a common discipline of action and thought, make possible and clear the way for common discourse. However, these ingredients are not exclusive to the covenantal faith community nor do they exclude the possibility and experience of people who communicate deeply despite the uncommonality and abysses that separate them. There is no public or private monopoly on transcendence. By permitting his typology to become a grotesque caricature of real people, he has weakened a valid critique of what a technological society can become if it becomes obsessed with extrinsic goals that do not take the whole person into account.

And what of the covenantal faith community? While subjecting majestic man to caustic criticism, the shortcomings of the man of faith pass unnoticed. One could ask Soloveitchik where indeed—with emphasis on deed—are his covenantal men who oscillate between the inner world of faith and the world of creation sharing equally the responsibilities of a living relation with God and with their fellow men? Is not the existing faith community which he urges majestic man to join a far, far cry from the community he so lavishly idealizes? Furthermore, must the covenantal faith be seen as a static, unchanging bastion of eternity? In the first place, the contention flies in the face of historic reality. Secondly, a tradition does not have to be impervious to time, place or circumstance to be an anchor to a transcendent vision for a confused society, a constellation of principles that give direction and enhance human struggle for self-worth and significance, a goad to human betterment. Consigning the covenantal faith to a sealed, unassailable sanctuary, is to lead to the very self-righteousness that Soloveitchik fears. Revelation that passes through fallible human minds and spirits is not free of imperfection and distortion. To withdraw from the criticism of others in the name of God's inscrutability or the immutability of the Torah, is to rob the faith community of the means to purify itself of the sedentary dross of unexamined lives.

But when all is said and done, we are richer for the seminal thought and whole-hearted faith of Soloveitchik. His analysis of the human condition, his juxtaposing and wedding of the creative, free, responsible individual with the man of faith who lives the eternal quest of a living relation with God and man, resonate in the inner recess of the questing spirit. I conclude with the words of Soloveitchik:

> The Jewish ideal is not the harmonious individual determined by the principle of man's essence, his metaphysical origin. It is existential, not social, political, or economic. The Torah bids man to combat . . . superficial, external crises. The ills of poverty, disease and war are debilitating and impair our spiritual freedom. The Torah, however, encourages man to submit to and embrace the experience of the depth crisis. Thereby does man truly grasp the reality of his condition and become stirred to great heights of the spirit. For this depth crisis there is no solution except prayer. Surface crisis can be overcome; the existential crisis can only be met by prayer. ("Sacred and Profane", 7)

BIBLIOGRAPHY

HARTMAN, David, *A Living Covenant*, New York and London, 1985.
LAING, R. D., *The Divided Self*, Victoria: Penguin Books, 1978.
SOLOVEITCHIK, Joseph B., "Ish haHalakha," published in *Talpiot* (New York) 1:3–4, 1944. Quoted from English translation by Lawrence Kaplan: *Halakhic Man*, Philadelphia, 1983.

_____, "Sacred and Profane," (based on lecture in 1945).

_____, "The Lonely Man of Faith," *Tradition* 7:2 (Summer 1965), 5–67.

_____, "Majesty and Humility," *Tradition* 17:2 (Spring 1978), 25–37 (based on a lecture given in 1973).

_____, "Catharsis," *Tradition* 17:2 (Spring 1978) 38–54 (based on a lecture given in 1962).

_____, "The Community," *Tradition* 17:2 (Spring 1978) 7–24 (based on a lecture given in 1976).

9. The Gate to God's Presence in Heschel, Buber, and Soloveitchik

Evan M. Zuesse

It is no easy thing to rethink a religious tradition. Despite a constellation of brilliant thinkers amongst the Jews in the last two hundred years, very few have been able to create a total and systematic rationale for Judaism. Those that have been created have inevitably made fundamental use of the best of contemporary European philosophical thought, and have been guides for the perplexed of their generation. They could not aspire to be such guides, did they not speak persuasively in the language of their time, and that also means using the language and assumptions of current thought. But at the same time, that current European thought has inevitably been a thought deeply influenced by Christian and other non-Judaic presuppositions, and there has always been the danger of miscomprehending the essential nature of Judaism in the process of interpreting it with such language. The task of Jewish thinkers down through the ages has always been to use the thought of their times to transcend that thought's limitations, and thus to refract something of the distinctive quality of Judaism, and

121

its dissenting message, to Jews of those generations. In the comments that follow, a number of major Jewish thinkers of this generation will be considered from this perspective. The value of this essay will not be in any pretense at originality, but simply in the opportunity it gives us to reconsider the significance and adequacy of thinkers whose greatness cannot be lessened by any criticisms of ours, and whose writings offer perhaps the most disciplined guidance to thinking Jews of our age. We cannot deal with all the major figures in modern Jewish thought; we have chosen instead to comment on the three figures who are perhaps the most significant intellectual leaders of the three chief forms of Judaism today: among Conservative Jews, Abraham Joshua Heschel, among Liberal or Reform Jews, Martin Buber, and among Orthodox Jews, Joseph Soloveitchik. Others might have been chosen; these are the paradigmatic ones in my own opinion.

Abraham Joshua Heschel

Abraham Joshua Heschel once began a typically illuminating discourse on the meaning of the Halakha with a reminiscence of his student days in Berlin (Heschel, 1977: 134ff.). It was, he said, a crucial time in his life. Although he was a descendant of great Hasidic saints, brought up and educated within mystical and traditional Judaism, and even expected to take over the role of saintly leader of one of the major eastern European Hasidic groups, Heschel inevitably suffered a kind of culture shock when he broke away from his wholly traditional environment to enroll at the University of Berlin to study philosophy. He had come to Berlin in quest of a way to integrate holiness into the whole of modern life, but he found that his professors did not even recognize the question. "My teachers were prisoners of a Greek-German way of thinking. They were fettered in categories which presupposed certain metaphysical assumptions which could never be proved. The questions I was moved by could not even be adequately phrased in categories of their thinking" (135f.).

This testimony of a fundamental incongruity between experiential traditional Judaism and modern (German) thought is of the utmost importance not only in regard to Heschel's experience and development, but in regard to the entire sweep of modern Jewish philosophy. One major reason for this is that to an astonishing degree, modern Jewish philosophy is, taken as a whole, a German phenomenon, and has been shaped by precisely the agendas and categories which Heschel found so alien; from Moses Mendelssohn at the very beginning of Jewish modernization right up to such giants of this century and even this generation as Hermann Cohen, Heschel himself, Martin Buber, Franz Rosenzweig, Leo Baeck, Emil Fackenheim and Joseph Soloveitchik, the greatest figures in modern Jewish thought grew up in or have been deeply shaped by German philosophy and cultural orientations, to such a degree, indeed, that Hermann Cohen, who came only in later years to a deep intellectual immersion in Jewish tradition, was only repeating many others when he spoke of a natural and almost predestined harmony between German and Jewish thought. To understand modern Jewish philosophy, in short, we must also understand the preoccupations of German philosophy.

Heschel tells us how the central concerns of German philosophy in his day were presented to him (we can replace the term "world" in his explanation by "reality" and even by "God"—the analysis remains valid):

> Kant, who held dominion over many minds had demonstrated that it is utterly impossible to attain knowledge of the world . . . because knowledge is always in the form of categories and these, in the last analysis, are only representational constructions for the purpose of apperceiving what is given. Objects possessing attributes, causes that work, are all mythical. We can only say that objective phenomena are regarded *as if* they behaved in such and such a way, and there is absolutely no justification for assuming any dogmatic attitude and changing the "as if" into a "that." Salomon Maimon was probably the first to sum up Kantian philosophy by saying that only *symbolic knowledge* is possible. (Italics in original: 134)

As Heschel goes on to remark, in the light of such assumptions, there can be no "valid conception of the supernatural in an objective sense, yet since for practical purposes it is useful to cherish the idea of God, let us retain that idea and claim that while our knowledge of God is not objectively true, it is still symbolically true"(135).

The dilemma is a profound one. It involves not only the question of the reality of God—or the lack of it—but also the question of how, assuming God's reality has been satisfactorily determined, we can *contact* God (or even dwell in any authentic reality). For if God and reality are only symbolically real, then so too are our contacts with both. There is actual reality (if the terminology be allowed) in neither God-as-known nor our living relationship with him.

Heschel's phrasing of the problem reflects the dominant views of the philosophy of religion in his student years, when the neo-Kantianism of Hermann Cohen's Marburg school shaped general discussion. Ernst Cassirer (who was also of Jewish background, but who knew very little of Judaism) exemplified the general approach to religion of this school in his *The Philosophy of Symbolic Forms*, which in its second volume described the history of religions in terms of symbolic thought. There were other schools of thought, however, which each reflected the fundamental impact of Kant's thought.

ʻ For example, a major alternative interpretation of Kant stressed the emotional or non-rational aspect of religion. If neither perception nor reason are able to bring us into direct contact with God or Being, feelings or intuitive experiences of a certain kind can. There might even be a special way of knowing that lies outside the rational limitations Kant imposed, or that constituted a unique category or mode of human experience not accounted for by Kant, that allowed a direct contact with God. Rudolf Otto, a Lutheran theologian, asserted that religion arises from the spontaneous recognition of the Wholly Other, which is directly experienced as Absolute, beyond all relativities, and shattering all other forms of knowing. It transcends rationality and even categories of time and space, and is known solely through ecstasies of awe and love. Such is the non-rational (faith) essence of religion, which appears in various ways in all religions and is imperfectly expressed in their theological teachings and ethical and liturgical systems, but which (Otto tells us) is found perfectly only in Christianity as presented by Luther (and interpreted by the Kantian Lutheran theologian Schleiermacher, Otto's own favorite guide). After all, Luther made very clear that neither reason nor ethical works provide any genuine access to "the holy." As we can see, and as was explicitly stated by Otto, this analysis of religion is a frank exercise in Christian "natural theology."[1] A prominent part of Otto's *Das Heilige* was devoted to showing how the Jewish understanding of the holy was a fumbling preliminary to the perfect Christian one: we are told of the "Old Testament" concept of the utter transcendence of the holy, before which mere human beings feel crushed and "sinful" (i.e., merely creaturely, impotent, overwhelmed and inadequate)—ancient Jewry symbolized all this in its alleged concepts of the dreadful wrath, severe justice, and awful loftiness of God.

It is interesting to see how deeply these thinkers influenced even a Heschel, certain though he was that their assumptions were inadequate for Jewish religious experience. In fact, it can be said that of all major modern Jewish thinkers, none are so similar to Rudolf Otto as Heschel. But just because of this similarity, the differences stand out the more clearly.

Heschel, like Otto, insists on the primacy of the non-rational and direct experience of God. God is found above all in the ecstatic sense of wonder and awe that we feel when we behold the universe, his creation, or when we pray directly to him. In his book subtitled "A Philosophy of Religion," we are told in the very first pages that the root of religion lies in "the sense of the ineffable." This "ineffable" points to the same qualities of awesome grandeur and gracious love that Otto has spoken of as "the holy" (and later Heschel will speak explicitly of "the holy"), but right in these first references there is a startling divergence from Otto (Heschel, 1951:5):

The ineffable inhabits the magnificent and the common, the grandiose and the tiny facts of reality alike. Some people sense this quality at distant intervals in extraordinary events; other sense it in the ordinary events, in every fold, in every nook; day after day, hour after hour. To them things are bereft of triteness; to them being does not mate with nonsense. . . . Slight and simple as things may be—a piece of paper, a morsel of bread, a word, a sign—they hide and guard a never-ending secret: A glimpse of God? Kinship with the spirit of being? An eternal flash of will?

Entirely like Otto, Heschel goes on to write of the difference between this "entrance to the essence" of religion from all paths that stress strict rationality. "Soul and reason are *not* the same," he exclaims (the emphasis is his own: 7). Only through "radical amazement" and wonder do we come to the realms of genuine knowledge of reality, realms not accessible to science as such. All of this sounds very familiar from Otto. The startling divergence lies in Heschel's stress on the possible ordinariness of the occasions and things that initiate us into the experience of "the holy." And, as we shall see, it is above all through the commandments that this ordinary non-ecstatic realm is raised to and preserved within the "holy."

It will be remembered that for Otto the experience of the holy, and the root of the "faith" of Christianity, lies quite outside of space and time, and is experienced in an overwhelming and shattering ecstasy of awe and dread, an experience of the utterly transcendent "Wholly Other"—*especially* in the "Old Testament" and in Judaism. But here, right at the start, Heschel emphasizes the love and graciousness of God as known in Judaism (which entirely undercuts Otto's historical schemas) and, even more remarkably, in faithfulness to the central thrust of Halakha, Heschel speaks of the ordinariness and non-otherworldly form of the holy, and goes on to draw attention to a "radical amazement" that includes the smallest things of everyday life. Moreover, if everything becomes symbolical of the ineffable, it would be incorrect to say that the ineffable is a synonym for the unknown, the abnormal or the enigmatic (as Otto would have it): quite the opposite: the world as a whole and in every normal and known detail refers to it. "The world in its grandeur is full of a spiritual radiance, for which we have neither name nor concept"(22). For Heschel, it would be quite true to say, the entire world should be understood as a symbolism of God, as if it were a great poem or song all parts of which refer to its creator—and of these parts or symbolisms humanity is especially precious because it epitomizes the rest and can become aware of precisely the symbolical and spiritual nature of reality. Judaism is the religion which consciously celebrates this, by a path of living that turns the whole of human life into a work of art and wonder, a passionate enactment of holiness, whose most dense form is precisely that of the commandments.[2] God himself can only be understood and contacted as a God of pathos, of intense "feeling"—the biblical God of the prophets is a passionate, living, experiential God, who cares about human beings, about the way that they relate to each other, and about the wonderfully poetical Creation he has made. We must understand God's engagement, his anger and his love equally from this experiential, yet symbolical basis (Heschel, 1962). Not only the prophets, but the simple Jews down through the ages made contact with this aspect of holiness through enacting God's will sympathically in the commandments. According to Heschel, Judaism as a whole is above all a religion of sympathy—a sympathy turned toward and echoing God and his love for Creation and for humanity.

So we find that Heschel goes far beyond Otto's concept of the "Wholly Other" ecstatic otherworldliness of the "holy," locating it instead in everyday life and in things, persons and events sanctified in deeds done with reverential intention, this in turn being grounded in a passionate relationship to an intimately present God who loves humanity intensely. The Commandments are obviously pivotal in this view of spirituality. Here, certainly, is a more authentic Judaism and "Old Testament" sense of "the holy" than any Otto knows.

Yet, we cannot help but notice even here, in the context of this persuasive, moving and exalted understanding of Judaism and of religion, that Heschel has echoed precisely that tendency of his time to find spirituality in *symbolisms* of God and reality, of which he complained when he encountered it in Berlin in his early student days. We may say that Heschel has both succumbed to his environment, and used it in order to overcome its limitations. In many ways, he succeeded. One must agree with Eugene Borowitz's comment that "Heschel's moving validation of a neo-traditional Judaism is unparalleled in twentieth-century Jewish thought" (Borowitz:183). However, the fact that some commentators on his philosophy of Judaism have complained of precisely his stress on emotional-spiritual feelings and poetic declamations rather than a patient and orderly philosophy of Judaism based on clear reason, indicates that perhaps not all limitations were overcome.[3] Of course, it is also true that the Hasidic and mystical kind of Judaism that Heschel grew up in was amenable to just such an emphasis on emotion and faith, so it cannot be said that his philosophy was unauthentic simply because it offers more appeals to the realm of feelings and spiritual-existential intuitions than is usual in Jewish philosophy. Like Yehuda ha-Levi's similar system in the Middle Ages, such appeals were even justified by Heschel's philosophy, and were thus reasonable.

The dualism between reality or Being and our world of relativeness that, as we have seen, goes back through Kant to a source in the New Testament/Hellenic division of spirit and flesh, crops up in other Jewish philosophers in the modern period, and very few were able to overcome those dualisms as fully as Heschel. One of the most obvious examples is that of Martin Buber.

Martin Buber

In one of his early works, *Daniel* (1913), Buber asserted that there were two different ways of relating to the world: "In each thing, there opens to you the door of the One if you bring with you the magic that unlocks it: the perfection of your direction (*Richtung*, orientation)."[4] By orienting or directing yourself properly in the world of things and relationships, you can break through to the "realization" (*Wirklichkeit*) of Being itself. "Orienting" is the mode of experience through which we order the world, discovering and following its rules and laws. "Realization" is the mode through which we penetrate its inner nature. It is beyond rules and laws. The dichotomous analysis was brought to its richest expression in a book written not long after the publication of *Daniel*, entitled *Ich und Du* (1923, translated into English under the title *I and Thou* in two different translations, 1938 and 1970). As is well known, Buber maintained that when we relate to the orderly world of things, we experience everything, and everyone, in "I-It" terms. The significant thing even about another person is how he or she relates to other things or interests. But when we spontaneously discover the other person (or animal or even inanimate thing) in his or her own specificity, in the depth of his or her single existence, in an "I-Thou" relationship, we are momentarily outside of all other relationships and are in a realm taken up solely by dialogue between two ineffable beings, where there are no fixed rules or laws, or even "world." The other person is important in him or herself, not in terms of some extrinsic relationship.

While Buber admitted that the I-It world of ordered relationships and varying laws of nature and of society were important, and had positive sides, his entire system seemed to deny it genuine moral value or even any final claim to truth. So, for example, Buber found no validity in any set ritual or binding moral law, and had to reject the entire formal sphere of Halakha that is so important in Judaism. Additionally, since God too can only be truly known in dialogue, in which the "I" encounters the "Eternal Thou" who makes all other "Thous" possible, and since this encounter occurs outside of any determinate world or structures, there can clearly be no notion of a literal revelation, or of any moral laws or explicitly defined teachings that were laid down by God. The Torah and prophets must be understood to express the world of the ineffable dialogue between God and humanity in symbolical language, and cannot be taken literally.

In such concepts, Buber seems to be giving an existentialist version, with some changes, of the Kantian notions of the chasm between true Being which can never be certainly and determinately known, and the world available to consciousness, the world of relationships, in which only proximate even if highly determinate truths can be known. For Buber, we can enter into contact with true and absolute being, only if we give our own whole being to it and break through the web of relative structures our consciousness has woven. In a way that does not after all differ very much from Otto's adaptation of Kant, Buber posits a special *a priori* category of perception, *sui generis* and supposedly engaging the whole self, ecstatic and outside of time and space, which can truly and non-rationally contact the "Other." It would even appear that Buber wrote *I and Thou* specifically as a reply to Otto, among others. We know that he intended it to be the first part, dealing with basic principles, of a general phenomenology of religions like Otto's.[5] He actually refers directly to Otto's theories in *I and Thou*: his comments are interesting and worth quoting here as indicative of the way a profoundly Jewish thinker felt bound to modify the Kantian assumptions he had nevertheless accepted, especially when they had led to the explicitly Lutheran conclusions of a Rudolf Otto (Buber, 1970: 127):

> One does not find God if one remains in the world; one does not find God if one leaves the world. Whoever goes forth to his You with his whole being and carries to it all the being of the world, finds him whom one cannot seek. Of course, God is "the wholly other"; but he is also the wholly same: the wholly present. Of course, he is the mysterium tremendum (the terminology Otto coined) that appears and overwhelms; but he is also the mystery of the obvious that is closer to me than my own I.

For Buber, unlike Otto, holiness was to be discovered in the ordinary things of life, and the everyday encounters, not only in the ecstatic flights to utter transcendence of all worldly things. This insight, which Buber owed to Hasidism, but even more deeply to Hasidism's halakhic roots, determined his entire modification of Kant's and Otto's perspective. The aim was to be wholly present at all moments of life, not at "spiritual" occasions but as a governing orientation, thus spiritualizing the whole of life. This was what Buber understood the *mitzvot*, the commandments, to be aiming for, even if he believed that, as rule and law, they were by definition not the sufficient means to attain the aim. Moreover, Buber even went on to criticize Schleiermacher's faith-oriented emphasis on the "feeling of absolute dependence" on "absolute Being" as the guarantor of being in actual contact with God, as well as Otto's specification of "creature-feeling" as the diagnostic evidence of this contact. "Feelings merely accompany the fact of the relationship which after all is established not in the soul but between an I and a You" (129). Stress on feelings and on the soul are too one-sided, and ignore the totality of the human relationship, as well as the call that comes from God to enter and dwell in his Creation, sharing it with God. Indeed, stressing feelings can end in stressing oneself, even if one pretends that one is feeling absolute dependence; while in emphasizing dependence as such, one is in danger of ignoring that what is required of one in dialogue is one's active involvement. One is addressed by God, and one has a response to make—a response that takes one into God's world. Contrary to Schleiermacher, ethics and action in the world are not a secondary and derivative sector unrelated to the essential religious "feeling of absolute dependence," but the actual form of the encounter between I and Thou. The Eternal Thou is experienced within every relationship to a particular Thou, for example.

Nevertheless, many commentators have criticized the one-sidedness and polarities of Buber's own thought, on the grounds that they do not do justice to the fullness of life and of the religious insights of Judaism.[6] The failure to understand the Halakha in a positive way is no doubt the chief symptom of this failure to break out completely from the Christian presuppositions underlying the Kantian categories.

Joseph Soloveitchik

In a short paper of this nature, it is not possible to review all even of the major Jewish philosophers of the modern period. I will end with a brief consideration of Joseph Soloveitchik, who more perhaps than any other contemporary Jewish philosopher may be said to embody Orthodox thought at its most vigorous. Certainly here, at least, we might expect to find a system of Jewish thought that does not repeat the Kantian dualistic dichotomies and oversimplifications.

Our expectation is disappointed. Indeed, Soloveitchik is much more obviously Kantian than, say, Heschel. He even approximates or exceeds Buber's Kantianism. Of course, it must be emphasized again that some indebtedness to Kant is inevitable and necessary in modern thought: the basic structure of modern philosophy has been shaped by this, and is inconceivable without it. The real question we must ask is how far any particular philosophy is limited by such structures, or uses them to transcend them, particularly when it is a question of gaining adequate insights into Judaism. So we must look more closely at Soloveitchik's thought to find the answer to this question of adequacy.

Unquestionably one of the greatest essays of Soloveitchik's is his discourse on Halakha (first appearing in Hebrew in 1944 as *Ish haHalakha*, and published in English as *Halakhic Man* in 1983). Aaron Lichtenstein, in an essay published in 1963 but still often referred to as the best summary of Soloveitchik's thought, wrote that his approach to halakha

> . . . emphasizes the integration of all parts of living into a unified, religious framework. It knows no dualism and recognizes no dichotomy between the religious and the secular. Each is distinct, but by no means disjunct. . . . Halakha does not permit the Jew to secularize life; it enjoins him from escaping it. The halakhic figure neither ignores the transcendental nor flees to it; he seeks to incorporate it within his own temporal existence. . . . Thus, while God alone can be recognized as an absolute good, all aspects of human activity attain vital significance as segments of a life committed in its totality to God. (Lichtenstein: 292).

Certainly, this sounds like Soloveitchik has overcome any split between spirit and flesh initiated by Christianity and subtly perpetuated by Kant. Yet, Lichtenstein commences his review of Soloveitchik's thought by stating that it begins with an awareness of the dual character of human existence, a duality which Lichtenstein claims is fundamental to Judaism: "Man is viewed from two aspects: he is both passive and active, cause and effect" (288). As Lichtenstein goes on immediately to admit, Soloveitchik borrows from Kierkegaard (who is a major influence on his general thought) a view that perhaps the "one definitive key to man's essential personality" is his spiritual loneliness—being alone before God, being what Kierkegaard calls "the Single One," utterly separated from all that connects him to nature or to his fellow human beings (288). Lichtenstein here no doubt is basing himself on Soloveitchik's remarkable essay, "The Lonely Man of Faith," first published in the journal *Tradition*, Vol. 7, No. 2, in 1965. In this essay, Soloveitchik even goes so far as to posit two Adams, two essential but radically different modes of human existence, suggested in the two accounts of Adam and Eve's creation in the Book of Genesis. In one of these primal modes, we engage with other human beings in an active and "creative" involvement with the world.[7] Our focus is both social and intellectual, directed to the many things of the world, which we work with and manipulate. But this is from a certain perspective merely a distraction from the other primal mode, the essential aloneness of each of us in our innermost being, where we stand bereft, helpless, laden with sinfulness and bewildered before the final realities of life and death, where our intellect and our worldly works do not help us and where our only aid and solace is our absolute dependence on God—our "faith." (The entire portrait, including the dualistic opposition of world of things with which we are active, and the lonely world of faith in which we are passive, also reflects the strong influence of Friedrich Schleiermacher.) Yet there is a way out for Adam the Second, for he seeks a community through which to mitigate his loneliness, a community composed of an "I," a "Thou" of human friendship and sympathy, and an authoritative and commanding "He," who reveals himself as the ultimate "Thou," God himself, creating the community through prophecy and prayer. The response from Adam the Second is self-sacrificial enactment of moral and ritual deeds, through which the personally addressed God is seen as embracing the entire universe and all living beings.

As with Buber, the basic vision seems to begin with a rather Lutheran and dualistic starting point, opposing passive subjectivity and even loneliness (the "faith" pole) with an active manipulation of the world that in itself can never win through to God and redemption. But, again like Buber, Soloveitchik allows the "lonely man of faith" a renewed access to community, to other human beings, and to God and redemption, through submission to a Torah perspective. The reference to "I" and "Thou" suggests that Soloveitchik is conscious of this echo, and even cognizant perhaps of Buber's critical response to Kierkegaard's insistence of the loneliness of the man of faith. In the essential encounter of the self with God, for Buber there can be no loneliness, for Buber sees the entire world implied in that encounter and indeed precisely this encounter makes it possible for Buber to meet in true recognition with all other Thous.[8] In confirmation of this, it is noteworthy that in the climatic moments of encounter with God in the Jewish liturgy, that is to say during the High Holy Day services, the confessions of sin are in the plural.

Soloveitchik suggest in places that the types of human situations that he evokes (e.g., Adam the First and Adam the Second) are not per se actual individuals, but to some degree coexist and mingle in all of us, or can be found more emphasized in some than in others. They are ideal types. In fact, it is because the pietist is constantly moving between one and the other polar type, that loneliness can never be escaped. Underlying this conception of ideal or essential types, however, is a typically Kantian theory, in this case as elaborated by Edmund Husserl, the founder of phenomenological theory in the first decades of this century.

The typologies in Soloveitchik's writings, besides, do not always appear as mere ideal constructions that can be mingled in ordinary life. At times they appear as radically opposed universes which, if mingled, can only be at the cost of their respective fundamental structures, their essences and not merely their forms. For example, in his majestic work, *Halakhic Man*, Soloveitchik structures the entire work around a striking opposition between "halakhic man" and the portrait of *homo religiosus*, "religious man," made known to us by Otto, Schleiermacher and Kierkegaard. Here he opposes the passive subjectivity of the latter to the activism and this-worldly, rational objectivity of the former. "This fundamental opposition between the ontological outlooks of *homo religiosus* and halakhic man is reflected in the very being of these two personalities; it pervades their entire characters" (Soloveitchik, 1983: 66). In that case, we have to do with a disharmonious conflict between the two types, if they should be experienced within the same person. As described by Soloveitchik, this conflict is indeed a persisting one. For example, the halakhic personality is an Adam the First as he reappears within the world of Torah, actively creating and manipulating ideal conceptions in a world of things and persons. *Homo religiosus*, on the other hand, seems to belong to an Adam the Second mentality.

It might well be argued that Soloveitchik is actually implying by his use of such typologies that human nature is per se internally contradictory and discontinuous. He actually asserts that there is constant movement between his types, however contradictory they may be, within actual persons. This may be so, but it would appear to be a strange way to approach a phenomenology of the Torah personality, seeing that the Torah grounds its call on an appeal to be whole, *tam*, before God. In Soloveitchik's perspective we have very little understanding of how this might be possible, or of the harmony Heschel and Buber perceive in Torah life. Apparently a simple, harmonious Torah personality is an ideal which even for the most deeply religious individuals also an impossibility.[9] This is one of the most striking and provocative themes of his writings. And even if it were possible, in terms of this philosophy it *would not be desirable*. As Pinchas Peli has remarked, in the introduction to his rendition to Soloveitchik's teachings on repentance,

> the depth of the personality . . . is measured according to criteria of the torments of duality, contradiction, doubts and struggles which issue in the "emergence of a personality shrouded in sanctity whose soul was purified in the smithy of perplexity and contradiction and refined in the fires of spiritual conflict."[10]

We must admit that Soloveitchik interprets very vividly some of the storm and stress we encounter in the Psalms, and perhaps his realism, however harsh and even narrow it may sometimes seem, is a welcome antidote to the sometimes perhaps too easy sentimentalism of both Buber and Heschel. What is needed to justify his approach, however, is a fully developed theory of human nature and its propensity to fragmentation, self-destruction and opposition, and disharmony. The closest he seems to have come to doing this is in his lectures "On Repentance" (cf. Peli, 1984b). We encounter here the reproduction in modern philosophical language of the world of the eastern European yeshiva Mitnaged (anti-Hasidic) Mussar religion (although modified by such Christian phenomenologies of sin and redemption as Kierkegaard's and Max Scheler's). The Mussar movement, in turn, was a late modulation, it seems to me, of the mood of asceticism and concern about sin engendered by Lurianic Kabbalah.[11] In any case, there is implicit in Soloveitchik's conception of human nature the most penetrating analysis of human evil to emerge from modern Jewish philosophy. Perhaps this is not remarkable for an Orthodox Jewish thinker. It has been the liberal wings of Judaism that have generally underestimated the capacity for evil and disharmony in human nature and history. Orthodoxy, with the solid rock of a faith in a truly transcendental yet commanding God to rest on, has been more able to look at human nature in an unflinching way.[12]

Yet the path forward visualized by Soloveitchik, for all his recognition of the multileveled complexity of human existence, is above all one of restriction, painful renunciations and a lofty sorrow. This is perhaps the dominant mood of his writings. As we have seen, the Torah and Talmudic ideal of wholeness is recognized, but is drastically undercut not only by the diverse typological identities seen as warring in the human, and especially the Jewish heart, but also by the actual idealization of suffering. "The permanent religious affinity, the 'living together' of God and man in one house, does not produce a calming or tranquilizing effect. On the contrary, 'the religious act is essentially one of suffering'."[13]

The Halakha is presented by Soloveitchik as the path to unification of the multiple personalities of the Jew. In fact, Halakha is the path to unification of all things, and above all of God with his world.

An individual does not become holy through metaphysical attachment to the hidden, nor through mystical union with the infinite . . . but, rather, through his corporeal existence, his bodily actions and *through fulfilling his task of realizing Halakha in the sense-world*. . . . Instead of raising up the lower world to higher realms, he brings down the higher realms to this lower world. . . . The realization of Halakha=the concentration of transcendence in this world=holiness=creation. (Kaplan: 56, supplying the italics and quoting various parts of *Halakhic Man* in his own translation)

But it is significant that what is meant by Halakha more generally in *Halakhic Man* is not so much an actional system, such as is insisted on in the above quotations, but above all an intellectual system (perhaps appropriately for a philosopher who is also an exemplar of the Mitnaged Yeshiva system of Eastern European Jewry). This highly intellectual and analytical Halakha is interestingly different from the more emotional, joyful and earthy Hasidic version we find in Heschel's philosophy.[14] Aside from the obviously strong Mitnaged yeshiva influence, however, a great deal of the intellectualization of the halakhic system, together with the typological and rationalistic approach of Soloveitchik in general, is due to the influence of the Kantian system, which finds the path to truth to life in a rationalistic parsing of reality, a turning away from the merely material world as being the source of error and confusion, replacing it with a search for cognitive-spiritual *a priori* structures and "essences" that float above and outside the material world and that from time to time achieve partial embodiment in the amorphous substance of things. The ultimate sources for such an idealism would seem to be both Christian and Hellenic. It is very understandable and appropriate that the outlook should be so persuasive to Western Christians. It is less appropriate that it should be adopted by Jews, even if it was Philo Judaeus who first showed the way two thousand years ago to accomplish precisely this kind of amalgamation of monotheism and Hellenic thought, including Stoicism, Pythagoreanism and Platonism.

Concluding Remarks

Philo's view of the Law was symptomatic of his fundamental attitude: as Scripture the Law was an allegorical presentation of virtue and reason, and as Commandments it was, among other things (including a divinely revealed socio-political structure), to be seen as a rational discipline, to restrict the passions and temper the mind, to direct it to higher things. After all, for Philo as for so many others ever since, rational and spiritual matters must be radically and clearly distinguished from material things and the passions. The goal of Judaism, to him, was to provide the possibility to ascend to God, rather than to allow the descent of God to this earth and this human encounter. Right at this crucial point, Philo went astray in his Neoplatonism, and departed from both biblical and Talmudic Judaism.[15] One of the striking things about those forms of Judaism is that the spirit cannot be distinguished so easily from the flesh, nor the spiritual from the material realms. The integral existence that they call for requires the genuine unification of both polarities, and no idealization of the splintered or the narrow person. The purpose of Torah observance, in the bible, and as each of the great modern thinkers we have discussed has affirmed, each in his own way, is to render existence in this world, and the passions, things, times and places of this world, "holy." There is no otherworldly or self-consciously "spiritual" goal or realm, for it is the body that is the form of the spirit; and the spirit that is the aware inwardness of the body.

To begin one's Jewish philosophy, therefore, with a stress on rational, cognitive, "spiritual" and intellectual issues is therefore to begin at a very labyrinthine, and perhaps even in some ways a wrong point of entry. Jewish philosophy, I believe, to be authentic should begin with an analysis of the body, which has been so notably neglected in long centuries of Western thought. The body in its fullness is the royal "gateway to the Palace," not the mind nor the "spirit" nor even certain cognitive "essences."

In a way, we are only ready to conceptualize this insight in this

generation in the phraseology of Western thought, for in this generation we have seen a kind of implosion and shattering of that tradition,
signaled by the rise of existentialism, linguistic analysis, a variety of
materialistic reductionisms and a general philosophical skepticism. So
it is now possible to phrase what I am trying to say in phenomenological and Kantian terms, even if it means a kind of ultimate overthrow of
Kantian categories and phenomenological essentialisms and typologies.

According to Edmund Husserl, founder of Phenomenology as a
philosophic school, there are two realms, Being-in-Itself, and Being-
for-Itself.[16] The dichotomy is the familiar Kantian one. Being-in-
Itself, the actual reality or being in its inwardness, can never be known
as such, for all that consciousness can know is Being-for-Itself, that is,
perspectives or aspects of reality that are refracted through consciousness. When we know something, we really only know an aspect of that
thing, as it relates to ourselves and our knowing. Consciousness is
essentially transitive, relational, bridging: all consciousness is
consciousness-of. Consciousness, the realm of Being-for-Itself, or as
we might also call it, Being-for-Others, dwells between things rather
than in them.

Husserl goes on to attempt to systematize the entire structure of
all possible knowing, so as to arrive by this route at the total framework of relative realities within which anything can exist at all: and
this would have final reality. We might be in error about this or that
perspective, but the coherence of all perspectives must be real. In
this bold, and even, according to Husserl, infinite and eternal task,
Husserl devotes all his attention to cognitions. The body is an uninvited guest, a "pivot" for the ego, but irrelevant to the quest that
consciousness is engaged in.

But what if the living body of the cognizer is already a Being-in-
Itself, whose *project* or expression is Being-for-Itself, that is, consciousness? Consciousness without a body, after all, is an impossibility,
even theoretically: in a world solely of relationships (which as we have
just seen is the only possible world for consciousness), if one cannot
take up a position, a specific location, an embodiment, one cannot

enter into relationships. The specific location of Being-for-Itself, con-sciousness, is always a particular body and identity. Only *as* Edmund Husserl, a very particular, assimilated German Jew, of a generation whose dreams were destroyed by World War II, could Husserl philos-ophize about universal "essences" and "a priori" modes of knowl-edge.[17]

But if the body is the foundation for any access to reality, we must ask how the body as body enters into reality. In the world of bodily action and perception there are many fleeting experiences and behav-iors, and many forms of error and transience. When the body experi-ences truth, the only way it has to seize it is to reenter that actional, experiential relationship by reenacting it. Repetition, and heightened, stylized behavior, point to true experiences rather than to false. Such reenactments delineate the norm, the true relationship, the right way of meeting and sustaining reality. The need for these repetitive reca-pitulations and embodiments of reality is all the greater when random ordinary behavior or merely personal desire and experience threaten to dissolve reality into happenstance. But what are such meditatively repetitive, consciously willed and stylized actions, if not *ritual*? An analysis of ritual and normativeness per se is therefore the most appropriate, or the most obvious starting point for analyzing the fundamental experiential realities, rendered into symbol, that con-front actual persons. Different experiential universes demand differ-ent ritual and normative enactments. This immediately brings us to a focus on Halakha, as the paradigmatic and authentic mode of the Jewish encounter with God—not in intellectual constructions, or personality typologies, but the direct and world-generating dialogue of ritual-ethical action.[18] Halakha would be important, from this perspective, not so much for the intellectual challenges its study affords, as for the experiential encounters with final realities, with other human beings and with God and holiness, and the realizations about the meaning of life it brings about in those who follows its paths. There are things experienced about reality, God and the world, through normative and ritual halakhic enactment, that can be experi-enced and understood in no other way.

Our discussion of Buber, Heschel and Soloveitchik has sought to show that right at this point their systems gain solid hold on the distinctive worldview of Judaism. Although the perspective from which the humble ritual-ethical embodiment and encounter is viewed is different in the case of each thinker, each one finds in this context his authentic foundation and unique contribution. The power and authenticity of Buber's thought, Heschel's thought and Soloveitchik's thought, as expressions of Judaism, arise above all from the faithfulness with which each of these great and quite different thinkers translates the worlds known through halakhic enactment into general philosophic discourse. From this arises, for example, Buber's clear repudiation of Otto's emphasis on the "Wholly Other" nature of the holy, his recognition of the holiness of the commonplace and everyday, and indeed his insistence on the possibility of real dialogue not only with other human beings, but also with the whole of a sanctified Creation, including animals and things. This, as well as the ethical sensitivity of Buber, reflects the resonances of halakhic experience and worldview in Buber's thought, and is the measure of its Jewish authenticity. Here, too, is the root of the incompatibility Heschel sensed as a student in Berlin between the traditional universe of Judaism and German Kantian thought. The otherworldliness and physical "irreality" (to adapt a Husserlian term) of that thought was contradicted by the simplest Hebrew blessing; Heschel tells in his account of his years in Berlin how the simple commandment to say the evening prayers, after a day of tormented and lonely wandering, philosophizing, and doubt, brought the living God back to him, and with that, also restored a real world (Heschel, 1977: 136–38). And in Soloveitchik's case too, it is halakhic behavior that is self-consciously and emphatically the source of that philosopher's originality.[19]

However, much the same can also be said of the other major Jewish thinkers of the modern period. Their power and originality, as well as their major contribution to contemporary Jewish thought, seems to lie above all in their treatment of what are in fact uniquely halakhic ethico-ritual realities, realities experienced *only by and through the body*, not by the mind nor the emotions alone. For example, perhaps

Franz Rosenzweig's most enduring achievement in *The Star of Redemption* was his philosophical and phenomenological analysis of the Jewish liturgical year, which transparently arose (as did his entire philosophy) out of his own shattering experience during a Yom Kippur service at a small shul (synagogue) in 1913. It is interesting that in a strictly cognitive and intellectual sense Rosenzweig already knew the ideas of that service, for he had gone to many High Holy Day services before, and the prayer book and liturgy were familiar to him. What was revelatory was the full physical immersion in the ritual itself, something which apparently the more formal and remote services he had previously attended did not invite. When Rosenzweig entered fully and with "all his limbs" into the rituals, as one bodily Jew along with others in traditional community, God was suddenly living and fully present to him, and so was Judaism. As our study of Jewish philosophy again suggests, the best and most solid foundation for all great insights can only be the humble physical realities of our too-much-disregarded bodily life.

NOTES

1. Cf. Otto, 1959, originally published in 1929 as *Das Heilige*. Ulf Drobin, in a penetrating analysis, shows the theological and specifically Protestant presuppositions not only of Otto, but of Schleiermacher, Heiler, Söderblum, and many other German philosophers of religion, in his brief essay, "Psychology, Philosophy, Theology, Epistemology: Some Reflections". (I am grateful to Professor David Westerlund of the University of Stockholm for this reference.) The insight that almost all the major theoreticians in the modern phenomenology and history of religions were involved in Christian natural theology is now well accepted. Cf., for example, Waardenburg.

2. Heschel, 1955, e.g., see especially Chapters 34 ("The Meaning of Observance"), and 40 ("The Deed Redeems").

3. See, for example, Borowitz: 178–83, where we also find criticism of the relative absence of the themes of peoplehood (a significant omission, considering Heschel's Conservative leanings), and of the conflict of personal autonomy with obedience to the Commandments; Berkovits: 192–

224 strongly criticizes the failure of Heschel to deal with the kinds of issues that medieval Jewish rationalists like Maimonides dealt with in their exposition of God and of Judaism, and in particular Berkovits doubts the "Jewishness" of the claim that one can participate in God's emotions: he calls it a shocking (and inadmissibly anthropomorphic) assertion about God and claim for humanity, and indebted much more to Christian theology than to Jewish. However, Arthur Cohen reminds us that Heschel was fully aware of the biblical, rabbinic and Maimonidean "as if," and that he explicitly denied making any statements about God in himself; cf. Cohen: 249–50.

4. Martin Buber, *Daniel, Gespräche von der Verwirklichung* (Leipzig, 1913), p. 13, as cited and translated by Friedman: 35f.

5. Kaufman: 49–50, gives the text of the larger work Buber intended *I and Thou* to be the first part of: immediately after it came a discourse on *"Urformen des religiösen Lebens"* (Original or Basic Forms of the Religious Life), including sections on Magic, Sacrifice, and so on.

6. Walter Kaufman, in the "Prologue" cited above in note 5, for example, commences his discussion with the biting comment, "Man's world is manifold, and his attitudes are manifold. What is manifold is often frightening because it is not neat and simple. Men prefer to forget how many possibilities are open to them. They like to be told that there are two worlds and two ways. This is comforting because it is so tidy. Almost always one way turns out to be common and the other one is celebrated as superior. Those who tell of two ways and praise one are recognized as prophets or great teachers. They save men from confusion and hard choices. . . . *Mundus vult decipi*: the world wants to be deceived. . . ." (p. 9). Kaufman even went on to make more direct criticisms at a conference at Fordham University on Buber in 1975, stating that *I and Thou* was seriously flawed and "approximates the oracular tone of false prophets" (as quoted by the *New York Times*, February 19, 1975)!

7. Kaplan: 44 and 60n.8, points out the influence of the neo-Kantian thought of Hermann Cohen on these formulations, and adds that Soloveitchik's doctoral dissertation was on *Das Reine Denken und die Seinkonstituierung bei Hermann Cohen* (Berlin: 1932).

8. Buber, 1970: 126–131, in which, not coincidentally, we find Buber's critique of Schleiermacher. Buber makes a detailed critique and appreciation of Kierkegaard in his important essay, "The Question to the Single

One," which draws out the implications of Buber's more dialogic and inclusive perspective in a way that applies as well to Soloveitchik: see "The Question to the Single One," in Buber, 1965: 40–82. The entire Kantian agenda, including Kierkegaard's rendition of it, is also dealt with explicitly and at illuminating length in another brilliant essay by Buber included in this collection, "What is Man?," pp. 118–208.

9. In his essay, *Uvikashtem misham* ("And you will seek from there," Deut. 4:29), (Soloveitschik, 1979) written in the 1940's, Soloveitchik sought to provide a philosophical analysis of the unification of the Torah personality. If rank subjectivism is the Scylla of seeking God in withdrawal from the world into absolute "Being," and artificial rationalist objectivism is the Charybdis of seeking God ("reality") in the world of multiplicity, there is a third way, exemplified by Maimonides' intellectual mysticism, in which through the study of the halakhic Torah given by God the Jew mentally actualizes what is neither objective nor subjective, the "noetic union" of all, thus cleaving to the will and mind of God. A luminous analysis of this important essay by Soloveitchik can be found in Ravitzky: 157–88. Despite such longings for union, however, the dominant theme in Soloveitchik's writings is the inevitability of the torn personality, on which see below.

10. Peli, 1984b: 13, quoting from the Hebrew version of Soloveitchik's *Halakhic Man*, p. 4. It is the goal of repentance of general halakhic life, according to this account, to crown the internal division and conflict by unifying it all with God. Halakhic man is not some unstable hybrid, but a person whose different horizons have been fused into something far more radiant than is imaginable by less complex religious devotees. Suffering enlarges the personality, according to Soloveitchik (he cites with approval the authorities Hegel, Kierkegaard, Karl Barth and Rudolf Otto, and concludes, in Peli's translation loc. cit.: "Inconsistency enriches existence, contradiction renews Creation, negation builds worlds and denial deepens and expands consciousness"). Suffering therefore is seen as having a positive function in Jewish religious psychology.

11. Soloveitchik was critical of the Mussar movement, but nevertheless seems to have been influenced by its ethical perfectionism, individualism, and sombre introspection; it may well be the case that a certain receptivity to the Mussar outlook helped acclimatize Soloveitchik to

similar traits in Kierkegaard. An excellent introduction to the world of Musar, and of the great Lithuanian *yeshivot*, is provided by two essays included in Goldin (1970), one by Louis Ginzberg, "Rabbi Israel Salanter," pp. 415–447, and the other by Gedalyahu Alon, "The Lithuanian Yeshivas," pp. 448–464.

12. Yet it is interesting that Lichtenstein, op. cit., an Orthodox disciple of Soloveitchik, largely ignores this aspect of his mentor's thinking, and presents what in the context of Soloveitchik's thought can only be called a glowing sentimentalization. And liberal thinkers have certainly also learned to confront evil: cf. Rubenstein, 1966.

13. Peli, 1984b: 15, summarizing Soloveitchik's views, and quoting from a response by Soloveitchik to a questioner at one of his lectures. In a footnote, Peli also refers the reader to his own essay, "On Suffering in the Thought of Rabbi J. B. Soloveitchik" (Peli, 1984a: 48–62).

14. As Kaplan observes, the model Soloveitchik seems to be using is that of the scientific personality or mathematician, as it has been elaborated by various modern philosophers (following Kantian precedents). But Kaplan also draws attention to modifications Soloveitchik introduced into this picture of the halkhic personality in later essays. According to this, at the summit of his studies the advanced halakhicist rediscovers and experiences the emotional, joyful aspect of the halkhic system as a divinely revealed and nurturing whole, given by God in her aspect as warm maternal protectress. Cf. Kaplan: 53–55.

15. Wolfson, while somewhat slurring over the differences between Philo and the Talmud in this regard, shows that Philo taught the superiority of extirpating the emotions and bodily desires, and the usefulness of the Law for achieving this aim or at least some mastery and transcendence of the merely material sphere; cf. Wolfson: II, 228ff.; 270ff.; also see Baer. On the similarities between this view and Paul's contrast of the bodily and the spiritual, see Saunders: 553ff. and the further references therein.

16. The following analysis repeats points made more fully in Zuesse, 1975: 518ff. (particularly citing Husserl, 1962).

17. For a fuller discussion, see Zuesse, 1985: 51–73; after noting that in his *Cartesian Meditations* (cf. Husserl, 1970), Husserl traced all consciousness back to a formless, contentless "ego," an ego that serves simply as a pivot for thought, I go on there (57) to remark that Husserl himself

confessed that this ego is given a location and pivot by the body: "Does not this suggest that the transcendental ego is simply the first efflux in consciousness of the inwardness of the body itself, that it is the most 'subjective' experience of the body? The pivot of the pivot, the soul of the soul, would then be the sentient flesh; the content of the 'contentless ego' is that physical person with the ski nose, bushy moustache and beard, vest and watch-chain . . . [i.e., Husserl himself] . . ., and we are plunged from the transcendental reduction back into the given world with all its existential and experiential facticities, in which the self is limited by a specific biography and skills, by particular other persons, by otherness, disease and death. In this case, a total transcendental reduction is certainly not possible, for an essential aspect of all thought at its foundation would then be embeddedness in a given world and embodiment. From the [Husserlian version of the] Buddhist *anatman* (no-self) we are thrown back into the [biblical] fusion of *nefesh* (life-soul) and *guf* (flesh); here arises the chasm between fundamentally different worldviews. Yet what a delicate distinction lies at their root!"

18. This is not to ignore the importance of the prophetic ecstatic encounters with God of Moses and the prophets, nor the mystical encounters of later Kabbalists. But the dichotomy between ritual-ethical action and such experiences has been far too overdrawn by commentators. In any case, the matter cannot be developed here, for want of space.

19. However, these reflections also suggest certain possible corrections of the above thinkers. If the body is so much a part of human reality, then there needs to be more awareness of the "Thou's" vulnerability to pain, disease, and death, and human finitude in general, in Buber's account of the I-Thou encounter: this in turn means that normative (and halakhic) obligation and concern with relationships with a wider world are essential parts of that encounter, and it does not transcend time and place. Heschel, similarly, might give more attention to our body's relationship with other persons, in physical community. And Soloveitchik could find in the unity and fullness of being of engaged bodily existence and encounter a way out of the tormented psychological and spiritual contradictions he discusses.

BIBLIOGRAPHY

BAER, Richard A., 1970, *Philo's Use of the Categories of Male and Female* Leiden: E. J. Brill.

BERKOVITS, Eliezer, 1974, *Major Themes in Modern Philosophies of Judaism.* New York: KTAV.

BOROWITZ, Eugene B., 1983, *Choices in Modern Jewish Thought: A Partisan Guide.* New York: Behrman House.

BUBER, Martin, 1965, *Between Man and Man*, translated by Ronald Gregor Smith. New York: Macmillan.

———, 1970, *I and Thou*, translated by Walter Kaufman. New York: Charles Scribner's Sons.

CASSIRER, Ernst, 1955, *The Philosophy of Symbolic Forms*, Vol. 2: *Mythical Thought*, translated by Ralph Manheim. New Haven and London: Yale University Press.

COHEN, Arthur, 1962, *The Natural and the Supernatural Jew.* New York: Random House.

DROBIN, Ulf, 1982, *Psychology, Philosophy, Theology, Epistemology: Some Reflections.* Studies Published by the Institute of Comparative Religion at the University of Stockholm, 3. Stockholm: Institute of Comparative Religion. Reprint from *Scripta Instituti Donneriani Aboensis*, XI, Upsala, 1982.

FRIEDMAN, Maurice S., 1960, *Martin Buber: The Life of Dialogue.* New York: Harper & Row.

GOLDIN, Judah (ed.), 1970, *The Jewish Expression.* New York: Bantam Books.

HESCHEL, Abraham Joshua, 1951, *Man Is Not Alone: A Philosophy of Religion.* New York: Harper & Row.

———, 1955, *God in Search of Man: A Philosophy of Judaism.* Philadelphia and New York: Jewish Publication Society of American and Meridian.

———, 1962, *The Prophets.* Philadelphia: Jewish Publication Society of America.

———, 1977, "Toward an Understanding of Halachah." In: *Conservative Judaism and Jewish Law*, edited by Seymour Siegel. Studies in Conservative Jewish Thought, I. New York: The Rabbinical Assembly and KTAV Publishing House.

HUSSERL, Edmund, 1962, *Ideas: General Introduction to Phenomenology*, translated by W. R. Boyce-Gibson. New York: Collier-Macmillan.

———, 1970, *Cartesian Meditations: An Introduction to Phenomenology*, translated by Dorian Cairns. The Hague: Martinus Nijhoff.

KAPLAN, Lawrence, 1973, "The Religious Philosophy of Rabbi Joseph Soloveitchik," *Tradition*, Vol. 14, No. 2 (Fall): 43–64.

KAUFMAN, Walter, 1970, "I and Thou: A Prologue," and "A Plan Martin Buber Abandoned." In *I and Thou*, by Martin Buber, translated by Walter Kaufman. New York: Charles Scribner's Sons. pp. 7–50.

LICHTENSTEIN, Aaron, 1963, "R. Joseph Soloveitchik." In *Great Jewish Thinkers of the Twentieth Century*, edited by Simon Noveck. B'nai B'rith Great Books Series: Vol. 3. New York: B'nai B'rith.

OTTO, Rudolf, 1959, *The Idea of the Holy*, translated by John W. Harvey. Baltimore: Penguin. Originally published as *Das Heilige*, 1929.

PELI, Pinchas H., 1984a, "On Suffering in the Thought of Rabbi J. B. Soloveitchik," *Da'at, A Journal of Jewish Philosophy and Kabbalah*, No. 12 (Winter): 48–62.

———, 1984b, *Soloveitchik on Repentance: The Thought and Oral Discourses of Rabbi Joseph B. Soloveitchik*. New York: Paulist Press.

RAVITZKY, Aviezer, 1986, "Rabbi J. B. Soloveitchik on Human Knowledge: Between Maimonidean and neo-Kantian Philosophy," *Modern Judaism*, 6, no. 2 (May): 157–88.

RUBENSTEIN, Richard L., 1966, *After Auschwitz: Radical Theology and Contemporary Judaism*. New York: Bobbs-Merrill.

SANDERS, E. P., 1977, *Paul and Palestinian Judaism*. London: SCM Press.

SOLOVEITCHIK, Joseph B., 1965, "The Lonely Man of Faith," *Tradition*, Vol. 7, No. 2 (Spring): 5–67.

———, 1979, *U-vikashtem misham*," in the same author's *Ish Hahalakhah-Galuy ve-nistar*, Jerusalem: World Zionist Organization.

———, 1983, *Halakhic Man*, translated by Lawrence Kaplan. Philadelphia: The Jewish Publication Society of America.

WAARDENBURG, Jacques, 1978, *Reflections on the Study of Religion*. Religion and Reason, 15. The Hague: Mouton.

WOLFSON, Harry Austryn, 1947, *Philo: Foundations of Religious Philosophy in Judaism, Christianity, and Islam*. 2 vols. Cambridge, MA and London: Harvard University Press.

ZUESSE, Evan M., 1975, "Meditation on Ritual," *Journal of the American Academy of Religion*, Vol. 43, No. 3: 517–30.

——, 1985, "The Role of Intentionality in the Phenomenology of Religion," *Journal of the American Academy of Religion*, Vol. 53, No. 1: 51–73.

10. Mordecai M. Kaplan and Henry Nelson Wieman

Emanuel S. Goldsmith

Mordecai M. Kaplan (1881–1983) and Henry Nelson Wieman (1884–1975) were two outstanding religious thinkers of the twentieth century. One a Jew and the other a Protestant, they were representatives of their respective traditions as well as pioneers on the frontier of the continuing human quest for the divine. Kaplan and Wieman were radical modernists who wholeheartedly embraced religious liberalism, naturalism, empiricism and process thought, and gave expression to the American spirit in theology and philosophy of religion. Defending their faiths from atheism and humanism, on the one hand, and from fundamentalism and literalism, on the other, their approaches were both reconstructive and innovative. They bequeathed to future generations rich legacies of understanding and insight which will continue to grow in significance as people search for new religious truths as well as for the relevance of their inherited traditions.

The childhood years of Kaplan in New York City and of Wieman in Missouri were similar in that while they grew up in intensely religious homes, the religiosity of their parents was probing, intellectual and non-dogmatic. They were thus able in later years to distinguish what they considered to be the deep and abiding concerns of religious conviction and devotion from religious formalism and institutionalism. Already as a child Kaplan realized that although Jewish religious observance was believed to have been dictated by God, its real significance was not intrinsic but lay in its ability to relate the Jew to the Jewish people. "Whether I was reciting the brief thanksgiving prayer on opening the eyes, or the prayer on going to bed, or various prayers and benedictions during the day, they all had one meaning for me—that of being a Jew."[1]

The major influence in Kaplan's life was his father. Rabbi Israel Kaplan was an adherent of the Lithuanian Mussar movement, founded by Rabbi Israel Salanter, which emphasized the ethical element in religion as of greater significance than piety or scholarship. While strictly observant, Kaplan's father was committed to intellectual honesty and tolerated his son's deviations from traditional standards and beliefs. When they studied Talmud together and Mordecai took exception to statements in the text or the commentaries, his father would pinch his son's cheek and say, "You don't let yourself be fooled, my son."[2]

The primary religious influence on Wieman was his mother who shaped his religious development by the strength of her faith.[3] Although his father was a Presbyterian minister, his parents did not indoctrinate him in their religion, and whatever he got from them seemed to be caught by contagion rather than taught. He did not, for example, automatically identify religion with the church. "The business of keeping the church going is the most religious religion there is. But it was never the religion of my mother or father, although he was a clergyman."[4]

Both Wieman and Kaplan recalled experiences in their formative years which were crucial for their religious development. While conducting a religious service together with fellow students when he was sixteen, Kaplan experienced a religious illumination. "The Psalms, which I had up to that time been in the habit of reciting mechanically as part of the daily prayers, suddenly became for me alight with meaning, and, for the first time, I experienced the reality of God."[5] On an April evening, during his senior year in college, Wieman sat alone in his room and looked out over the Missouri River. Suddenly it came over him that he wanted to devote his life not to journalism, as he had been planning, but to the philosophy of religion. "The new purpose took hold of me with overwhelming force and satisfaction . . . this new idea seemed to release an urge that had been blocked and I was joyously exuberant over this new plan."[6]

Not having been taught to identify religion with particular beliefs or institutions, Wieman felt no distress when challenged to alter his beliefs by new ideas such as Darwin's theory of evolution.[7] Kaplan, on the other hand, was troubled by the problems which modern thought posed to traditional religion and specifically to the writings of the medieval Jewish theologians in which he sought answers to his perplexities. He became aware of the fact that the medieval theologians lacked a historical sense and an awareness of evolution in religion. His faith in the Mosaic authorship of the Torah and in the historicity of the biblical miracles was eventually undermined and replaced by an evolutionary and historical approach.[8]

Kaplan and Wieman began their work during the heyday of American religious liberalism which lasted from the turn of the century until the beginning of the Second World War. In addition to the growth of modern science, a major factor in the rise of liberalism was the development of modern historical and literary research of religion and the Bible. Although exposed to modern religious scholarship, neither Kaplan nor Wieman was particularly attracted to textual or historical study. During a year of study in Germany, Wieman heard the great religious historians Wilhelm Windelband and Ernst Troeltsch. He felt that Windelband's systematizing and classifying was done at the expense of depth and constructiveness. His reaction to Troeltsch was that despite the great importance of such historical study it could not provide any direction for living.[9] Kaplan's attitude to modern Jewish scholarship was similar, and his scholarly recension of an ethical treatise by Moshe Hayyim Luzzatto appears to have been his sole foray into the world of textual scholarship. He was generally distrustful of those scholars who live themselves so thoroughly into the past that it functions for them as a continuing authority with which they defy the present and criticize any changes dictated by practical or rational considerations.[10]

The religious liberals of the early twentieth century continued the work of the Enlightenment and led religion into the worlds of modern science, philosophy and history. They domesticated modern religious ideas and carried forward the "confrontation between traditional orthodoxies and the new grounds for religious skepticism exposed during the nineteenth century."[11] American religious liberalism, in particular, was characterized by ethical passion and a preoccupation with religious experience. Its underlying motifs were continuity or emphasis on the immanence rather than the transcendence of God, autonomy or the centrality of personal religious experience rather than the appeal to external authority, and dynamism or the stress on evolution in nature and history rather than the traditional appeal to static categories.[12]

While clearly within the broadstream of American religious liberalism, Wieman and Kaplan were critical of certain liberal presuppositions. As modernistic liberals and radical modernizers they took scientific method, scholarly discipline, empirical fact and prevailing forms of philosophy as their point of departure.[13] Although aware of much in Judaism and Christianity that should be retained in modern times, they felt that their traditions had to be evaluated in the light of modern science, philosophy, psychology and sociology. Nothing was to be adhered to unless its relevance could be made apparent.[14] As modernists they advocated "the conscious, intended adaptation of religious ideas to modern culture."[15] For them, God was immanent in cultural evolution, and society was progressively moving toward realization of the kingdom of God even if such a goal might never actually be attained.[16]

In the period under discussion, liberalism was represented in the

Jewish community chiefly by the Reform movement. Reform taught that Judaism had attained the highest development of the God-idea and was therefore superior to all other religions. Kaplan felt that such a claim could not be substantiated by historical fact. Reform also stressed ethical commitment to the detriment of ritual practice. Kaplan chided it for having thus reduced Judaism to a philosophy of religion. In addition, Reform renounced Jewish nationalism and insisted that the Jews were merely a religious community. Kaplan accused it of thereby severing Judaism from the texture of Jewish experience and of failure to understand the full implication of religion and community. A community, according to him, was not merely a society. A community implied living in common as well as believing in common. The Reform movement, he contended, had failed to assimilate recent studies of the nature and history of religion, and its theology and sociology were hopelessly anachronistic. It had given free scope to intellectual inquiry without taking advantage of that freedom to understand the nature and purpose of religion and peoplehood.[17] The main function of religion, as Kaplan saw it, was to enable a group to adjust to its environment and make the most of its life. "The scientific spirit has invaded the entire domain of human thinking. Even theology is giving way to the science of religion to which it bears the same relation as alchemy to chemistry."[18]

Wieman's major quarrel with Protestant religious liberalism, like Kaplan's with Reform Judaism, was based on what he perceived to be its misunderstanding of the true nature of religion. He attacked what he saw as its subjectivism and sentimentalism. These, he felt, were the results of an inadequate understanding of the nature of religious experience and a failure to treat such experience scientifically.[19] To him, religious experience "when not controlled and directed by devotion to something well-defined and distinguished and assuredly known to be the present source of human good" was "futile sentimentalism" and "promiscuity in religious living."[20] Belief in what seemed helpful without other evidence was to him a religion of wishful fancy. He sought objective evidence of God in nature and human life.[21] He advocated a theocentric faith in which the actuality of God rather than human ideas about God would be object of salvation.

Despite their reservations about religious liberalism, Kaplan and Wieman were, broadly speaking, members of the religious liberal camp. Kaplan, for example, while concerned with the preservation of those elements of the Jewish past which had contemporary significance, and with the integrity and continuity of Jewish civilization, also insisted on "the responsibility of the living generation to evaluate tradition and to reject what is not relevant to contemporary needs, or in accord with the best in modern thought."[22] Liberal religion, said Wieman, had to oppose religion which assumes that the problems of human life have been solved by the religious personalities and traditions of the past. It had to be based on questions rather than answers, and any answers it provided had to be seen as tentative. It had to be committed "not to a belief but to the actuality which a belief seeks to apprehend; not to a problem solved but to a problem in process of being solved; not to an answer given but to a question being asked and an answer found more or less adequate to the question."[23] Liberal religion was faith that demanded tests of reason for its affirmations. "As in science, every discovery only opens the way for further inquiry."[24]

Generally speaking, religious liberalism emphasized subjective belief and appealed to religious experience for evidence of God. This emphasis, however, frequently led to the denial of the objective reality of God. Along with their opposition to idealism and its tendency to objectify subjective human ideals, Wieman and Kaplan were also opposed to the extreme forms of humanism which deny all objective reality to the divine aspects of experience. "Does the idealism of humanism give us the deepest and most characteristic quality of religion which enables it to pour into human life something of great value which cannot be got in morality or art or politics or industry or home life or anywhere else?" asked Wieman.[25]

> Human effort can be efficacious in bringing a desired possibility to pass only when there is some order in which and with which men can work

to that end . . . God is that order of existence and possibility which includes the possibility of greatest value to be attained, which makes it a possibility and in adjustment to which human effort is efficacious in achieving it, but without which human effort would be entirely futile and foolish.[26]

Kaplan deemed the humanistic interpretation of life inadequate because of its failure to express or foster the feeling that man's ethical aspirations are part of a cosmic urge. "Without the conviction that the world contains all that is necessary for human salvation, the assumptions necessary for ethical living remain cold hypotheses lacking all dynamic power."[27] Spiritual religion differs from humanism in its assumption that the cosmos is in rapport with the human quest for fulfillment. It stresses the fact that "the universe is not only interrelated but divine, in that it is constituted to help man in his striving after salvation."[28] Despite these misgivings, however, Kaplan and Wieman are properly designated religious humanists since both accorded centrality in religion to the human need for salvation or transformation and both rejected supernaturalism.

Kaplan and Wieman belonged to that sector of American religious liberalism which embraced theistic or religious naturalism. They conceded that naturalism had formerly been incompatible with religion because it reduced all life and thought to operations of matter and physicochemical causes, and left no room for belief in the reality of God and spiritual values.[29] In countering belief in a supernatural power in a realm beyond space and time, the older naturalism had failed to point to the creative, transforming or spiritual element inherent in the midst of actual events in the temporal world. The type of naturalism which Wieman and Kaplan espoused recognized qualitative distinctions between lower and higher orders of being. It allowed for creative or emergent evolution and for the autonomous functioning of mind and spirit. It conceived of truth, justice and love as operating in their own right and helping to bring order out of chaos.[30] People could thus have a faith and devotion to "a power resident in events, that transforms the world in ways better than the

human mind can imagine. . . . This power demands of man not only
the faith of self-giving, but also obedience to the moral law and the
practical setting up of all conditions within his ability that facilitate the
transformation of creativity."[31]

Wieman and Kaplan were also empirical theologians who sought an
anchor for religious faith independent of revelation and tradition, and
found it in the scientific methods of reason, observation and experi-
mentation. The empirical method in theology bases all claims to, and
interpretations of, knowledge on personal experience. Such experience may embrace all that has been "enjoyed and suffered." Empirical theology also insists on a method of religious inquiry which is
accessible to all. "Recent empiricism," as James S. Martin, Jr., points
out,

> while retaining the notion that scientific knowledge must begin and end
> with public experience, has not conceived of such experience narrowly
> in terms of mere sensation and association. Affective, volitional and
> valuational elements are seen to be parts of the whole. And the signifi-
> cance of experimentation, or experimentalism, as the most fruitful
> method for exploration and organization of experience has been em-
> phasized.[32]

Wieman therefore insisted that God must be found in human life and
that reason must serve as a guide to the classification and testing of
religious concepts. To Wieman, "the canons of rational consistency
are important," writes Daniel D. Williams, "not because all experience can be presented in a rational scheme, but as man's protection
against illusion, nonsense and the imposition of untestable doctrines
upon his religious search for truth."[33]

For Kaplan, the effect of trying to preserve Jewish religion in its
traditional form, without adequately reckoning with modern experience, was to make Jewish religion an anachronism in the modern
world. Jewish religion had to be based "not on what our ancestors
have told of their experience with God, but on our own experience
with God."[34] His study of the evolution of Jewish religion led him to

realize that "although medieval Jewish theology believed it was merely reaffirming the Jew's allegiance to traditional beliefs, it indirectly paid sufficient homage to reason to prepare the way for a type of religion in which reason—in a sense sufficiently large to include our deeper insights and intuitions—is the only guide and authority."[35] To Kaplan, any conception of God based on delusion partook of idolatry. Anti-intellectualism and irrationalism in the form of romanticism and mysticism were to him distortions of truth and the sense of reality.[36]

Kaplan and Wieman were process theologians influenced by the thought of such philosophers as Henri Bergson, Samuel Alexander, C. Lloyd Morgan, John E. Boodin, George Herbert Mead and Alfred North Whitehead. Process philosophy emphasizes both process or becoming and relations or relativity. It contends that the entire universe is in a state of change or process and stresses the theme of relationship.[37] Time, change, becoming, growth, organicity and creativity are terms which it uses frequently. Wieman has been called "the theologian par excellence of man's experiential encounter with the concrete actuality of God's being as this issues in creative, transformative and redemptive processes."[38] According to Wieman, it is only God *in* human life, rather than at the beginning, bottom, top or end of it, who can be a matter of religious concern. It is only "when God is sought and found in the midst of the concrete situation where we are that he can be known through action." Action, Wieman emphasized, "is the only way in which we come to know anything in truth, but especially any reality in its character of commanding our supreme devotion and absolute self-commitment."[39] Kaplan emphasized that modern scientific and philosophic thought views all of reality as dynamic and as energy in action. To speak of God as Process is "to select, out of the infinite processes in the universe, that complex of forces and relationships which makes for the highest fulfillment of man as a human being and identify it by the term 'God.' "[40]

Wieman and Kaplan also shared a deep concern with the concept of value. Religion is actually concerned with value in two senses. It involves the choice, appreciation and adoration of value or the source of value, and it posits a faith in the universe as hospitable to value.[41]

Kaplan placed the term "God" in the category of value which is related to wisdom rather than in the category of fact which is related to reason and intelligence. Values, he insisted, are actually as real as visible and tangible facts.[42] "As psychic and social facts or realities, values are far more potent as fact makers or factors, in the sense of producing results. The God concept, properly understood as a factor in ordering the life of men and nations, is the most potent and creative factor in human existence."[43]

Wieman contended that as a supreme value, God is a perceptible natural process.[44] The term "God" is a name for the growth of meaning and value in the world and values are the data by which God is sought and found. Although God is always greater than "the specific objects of human desire and aversion," God and the highest human values are identical.[45] He warned that "the creative source of value must come first in man's devotion, while the specific values apprehended through the narrow slit of human awareness must come second, if we are to find the way of our deliverance and the way of human fulfillment."[46] John E. Smith observes that Wieman's position rests on two central theses. "His claim that God is truly present in perceived experience is intended to avoid reducing God to a mere concept or ideal. His interpretation of God as the source of human good or value, on the other hand, seeks to avoid confusing God with the whole of reality."[47]

The approaches of Wieman and Kaplan were not only axiological or concerned with values but also soteriological or concerned with salvation. As theologians they introduced concepts such as salvation, redemption, deliverance, transformation and metamorphosis into empirical and process thought. To both of them, salvation is a this-worldly social as well as individual reality which must be understood in terms of human needs. For Wieman, salvation is the life of aspiration in which the deepest need of human nature finds fulfillment. This need is "the need of bringing to fulfillment that multiplication of responses which arise in a man over and above his established habits. . . . It is to interact with ever more of the world round about him."[48] Modern persons can therefore find their salvation only through the social world in which they participate, and social recon-struction is the modern road to salvation.[49] Psychologically, salvation is emergence

> from inner conflict or stagnation to progressive integration of per-sonality; from personal powers confined to personal powers released; from a disjunct personality to a conjunct one; from a sense of insecurity to a profound and indestructible peace; from specific objectives that imprison and perish, to a total objective that is eternal; from bondage to an established social pattern of life, to a pattern that opens out into an illimitable realm of possible value and meaning.[50]

The salvation of society involves rearranging institutions, ideals and customs in order to "restore mutual support and release growth of meaning."[51] The salvation of the individual and the salvation of soci-ety are interrelated. "The salvation sought is the salvation of man, psychologically, socially, historically. It is the salvation of human life in its total movement of history, society and individual existence.[52]

Religion's major responsibility, according to Wieman, is to point to the way of salvation.[53] The salvation which affords deepest satisfac-tion and maximum realization of human potentialities is found in a creativity which reconstructs personality, society and history by gener-ating insights and expanding horizons. It operates through creative intercommunication between individuals, peoples and cultures. This creativity expands the range of what an individual can know, control, appreciate as good and distinguish as evil, and the depth and scope of what he can appreciate and understand about himself and about the unique individuality of other persons and peoples.[54]

Religion, according to Kaplan, is man's conscious quest for salva-tion or the achievement of his human destiny.[55] The proper task of religion is not to prove the existence of God but to assist people in their quest for self-fulfillment or salvation.[56] Salvation is "the achieve-ment of such personality in the individual and of such society in the collective, as to augment the measure of integrity, responsibility and creativity in the world."[57] It is the maximum fulfillment of those capacities which entitle people to be described as created in the Divine image.[58] It is the effort to improve oneself and one's environment and as such is prophetic of human destiny and a manifestation of the divine in human life.[59] It is the capacity to play a conscious role in the evolution of self as well as the urge to transformation and metamorphosis.[60]

The concept of salvation, according to Kaplan, is rooted in the objective psychological need to be needed, which is experienced as the need to be accepted and loved. To be needed a person must be honest, creative, just and ready to serve. Every person may be creative because insofar as he produces more than he consumes he contributes to making life worthwhile for all.[61] The need to be needed applies to nations as well as to individuals. To achieve salvation, human beings must strive for world peace, ethical nationhood and individual happiness.[62] For the individual, salvation also consists of the satisfaction of the three primary needs: health, love and creativity. For society, salvation involves seeing to it that every person has the economic and cultural opportunities necessary for maximum self-fulfillment.[63]

The word "God" may become a device with which to conceal from oneself and from others the true character of one's faith.[64] Wieman and Kaplan sought to specify the distinguishing characteristics of God. For Wieman, the word "God" refers to a kind of communication:

> the kind which creates appreciative understanding of the individuality of persons and peoples when they allow it to operate in their lives, creating society, sustaining all these in their being and increasing the values in them, when required conditions are present. This operative presence creates in each individual his capacity to love and appreciate and understand the individuality of others.[65]

Such communication occurs between persons all the time to some degree. But to be radically transforming, it must rise to a high level and overcome the counter-processes which ordinarily obstruct and suppress it. When it rises to a level of power and dominance, it endows life with all of its great values.[66]

God is the process of creative good or creativity which, in the form of creative interchange and internal integration, operates to transform human life in a way that it could not do by itself. It delivers human life from evil and conveys it to the greatest good which human life can ever attain.[67] Wieman insisted that God can never be a person or a personality. "It is a logical fallacy to call God a person if any of his essential powers are different in kind from those essential to, and definitive of, the human being. This is so because the established meaning of the word 'personality' is to designate the characteristics which are distinctive and essential to the human being."[68] There is a creativity which personality may undergo but not perform. It is this creativity which progressively creates personality through community.

> Either God exercises the power of creativity progressively creating personality, in which case he cannot be a personality because he is then exercising the creativity no person can exercise but can only undergo; or else, if he is a personality he is himself a creature of this creativity. A God who is a creature of an ontologically prior creativity is properly called an idol.[69]

Creative interchange can be readily observed in the growth of young children where it creates mind, personality and, through "symbolized meanings," a community with others.[70] It is in the form of symbolized meanings conveyed by language that values reach the human mind. Language may be distinguished from the signs to which lower animals respond by its ability to carry symbolized meanings that can expand indefinitely in terms of values, knowledge, skills and power.[71] Creative interchange may be said to create the universe since it makes possible whatever experience of the universe people can have. "It creates the human mind and in that way creates the world relative to the human mind."[72] Because it creates us and sustains us at the human level and gives us all the values which human beings can have, creative interchange is the one basic and most precious good which all human beings share together.[73]

To Kaplan, nature's God or Godhood is identical with the totality of creative processes in man and nature which make for self-transcendence and self-perfection.[74] "Divinity is that aspect of the whole of nature, both in the universe and in man, which impels mankind to create a better and happier world and every individual to make the most of his own life."[75] God is "the functioning in nature of the eternally creative process, which, by bringing order out of chaos and good out of evil, actuates man to self-fulfillment."[76]

Kaplan sought to divorce the God-idea from mythology, anthropomorphism and supernaturalism, and identify it with "all human conduct that strives for the creative survival of the human species in a warless world."[77] Since we can now understand the moral aspect of social existence which impels us to fulfill ourselves as human beings, we can freely reject the supernatural elements of traditional elements of traditional religion.[78] We can find God in the urge to truth, honesty, empathy, loyalty, justice, freedom and goodwill.[79] Religion must be purged of: 1) "an attitude of credulity which renders the mind susceptible to irrational and superstitious beliefs in luck, fate or sinister consequences. . ."; 2) "the belief that salvation is the exclusive prerogative of one's own religion . . ."; 3) "intellectual fixation on some past stage in the history of one's religion as one of divine revelation, and the nostalgic hope for a return to that period. . ."; 4) "inability to think of God in any but anthropomorphic or anthropopathic terms. . ."; 5) "inability to identify divinity with the natural processes of body or mind. . ."; 6) "belief in divine reward and punishment not only for social sins but also for ritual transgressions and unbelief. . ."; 7) "otherworldliness or the assumption that man cannot possibly achieve his destiny in the world. . ."; 8) "the dichotomy of body and soul as a rationale for asceticism which is pleasing to God. . ."; 9) "abnormal mysticism which is a perversion of normal mysticism. . ."[80]

Although Kaplan emphasized moral responsibility and conscience as the principal manifestations of Godhood in human life, he sought to prove that ethical traits are the subjective expressions of objective processes in nature. "The theory of reciprocal responsibility is the conscious human manifestation of the principle whereby everything in nature is both cause and effect of everything else. It corresponds with the universal law of polarity whereby everything in the universe, from the minutest electron to the vastest star, is both self-active and interactive, independent and interdependent."[81] "The cosmic process of universal reciprocity outside the human mind comes to be God only when it is experienced as cosmic interdependence, and, in the world, as moral responsibility."[82] Human nature is an extension of cosmic processes, while conscience, which dictates to man what he should do and induces remorse for failure, is actually the "semi-conscious intellectual effort to experience Divinity without recourse to anthropomorphic terms, rational propositions or mystic ecstasy."[83]

Kaplan stressed the significance of group or public religion as essentially an expression of response to human needs. Group religion is an aspect of wisdom or the concern with value and as such responds to the need to be needed. The need to be needed is identical with the need to transcend oneself or to experience the holiness of life. Transcendence or holiness is actually the human equivalent of what in nature is known as organicity or the process by which anything is more than the sum of its parts. God is the incremental plus of organic human society. "The process of organicity, functioning *self-consciously* in organic human societies is God, as the power that makes for salvation."[84] The God of Israel "represents the power of salvation which the collective self-consciousness generates by means of its organic function, and which is inherently akin to that which makes the cosmos or nature as a whole, possible."[85]

To Kaplan, the idea of God is a correlate of the idea of salvation or self-fulfillment. It reflects awareness of the organicity of the universe and assumes that there is enough in the world to meet men's needs but not enough to satiate their lusts and greeds.[86] Historically, the term "god" denoted any value or good that answered a need. "The unique God denotes the fulfillment of all human needs."[87] Such fulfillment depends on the functioning of conscience and moral responsibility. Religion is not a response to an intellectual need but to the human need to be needed. "It is not a matter of reflection but a matter of responsibility."[88] The term "God" is not a substantive but a functional noun denoting something exceptional and therefore transcendental or transnatural. It denotes the experience of holiness, which is related to the functioning of conscience.[89]

Wieman and Kaplan both grappled significantly with the problem of evil. By denying the traditional conception of divine omnipotence, they were able to rescue divine beneficence without resorting to, and glorifying in, paradox. Wieman stated unequivocally that although creativity creates mind, culture and history, it does not create the monstrous evils in the world. Evil results from counterprocesses and obstructions to creativity.[90] Creative interchange creates all the positive values of human existence but the self-destructive processes result from what obstructs creativity and operates in opposition to it.[91] Most important, whatever evil exists, people can always choose between better or worse. The responsibility to know what is better and to commit oneself to it devolves upon all of us. "Whether the good is mighty or weak over against the evil, it is the best there is and blessedness is found in living for it even in error and defeat."[92]

For Kaplan evil was religion's worst quandary and the source of its crisis in the modern world. Theology's attempt to understand evil intellectually and to resign people to it actually contributes to the worsening of the human situation. Religion is too preoccupied with justifying "God's ways" and preaching resignation instead of actively seeking an end to exploitation and war. The various attempts to account for evil are erroneous because they derive from the incorrect notion that God is a being like man. For Kaplan, insofar as Godhood is the correlate of humanity's efforts to improve human life, God is a process. The creativity manifest in human responsibility, integrity and loyalty or love constitutes the Godhood or Divinity of the cosmos. This perspective shifts attention from metaphysical speculation to man's inhumanity to man.[93] "If God, conceived as function, denotes whatever is of ultimate value to mankind, he cannot be represented as a personal Being infinite in power and goodness, which is a contradiction in terms."[94] Theodicies which attempt to justify God's ways are meaningless and replete with inconsistencies. "Nature is infinite chaos, with all its evils forever being vanquished by creativity, which is God as infinite goodness . . . The power of God is inexhaustible but not infinite."[95] Kaplan's position was based on his analysis of the empirically verifiable functioning of conscience. The function of conscience, the "pain of the human spirit," is not to promote speculation about God or reconcile humanity to man-made evil but to eliminate the causes of such evil and help bring about God's kingdom on earth. Conscience is thus also the revelation of God in the human spirit.[96]

Kaplan and Wieman gave a great deal of thought to the practical aspects of religion and especially to religious education and worship. Kaplan spoke of the creative expansion of Torah based on a conception of this-worldly salvation. It would have to deal, from the standpoint of ethics and religion, "with all those higher needs of the human spirit which have come to be better understood by reason of the general advances in the knowledge of human nature."[97] The primary purpose of education should be to get people to want only what they absolutely need physically, socially and spiritually. As a lifelong process, Jewish education should deal with the subject of ecology and include topics such as the elimination of war, ethical nationhood and individual freedom.[98] Kaplan was disturbed by the fact that present-day organized Jewish life gives little encouragement to the consideration of religion from an intellectual point of view. It is therefore necessary to stimulate interest in such problems as are dealt with in theology and philosophy of religion, and to cultivate religion as an integral element in human culture.[99]

In order for Jewish education to be a source of self-fulfillment, it has to deal with the fact that the human mind evolves, as people's needs multiply and means are found to satisfy those needs. Religious traditions must therefore be transmitted not in their own terms but in terms that make them contemporaneous and subject to the process of conscious ongoing interpretation.[100] Moreover, "the Jew as an individual must reckon with his individuality, with a sense of freedom which he must not renounce nor even play down. He must insist upon his right to do his own thinking and to refuse to be brainwashed."

Jewish education should emphasize wisdom rather than faith since "the very nature of religion and God can be demonstrated as having greater validity in terms of human experience, instead of in terms of faith, which is experience by proxy."[101]

Wieman stressed the need to understand religion not only as a set of answers but also as a question or problem which is part of the totality of human life and which we may not escape even if we reject all answers thus far given. Religion must therefore be taught in the same way that every other subject is taught.[102] The Bible, for example, must be approached neither as a book of answers to religious questions nor as literature but as a book of inquiry containing the history of a religiously gifted people. Answers found in the Bible should be treated as incomplete and subject to correction.[103] The problem of religion should be viewed both in its social context and as internal to individual personality.[104]

Wieman wrote that

> empirical theology opens the way for hope, because it can show that if creativity and its demands are studied and searched, and if its demands are accepted, it can and will transform human life toward the greater and deeper satisfactions of life and save man from self-destruction and from the mechanization of life which occurs when action is not inspired and guided by appreciation of individuality . . . Creativity at the human level operates as people learn from one another and then are transformed by the unconscious integration in each individual of what he gets from others.[105]

Mutual learning takes place on the superficial level of knowledge, skills and techniques, as well as on the deeper level of creative interchange. Such mutual learning in depth, "creative interchange which creates appreciative understanding at the deeper levels, must itself become our ruling loyalty and dominant motivation."[106]

Kaplan believed that worship fulfills essential needs of human nature by affirming the meaning of life and the primacy of moral and spiritual values and by giving reality, purpose and self-consciousness to the collective spirit of a people. It provides a glimpse into the unity, creativity and worthwhileness of life.[107] According to him, "prayer aims at deriving from the Process that constitutes God, the power that would strengthen the forces and relationships by which we fulfill ourselves as persons."[108] Nevertheless, Kaplan advocated emphasizing the study rather than the prayer element in worship. Worship, he felt, should be used to study God's laws in nature and in human life.[109]

The deep personal needs of the religious man, according to Wieman, are for "salvation and transformation, for deep communion and appreciative understanding, for answered prayer and the kingdom of love. . . . It can be demonstrated how creativity meets these needs; it cannot be demonstrated how a supernatural person and almighty power does so."[110] The purpose of worship is to keep the religious problem in the forefront of human life.[111] In prayer we attempt to renew and deepen our commitment and to submit ourselves more completely to the direction and control of what can creatively transform us.[112] When one worships profoundly and sincerely, with his personality organized around his prayer, the prayer becomes an ingredient in the experience of creative interchange and transformation. "The outcome of this creative transformation will have a character it would not have if this petition had not been an ingredient in the total process of creativity. In this way prayer can be truly effective in producing consequences."[113] Thus, prayer may be defined as "that voluntarily established attitude of the personality which enables connections of value to grow far beyond the scope of ordinary instrumentalities of consciousness" and "enables the work of God to go on more abundantly and blessedly."[114]

Wieman and Kaplan did not fail to apply their approaches to the attitudes of their respective religions to other faiths. "The value of the Christian message," said Wieman,

lies in what it can contribute to promoting creative interchange between parent and child, husband and wife, human associations of all kinds, cultures and peoples. When not applied to human living in this way, the Christian message becomes a tyranny of dogma, a barrier to creative interchange, and source of great evil, as history demon-strates.[115]

Diverse temperaments, traditions and regional interest require differ-ent forms of religion. The different forms of religion need not be reduced to one form only. But if conflicting interests are to be brought into greater interdependence, the various forms of religion must have a ruling commitment to creative interchange which can bring con-flicts under control.[116]

Kaplan wrote of the *sancta* of a people or church as the persons, events, texts, places, etc., through which it helps those who belong to it achieve salvation. The *sancta* of each people or church naturally mean more to its members than to those of any other group. Whether the *sancta* of one group are more ethical or spiritual than the *sancta* of another group is beside the point. "The fact is that such comparison is not only odious but unwarranted, because the *sancta* of no religion or civilization are so fixed or static as to be incapable of development and revaluation."[117] Since every religion aspires to be a means of salvation to its own people or church, the assumption that one's own religion is the only religion is obsolete. No religion can be absolutely more or less true than another. "Though, at some particu-lar time or place, one religion may be more helpful to its own adherents than another religion is to the adherents of that religion, that condition may be reversed before long."[118] Each religion exists in its own right and has no need to justify itself by asserting its superiority over other religions.

> If a devout Christian tells me that he finds in the adoration of the personality of Jesus all the inspiration that he requires for living a life that satisfies his spiritual needs, I cannot as a Jew say this attitude is not true, although I am so conditioned that I could not possibly find it true in my own experience. On the other hand, if I say to him that I can find in the Torah literature of the Jew the reflection of an attitude toward life more satisfying than any I could find in the New Testa-ment or elsewhere, I, too, am speaking the truth, and my religion is as true as his.[119]

Each religion exists in its own right and should not have to justify its existence by any assertion of superiority.

Thus, for both Kaplan and Wieman the future of interfaith goodwill depends on something other than tolerance between groups. The way to deal with diversity is for each faith to heed the voice of conscience and the dictates of moral responsibility, and to relate to other faiths in the spirit of creative intercommunication and mutual learning in depth. It is a tribute to the diversity and openness of American society that these two religious thinkers of diverse traditions could not only come to know and appreciate each other's work but to publicly acknowledge their mutual admiration and respect. Kaplan was a diligent student of Wieman's writings and recommended them to his students. In the classes in philosophy of religion which he taught at the Jewish Theological Seminary he sometimes utilized Wieman's books as texts. Wieman, for his part, said that he was certain that Kaplan's thought was on the right track and that, sooner or later, the dominant form of religion by which people find salvation would be developed along the lines indicated by Kaplan.[120]

The ideological convergence of the Judaism of Mordecai M. Kaplan and the Christianity of Henry Nelson Wieman constitutes a significant development in American religious thought. The two thinkers remained remarkably loyal to the presuppositions of modernist liberalism during careers which extended beyond the emergence of crisis theology, neo-Orthodoxy, existentialism and death-of-God theology. While their thoughts continued to evolve and to absorb insights from new developments in philosophy and the social sciences, the two thinkers remained firmly rooted in the basic outlooks they developed quite early in their careers. Refusing to succumb to despair about human nature and the possibility of progress, they continued to affirm the interdependence of religion and culture and to require of their respective faiths both intellectual honesty and moral action consonant with belief.[121] In the tradition of a significant sector of American religious thinking, they were "free theologians" seeking both self-understanding and insight into the issues of their day through creative thinking about God.[122] They grappled critically and imaginatively with human experience so that it might provide new religious vision and hope. Such reflection has often played a unifying and constructive role in the history of religion. The ideologies of Kaplan and Wieman may indeed play such a role in the future.

NOTES

1. Mordecai M. Kaplan, "The Way I Have Come," *Mordecai M. Kaplan: An Evaluation*, ed. I. Eisenstein and E. Kohn, New York, 1952, p. 287.
2. Mordecai M. Kaplan, "The Influences That Have Shaped My Life," *Reconstructionist*, Vol. 8, No. 10 (June 26, 1942), p. 30.
3. Henry Nelson Wieman, "Intellectual Autobiography," *The Empirical Theology of Henry Nelson Wieman*, ed. R. W. Bretall, New York, 1963, p. 6.
4. Henry Nelson Wieman, "Theocentric Religion," *Contemporary American Theology*, ed. V. Ferm, New York, 1932, Vol. 1, p. 340.
5. Kaplan, "The Influences That Have Shaped My Life," p. 29.
6. Wieman, "Theocentric Religion," p. 342.
7. Ibid., p. 341.
8. Kaplan, "The Way I Have Come," p. 287.
9. Wieman, "Theocentric Religion," 343f.
10. Mordecai M. Kaplan, *The Greater Judaism in the Making*, New York, 1960, p. 353.
11. Sidney E. Ahlstrom, *A Religious History of the American People*, New York, 1983, p. 783.
12. Kenneth Cauthen, *The Impact of American Religious Liberalism*, New York, 1962, p. 25.
13. Ahlstrom, op. cit., p. 782f.
14. Cauthen, op. cit., p. 29.
15. William R. Hutchison, *The Modernist Impulse in American Protestantism*, Cambridge, MA, 1976, p. 2.
16. op. cit., p. 2.
17. Mordecai M. Kaplan, *Judaism as a Civilization*, New York, 1934, p. 115.
18. Mordecai M. Kaplan, "The Future of Judaism," *The Menorah Journal*, Vol. 2, No. 3 (June 1916), p. 169.
19. Henry Nelson Wieman (with Walter M. Horton) *The Growth of Religion*, Chicago, 1938, p. 248.

20. Henry Nelson Wieman, "Neo-Orthodoxy and Contemporary Religious Reaction," *Religious Liberals Reply*, ed. H. N. Wieman, et al., Boston, 1947, p. 6f.

21. Henry Nelson Wieman, *The Issues of Life*, New York 1930, p. 168f; cf. Wieman, "Theocentric Religion," p. 346.

22. Mordecai M. Kaplan, *Questions Jews Ask: Reconstructionist Answers*, New York, 1956, p. 443.

23. Henry Nelson Wieman, *Intellectual Foundation of Faith*, New York, 1961, p. 2.

24. Ibid., pp. 2, 201.

25. Wieman, *The Growth of Religion*, p. 251.

26. Wieman, *The Issues of Life*, p. 163.

27. Mordecai M. Kaplan, *The Meaning of God in Modern Jewish Religion*, New York, 1936, p. 245.

28. Mordecai M. Kaplan, *The Future of the American Jew*, New York, 1949, p. 193.

29. Kaplan, *Questions Jews Ask*, p. 95.

30. Ibid., p. 95.

31. Henry Nelson Wieman, *The Directive in History*, Boston, 1949, p. 59.

32. James A. Martin, Jr., *Empirical Philosophies of Religion*, New York, 1945, p. 2.

33. Daniel D. Williams, "Wieman as a Christian Theologian," *The Empirical Theology of Henry Nelson Wieman*, ed. R. Brettall, p. 79.

34. Kaplan, *The Future of the American Jew*, p. 210.

35. Kaplan, *Judaism as a Civilization*, p. 382.

36. Mordecai M. Kaplan, *The Religion of Ethical Nationhood*, New York, 1970, p. 66.

37. Charles Hartshorne, "Introduction," *Philosophers of Process*, ed. D. Browning, New York, 1965, p. v; cf. James R. Gray, *Modern Process Thought*, Washington, D.C., 1982, p. xi.

38. Bernard E. Loomer, "Wieman's Stature as a Contemporary Theologian," *The Empirical Theology of Henry Nelson Wieman*, ed. R. Bretall, p. 395.

39. Wieman, *The Growth of Religion*, p. 347.

40. Kaplan, *Questions Jews Ask*, p. 103.

41. Edgar S. Brightman, *A Philosophy of Religion*, New York, 1940, p. 86.

42. Kaplan, *The Religion of Ethical Nationhood*, p. 48.
43. op. cit., p. 23.
44. James A. Martin, Jr., op. cit., p. 6.
45. Wieman, *The Growth of Religion*, p. 267.
46. Henry Nelson Wieman, *The Source of Human Good*, Chicago, 1946, p. 39.
47. John E. Smith, "Philosophy of Religion," *Religion*, ed. P. Ramsey, Englewood Cliffs, NJ, 1965, p. 380.
48. Henry Nelson Wieman, *The Wrestle of Religion with Truth*, New York, 1927, p. 123f.
49. Henry Nelson Wieman, *Normative Psychology of Religion* (with R. W. Wieman), New York, 1935, p. 99f.
50. op. cit., p. 171.
51. op. cit., p. 172.
52. Wieman, *Intellectual Foundation of Faith*, p. 169.
53. op. cit., p. 80.
54. op. cit., p. 7f.
55. Kaplan, *The Future of the American Jew*, p. 172.
56. Kaplan, *The Religion of Ethical Nationhood*, p. 21.
57. Mordecai M. Kaplan, "Religion in a New Key," *Reconstructionist*, vol. 26, no. 1 (February 19, 1960), p. 17.
58. Kaplan, *Questions Jews Ask*, p. 126.
59. Ibid., p. 480.
60. Kaplan, "Religion in a New Key," p. 18.
61. Kaplan, *The Religion of Ethical Nationhood*, p. 49.
62. Mordecai M. Kaplan, *If Not Now, When?* (with Arthur A. Cohen), New York, 1973, p. 80.
63. Kaplan, *The Future of the American Jew*, p. 206.
64. Wieman, *Intellectual Foundation of Faith*, p. 47.
65. Ibid., p. 53.
66. Ibid., p. 55.
67. Ibid., p. 53.
68. Ibid., p. 58.
69. Ibid., p. 66.
70. Henry Nelson Wieman, "Appendix," *Creative Interchange*, ed. J. A. Broyer and W. S. Minor, Carbondale, IL, 1982, p. 447.
71. Ibid., p. 447.

72. Henry Nelson Wieman, *Man's Ultimate Commitment*, Carbondale, IL, 1958, p. 31.
73. Wieman, "Appendix," p. 447.
74. Kaplan, *The Religion of Ethical Nationhood*, p. 109.
75. Ibid., p. 75.
76. Ibid., p. 10.
77. Ibid., p. 82.
78. Ibid., p. 70.
79. Mordecai M. Kaplan, "Between Two Worlds," *Varieties of Jewish Belief*, ed. I. Eisenstein, New York, 1966, p. 141.
80. Kaplan, *The Religion of Ethical Nationhood*, p. 86f.
81. op. cit., p. 34f.
82. op. cit., p. 48.
83. op. cit., p. 71.
84. Kaplan, *If Not Now, When?*, p. 38.
85. Mordecai M. Kaplan, "Our God as Our Collective Conscience," *Reconstructionist*, Vol. 41, No. 1 (February 1975), p. 14.
86. Kaplan, *If Not Now, When?*, p. 14.
87. op. cit., p. 79.
88. op. cit., p. 119.
89. op. cit., p. 89.
90. Wieman, "Appendix," p. 446.
91. Ibid., p. 446.
92. Wieman, *Intellectual Foundation of Faith*, p. 120f.
93. Mordecai M. Kaplan, "The Unresolved Problem of Evil," *Reconstructionist*, Vol. 29, No. 7 (May 17, 1963) pp. 6–11; No. 8 (May 31, 1963), pp. 11–16.
94. Kaplan, *The Religion of Ethical Nationhood*, p. 51.
95. Ibid., p. 51.
96. Kaplan, "The Unresolved Problem of Evil," *Reconstructionist*, May 31, 1963, p. 15.
97. Kaplan, *Questions Jews Ask*, p. 389.
98. Mordecai M. Kaplan, "Jewish Consciousness," *Reconstructionist*, Vol. 38, No. 6 (September 22, 1972), p. 11.
99. Kaplan, *The Future of the American Jew*, p. 166f.
100. Kaplan, *If Not Now, When?*, p. 98.
101. Ibid., p. 55, p. 96.

102. Wieman, *Man's Ultimate Commitment*, p. 196.
103. Ibid., p. 200.
104. Wieman, *Intellectual Foundation of Faith*, p. 181.
105. Henry Nelson Wieman, "Reply to Williams," *The Empirical Theology of Henry Nelson Wieman* ed. R. W. Bretall, p. 102.
106. op. cit., p. 104.
107. Kaplan, *Judaism as a Civilization*, p. 347.
108. Kaplan, *Questions Jews Ask*, p. 104.
109. Mordecai M. Kaplan, *Not So Random Thoughts*, New York, 1966, p. 210.
110. Wieman, *Man's Ultimate Commitment*, p. 178.
111. Wieman, *Intellectual Foundation of Faith*, p. 21.
112. op. cit., p. 71.
113. op. cit., p. 77f.
114. Wieman, *The Growth of Religion*, p. 380.
115. Henry Nelson Wieman, *Religious Inquiry*, Boston, 1968, p. 21.
116. op. cit., p. 33f.
117. Mordecai M. Kaplan, *Judaism Without Supernaturalism*, New York, 1958, p. 74.
118. op. cit., p. 75.
119. Mordecai M. Kaplan, *Judaism in Transition*, New York, 1936, p. 282.
120. Henry Nelson Wieman, "Mordecai M. Kaplan's Idea of God," *Mordecai M. Kaplan: An Evaluation*, ed. I. Eisenstein and E. Kohn, p. 210.
121. Hutchison, op. cit., p. 310.
122. Frederick Sontag and John K. Roth, *The American Religious Experience*, New York, 1972, p. 340.

11. Primo Levi: Elemental Survivor

Richard L. Rubenstein

The preeminent witness to the Holocaust is, of course, Elie Wiesel. Nevertheless, in recent years a very different witness to Auschwitz of perhaps equal importance has gained international recognition, the late Primo Levi. Although Levi was a person of towering importance in his native Italy—Italian school children study his writings—and in the Italian Jewish community, he never achieved the kind of almost sanctified status accorded to Nobel Laureate Wiesel by the world Jewish community and even by many thoughtful Christians.[1] Levi and Wiesel came from radically different Jewish backgrounds. Levi was an assimilated Jew from Turin who had received his doctorate in chemistry two years before he was taken to Auschwitz. Even in the most extreme situations, Levi steadfastly refused the consolations of religious tradition. He has described the one and only moment in which he experienced "the temptation ... to seek refuge in prayer." In October 1944, as he stood naked waiting for an SS "commission" to glance at him and instantaneously decide whether to condemn him to be gassed or permit him to continue to work as an Auschwitz

177

slave, Levi felt the need for "help and asylum," but immediately overcame it:

> then, despite my anguish, equanimity prevailed: you do not change the rules of the game at the end of the match, nor when you are losing. A prayer under these conditions would have been not only absurd . . . but blasphemous, obscene, laden with the greatest impiety of which a nonbeliever is capable. I rejected that temptation: I knew that otherwise were I to survive, I would have to be ashamed of it.[2]

By contrast, Wiesel's background was that of a Jew wholly immersed in the traditional Judaism of Eastern Europe. Wiesel has given us a verbal picture of young Eli as a boy of twelve in his native Sighet: "I believed profoundly. During the day I studied the Talmud and at night I ran to the synagogue to weep over the destruction of Jerusalem."[3]

The dissonance between Wiesel's Auschwitz experience and his faith in the just and providential God of Israel left him unable to believe yet unable not to believe. Wiesel is reported to have said, "If I told you I believed in God, I would be lying; if I told you I did not believe in God, I would be lying."[4] Undoubtedly, much of Wiesel's unique ability to speak to and on behalf of thoughtful religious believers, both Jewish and Christian, lies precisely in his profound theological ambivalence.[5]

Unlike Wiesel, Levi's cultural background was fundamentally the literature of his native language, Italian. His experience at Auschwitz instilled in him a strong curiosity about and an appreciation of the culture of Eastern European Judaism. Nevertheless, he tells us, "it was not my culture."[6] As a young man Levi was far more conversant with Dante Alighieri's *Divina Comedia* than with any work of either biblical or rabbinic Judaism. According to critic Clive James, "Levi often echoes Dante."[7] Indeed, as James points out, one of the difficulties in reading Levi in translation is that the allusions to Dante, which are taken for granted in Italian, are lost in English. No one would ever worry about allusions to Dante being lost in the translating of Wiesel.

Levi has described his family background in the first chapter in his book, *The Periodic Table*. Each chapter of *The Periodic Table* is given the name of a chemical element which Levi employs as a metaphor for a particular human characteristic or experience. The chapter describing his background is entitled "Argon," an inert gas. According to Levi, argon is one of three gases that are "so inert, so satisfied with their condition, that they do not interfere in any chemical reaction, do not combine with any other element, and precisely for this reason have gone undetected for centuries."[8] Levi tells us that his ancestors and their descendants were like the gas. Hard workers, "they were inert in their inner spirits, inclined to disinterested speculation, witty discourses, elegant, sophisticated, and gratuitous discussion . . . all the deeds attributed to them . . . have in common a touch of the static, an attitude of dignified abstention, of voluntary (or accepted) relegation to the margins of the great rivers of life."[9] Using the metaphor of an inert gas, Levi offers a succinct description of the apolitical way of life of a merchant and professional class separated from the indigenous majority in both belief and origin.

Levi's ancestors arrived in the agricultural regions of Piedmont around 1500. According to Levi, "they were never much loved or hated," but there was enough mutual suspicion to have kept them distinct from the rest of the population until late in the nineteenth century. Relatively few in number, the Piedmontese Jews had their own familial and linguistic subculture which Levi describes in some detail in *The Periodic Table*. Although Levi had a Bar Mitzvah, his sense of Jewishness was minimal and pro forma until the racial laws of 1938. Levi has written:

> Like most Jews of ancient Italian descent, my parents and grandparents . . . had thoroughly assimilated the language, customs and ethical attitudes of the country. Religion did not count much in my family . . . Nevertheless, both in my family and among Jews in general, the sense that we were Jewish was not entirely lost. It was manifest in the observation of a number of family rituals (especially the holidays of Rosh Hashanah, Passover, and Purim). . . .[10]

Levi himself was born in 1919 in the industrial city of Turin. He studied to be a chemist at the University of Turin, receiving his doctorate in 1941. However, Levi's motives for studying chemistry were very different from those of his classmates. For Levi the study of chemistry and physics was the key to understanding the universe. For Rita, a Christian student with whom Levi had with difficulty become friends, "the university was not at all the Temple of Knowledge: it was a thorny and difficult path that led to a degree, a job and regular pay."

With the enactment of Mussolini's anti-Semitic racial laws in 1938, Levi came to understand how different he was from Rita and his classmates. Levi describes his growing awareness of his Jewish identity in the chapters of *The Periodic Table* entitled "Iron" and "Zinc." In the chapter, "Zinc," Levi describes his personal response to the atmosphere in Italy during the period when the racial laws were enacted. There was much Fascist propaganda about racial purity and of the Jews as impurities in the pure body of the Italian people. Imitating Goebbels, the Fascists initiated the publication of the anti-Semitic magazine, *Defense of the Race*. Levi writes that zinc is only capable of reacting with acids if certain impurities are present in it. If it is too pure no reaction takes place. Impure zinc became for Levi a metaphor for his Jewish identity:

> I am the impurity that makes the zinc react, I am the grain of salt or mustard. Impurity, certainly, since just during those months the publication of the magazine *Defense of the Race* had begun, and there was much talk about purity, and I had begun to be proud of being impure. In truth, until precisely those months it had not meant much to me that I was a Jew: within myself and in my contacts with my Christian friends, I had always considered my origin an almost neglible but curious fact, albeit a curious one: a small amusing anomaly, like having a crooked nose, or freckles. A Jew is one who does not put up a tree at Christmas; who should not eat salami, but who eats it all the same; who learned a bit of Hebrew at thirteen years of age, and then forgot it. According to the magazine mentioned before, a Jew is stingy and astute. But I was neither particularly stingy nor astute; nor had my father been."[11]

Elsewhere, Levi has written that this passage reflected accurately the state of mind of most Italian Jews at the time.[12]

When Mussolini's racial laws went into effect, neither Levi's teachers nor his classmates were overtly hostile. However, Levi recalls, ". . . I could feel them withdraw and, following an ancient pattern, I withdrew as well: every look exchanged between me and them was accompanied by a minuscule but perceptible flash of mistrust and suspicion. What do you think of me? . . . The same as six months ago, your equal who does not go to Mass, or the Jew who, as Dante put it, 'in your midst laughs at you'?"[13]

In spite of his isolation, he became friends with Sandro Delmastro, a Christian student whose family had been tinkers and blacksmiths for generations. Hence, the title "Iron." Like Primo, Sandro was also a loner, and originally this was the basis of their bond. Unlike Primo, Sandro had decided on a career in chemistry because he wanted "a trade that dealt with things one can see and touch. . . ."[14] However, Levi's enthusiasm for both literature and science proved contagious and Sandro became a voracious reader. In the course of one conversation, Primo told Sandro that chemistry and physics are the "antidote to Fascism . . . because they were clear and distinct and verifiable at every step, and not a tissue of lies and emptiness, like the radio and newspapers."[15] Levi's commitment to that which is "clear and distinct and verifiable at every step" was to remain an enduring characteristic of his life and work. It constitutes a fundamental difference between his testimony and that of Elie Wiesel for whom ambiguity and paradox are essential, especially when Wiesel addresses the theological issues present in the Holocaust.

Levi's capacity for dispassionate analysis stood him in good stead in chemistry. It also contributed materially to his survival in Auschwitz. The same quality is always present in his writing. He never sensationalizes; he almost never lets his own feelings intrude on the cool accuracy of his descriptions of many of the most degrading, anti-human experiences to which men and women have ever been subjected. Refraining from anger, Levi shifts the burden of anger and indignation to his readers for whom it is inescapable. Levi has stated that he deliberately refrained from formulating judgments in *Survival in Auschwitz* because he felt it was wrong for the witness to take the place of the judgment. Nevertheless, he tells us, while he suspended explicit judgments "his implicit judgments are clearly there."[16]

The racial laws prevented Levi from finding employment at a level appropriate to his training. He took odd jobs in a varnish factory and then in a nickel mine. In the fall of 1942 he left Turin for Milan where he first became aware of Italian resistance to Fascism. On July 25, 1943, Fascism collapsed. On September 8th, the Nazis occupied Milan. At this point Levi decided to join a partisan group in the hills of Piedmont. Concerning his unit, Levi has written: "We were cold and hungry, we were the most disarmed partisans in the Piedmont, and probably the most unprepared."[17] Sandro also joined the Resistance but was captured by the Fascists and executed in April 1944. Levi's terse description of Sandro's end is one of the few places in his writings where his anger is manifest:

> in April of 1944 he was captured by the Fascists, did not surrender, and tried to escape from the Fascist party house in Cuneo. He was killed with a tommygun burst in the back of the neck by a monstrous child executioner, one of those wretched murderers of fifteen whom Mussolini's Republic of Salo recruited in the reformatories. His body was abandoned in the road for a long time, because the Fascists had forbidden the population to bury him.[18]

Levi's Resistance group did not last long. His first book, *Survival in Auschwitz (Se questo è un uomo)*, begins:

> I was captured by the Fascist Militia on December 13, 1943. I was twenty-four, with little wisdom, no experience . . . At the time I had not yet been taught the doctrine I was later to learn so hurriedly in the Lager: that man is bound to pursue his own ends by all possible means, while he who errs but once pays dearly."[19]

Interrogated by Fascist militia, Levi admitted to being Jewish. In *The Periodic Table*, Levi writes that he did so "partly because I was tired, partly out of an irrational digging in of pride."[20] As a Jew he was sent to an internment camp for Italian Jews at Fossoli, near Modena, in January 1944. On February 20, 1944, the Germans took over the camp. On February 21, Levi and the other internees learned that they would all, men, women and children, be taken from the camp the next day. Levi understood the departure to be a death sentence, as did most of the others.

The next morning the group was assembled by the Germans for roll call. At the end of roll call the German officer asked, "Wieviel Stück?" and was informed that there were 650 pieces. In the eyes of his captors, the Jews were no longer human beings but "cheaper merchandise" to be eliminated in an industrial installation for human waste disposal. The 650 Jews were sent to Poland in twelve freight trains. Levi was lucky; there were only forty-five people in his wagon. There were eighty in Elie Wiesel's wagon. At every stop the victims begged for water to no avail. As the train reached Poland and the cold became unbearable, they stopped begging for food. The victims felt that they were now "on the other side," cast out of any contact with the rest of humanity.

Suddenly the wagon door opened. The group was speedily divided into those judged capable of working for Hitler's Reich and those who were to be exterminated without delay. In Levi's convoy ninety-six men and twenty-nine women were selected as slaves to work in the camps of Auschwitz-Monowitz and Auschwitz-Birkenau. Within less than two days the remaining 525 were all murdered. "Thus, in an instant, our women, our parents, our children disappeared."

Levi and the others who had been given an undefined respite from immediate extermination were transported to Auschwitz-Monowitz, an *Arbeitslager*, a slave-labor camp adjacent to the extermination camp. Monowitz was the site of a new form of profit-making corporate enterprise, the I. G. Farben factory for the production of synthetic rubber or Buna.[21] Upon entering, the prisoners were subjected to a calculated routine of systematic degradation intended to strip them of all dignity and to impress upon them their absolute rightlessness.

Their condition is perhaps best epitomized by an incident which occurred at the very beginning of Levi's incarceration in the *Arbeitslager*. No water was provided for the four-day journey from Italy to Auschwitz. By the time Levi arrived at Monowitz and went through the entry ritual of being stripped, beaten, disinfected and provided with thin rags to protect his body from the bitterly harsh Polish winter, he was tortured with thirst. Seeing an icicle outside a window, he opened the window and broke off the icicle. The icicle was immediately snatched from him by a Lager guard. Puzzled, Levi asked, "*Warum?*" The guard replied, "*Hier ist kein Warum.*"

Overnight Levi and his fellows had been transformed into the phantomlike prisoners they had seen on their arrival. Levi describes the transformation:

> Imagine now a man who is deprived of everyone he loves, and at the same time of his house, his habits, his clothes, in short, of everything he possesses: he will be a hollow man, reduced to suffering and needs, forgetful of dignity and restraint, for he who loses all often easily loses himself. He will be a man whose life and death can be lightly decided with no sense of human affinity, in the most fortunate cases on the basis of a pure judgment of utility. It is in this way that one can understand the double sense of the term "extermination camp," and it is now clear what we seek to express with the phrase: "to lie on the bottom."[22]

Levi had become *Haftling* number 174517 with the number indelibly tattooed on his left arm. Apart from the indispensable ingredient of luck, survival depended on Levi's ability to learn how to cope with an artificially created Hobbesian state of nature, an incessant war of all against all. The system was a "pitiless process of natural selection" calculated to kill the average slave worker at Monowitz within three months of arrival. Apart from the degrading absolute contempt with which the prisoners, especially the Jews, were treated, it was impossible to survive on either the food ration or the clothing distributed to the prisoners. Without theft, barter or the ability to become a "Prominent," or be assigned a special task, survival was impossible.

Levi has given a brief description of those who failed the test of survival, the "mussulmen":

> To sink is the easiest of matters; it is enough to carry out all the orders one receives, to eat only the ration, to observe the discipline of the work and the camp. Experience showed that only exceptionally could one survive more than three months in this way. All the mussulmans who finished in the gas chambers have the same story, or more exactly, have no story; they follow the same slope down to the bottom, like streams that run down to the sea. On their entry into the camp, through basic incapacity, or by misfortune, or through some banal incident, they are overcome before they can adapt themselves; they are beaten by time, they do not begin to learn German, to disentangle the infernal knot of laws and prohibitions until their body is already in decay, and nothing can save them from selections or from death by exhaustion. Their life is short, but their number is endless: they, the *Musselmanner*, the drowned, form the backbone of the camp, an anonymous mass, continually renewed and always identical, of non-men who march and labor in silence, the divine spark dead within them, already too empty to really suffer. One hesitates to call them living: one hesitates to call their death death, in the face of which they have no fear, as they are too tired to understand . . . if I could enclose all the evil of our time in one image, I would choose this image which is familiar to me: an emaciated man, with head dropped and shoulders curved, on whose face and in whose eyes not a trace of a thought is to be seen.[23]

I know few, if any, writings which convey the immeasurable harshness and the horror of what passed for life in the camps as effectively as does the above. In his utter honesty and his undeviating commitment to factuality, Levi describes how those incorporated into the Nazi camp system could only survive by becoming in some measure part of the system. Inside the Lager, the Germans had created a society of total domination, an intensified version of the hierarchical structure of the totalitarian state. At each level of the hierarchy, with the SS at the top and the various ranks of prisoner-collaborators with derivative authority or specialized function, the domination of those above was always absolute over those beneath. In the camps as outside, there were "grey, ambiguous persons ready to compromise."[24]

Levi calls these prisoner-collaborators "grey-zoners." He contemptuously rejects the irresponsible and malicious statement of Liliana Cavani, the director of the film, *The Night Porter*, "We are all victims or murderers, and we accept these roles voluntarily." Levi did not deny that survival involved some measure of guilt, if only the indispensable rejection of altruism for the sake of survival. Nevertheless, in almost all cases even the collaborators had no choice. Abruptly deprived of anything resembling a normal human environment, their daily struggle "against hunger, cold, fatigue and blows" left no room for moral choices if they were to survive.[25]

Levi cites as an extreme case of collaboration the *Sonderkommando* who consisted largely of Jews assigned the task of maintaining order among the new arrivals about to be gassed, of removing the corpses, then of removing from the dead gold teeth and hair, of collecting their clothes, cremating their bodies and disposing of the ashes. While they lived they had enough to eat. Periodically, the SS would murder the whole group and create a new squad with fresh replacements. The latter were recruited as they stepped off the freight trains at Auschwitz, disoriented and exhausted from the journey. At that point they had no will to resist.

Levi sees contradictory impulses at work in the SS decision to utilize the *Sonderkommando* as they did. On the one hand, it was a "paroxysm of perfidiousness and hatred" in which the Jews must be shown to be a "sub-race," sub-humans who will bow to the most extreme humiliation even to the point of putting their own into the ovens and destroying themselves.[26] At the same time, there were some among the SS who were relieved to assign the dirtiest aspects of the slaughter to be done by others.

Levi nevertheless insists that there was nothing distinctively Jewish about the behavior of the *Sonderkommando*. Prisoners of every nationality did not behave any differently. Levi holds that creating these squads was "National Socialism's most demonic crime." Apart from any pragmatic motives, Levi discerns an attempt to shift the burden of guilt from the perpetrators to the victims who were "deprived of even the solace of innocence." According to Levi, the existence of the *Sonderkommando* contained a message. The Germans were saying to their victims: "We, the master race, are your destroyers, but you are no better than we are; if we so wish, and we do so wish, we can destroy not only your bodies but also your souls, just as we have destroyed ours."[27]

Yet, if the creation of the *Sonderkommando* was a demonic crime, Levi nevertheless insists that we must suspend judgment in considering their behavior. He asks his readers to consider why these men were under a *Befehlnotstand*, a compulsion to obey orders:

> I would invite anyone who dares pass judgment to carry out upon himself, with sincerity, a conceptual experiment: let him imagine, if he can, that he has lived for months and for years in a ghetto, tormented by chronic hunger, fatigue, promiscuity and humiliation; that he has seen die around him, one by one, his beloved; that he is cut off from the world, unable to receive or transmit news; that, finally, he is loaded onto a train eighty or a hundred people to a boxcar; that he travels towards the unknown, blindly, for sleepless days and nights; and that he is at last flung inside the walls of an indecipherable inferno. This, it seems to me, is the true *Befehlnotstand*.[28]

When Levi reflected upon human nature after his Auschwitz experience, he expressed the belief that when every civilized institution is removed, man is not fundamentally brutal or egoistic. Nevertheless, "in the face of driving necessity and physical disabilities many social habits and instincts are reduced to silence."[29]

Levi's own survival was partly made possible because he had taught himself enough German to obey commands and was a trained chemist who, after months in the camp, came to be regarded as useful to I. G. Farben in manufacturing Buna or synthetic rubber. His scientific training also enabled him to grasp his human and social environment as it was rather than as he might have wished it to be. He refused to fabricate his own truths as did so many others. Chemists deal with elements whose laws must be obeyed rather than invented. Levi's capacity for dispassionate scientific analysis undoubtedly helped him to survive when he was suddenly thrust into the hell of Auschwitz. Yet another element in his survival was his friendship with two Italians, Alberto, a fellow *Haftling*, and Lorenzo, an Italian civilian worker at the Buna installation whom Levi met by chance. Levi was assigned to Alfredo's block after a two-week stay in the *Ka-Be*, the *Krankenbau*, that passed for an infirmary. Levi and Alberto shared rations and supported each other in their quest for survival. Lorenzo's friendship was of even greater importance. Lorenzo became Levi's protector and brought him a piece of bread and what was left of his ration every day for six months. Lorenzo's conduct was atypical of the civilian behavior toward the *Haftlinge* in the camp. The civilians saw the degraded and disfigured slaves as deserving of their fate even when they threw them potatoes or bread. Above all, Lorenzo treated Levi as a human being and it was that treatment which Levi believes kept him alive:

> I believe that it was really due to Lorenzo that I am alive today; and not so much for his material aid, as for his having constantly reminded me by his presence, by his natural and plain manner of being good, that there still existed a just world outside our own . . . a remote possibility of good, but for which it was worth surviving.[30]

There was yet another reason why Levi survived, sheer accident. On January 11, 1945, Levi came down with scarlet fever and was sent to the *Ka-Be*. On January 18th, the Germans evacuated the entire camp except those in the infirmary. Levi estimates that there were about 20,000 people on the evacuation march almost all of whom, including Alberto, died. Levi survived because of his illness.

According to Levi the people he describes in the Lager from the SS down to "the indifferent slave *Haftlinge* are not men," all the grades of the mad hierarchy created by the Germans paradoxically fraternize in a uniform internal desolation."[31] Nevertheless, Lorenzo was a man of whom Levi could say, "Thanks to Lorenzo, I managed not to forget that I myself was a man." Lorenzo was the slender thread connecting Levi to humanity.

By October 1944, the Lager had become overcrowded with two thousand extra "guests" inhabiting the huts. The Germans had a simple solution to the overcrowding, a *Selekcja*, in which the physically fit or those otherwise useful would remain and the others gassed. The entire camp was made to file naked past an SS subaltern who by an instantaneous glance made the decision for life or death. It took no more than three or four minutes to decide the fate of two hundred men in a hut and the 12,000 inmates of the Lager in an afternoon. Levi survived the *Selekcja*. After it is over, Levi notices another prisoner, Kuhn, swaying backwards and forwards, praying aloud, thanking God that he was not chosen to be gassed. This infuriates Levi who asks himself how Kuhn can offer thanks when next to him Beppo the Greek knows that he will be gassed in two days. Levi asks:

> Does not Kuhn fail to understand that what has happened today is an abomination, which no propitiary prayer, no pardon, no expiation by the guilty, which nothing at all in the power of man can ever clean again. *If I was* (sic) *God, I would spit at Kuhn's prayer.*[32] (Italics added)

The question of God and the Holocaust never agonizes Levi as it does Wiesel. He has written that he entered the Lager as a non-believer and he has remained a non-believer throughout his life. The experience of the Lager prevented him from "conceiving of any form of providence or transcendent justice."

Even before Auschwitz Levi saw no reason for believing in a providential God of Israel. In January 1941 he came together with a group of friends in the gym of the Turin Talmud Torah to study the bible. Through their study they came to recognize in Ahasuerus and Nebuchadnezzar the oppressors of the Jewish people of their own time. Nevertheless, they could not find the God of the Bible:

> But where was Kadosh Barukhu, "the Holy One, blessed be He"; he who breaks the slaves' chains and submerges the Egyptian chariots? He who dictated the Law to Moses, and inspired the liberators Ezra and Nehemiah, no longer inspired anyone; the sky above us was silent and

empty: he allowed the Polish ghettos to be exterminated, and slowly, confusedly, the idea was making headway in us that we had no allies we could count on, neither on earth nor in heaven. . . ."[33]

After the war, after Levi had returned to Italy, a friend who was a believer visited him and told him that his survival was not a matter of chance or of fortunate circumstances, but of Providence. Levi was told by his friend that he, Levi the non-believer, was one of the elect, touched by grace, saved by God to bear witness by writing about Auschwitz.

Recollecting this encounter almost forty years later, the following took place between Levi and Fernando Camon:

Levi: ". . . And this, I must confess, seemed to me like a blasphemy, that God should grant privileges, saving one person and condemning someone else. I must say the experience of Auschwitz has been such as to sweep away any remnant of religious education I may have had."

Camon: "Meaning that Auschwitz is proof of the nonexistence of God?"

Levi: "There is Auschwitz so there cannot be God."

That, however, was not quite Levi's final word. On the typescript of Camon's manuscript, he added, "I don't find a solution to this dilemma. I keep looking, but I don't find it."[34]

There are many reasons why Levi never had the kind of impact on the Jewish community and, for that matter, on religiously committed Christians interested in the Holocaust that Elie Wiesel has had. The Jewish world has been impaled on the horns of an impossible dilemma by the Holocaust. If the traditional God of Israel, the just and providential God of the covenant at Sinai, is affirmed, then Auschwitz is his handiwork and Israel is either the Christlike offering for a sinful world or the object of the bottomless wrath of an angry and punitive God. If, on the contrary, no human beings anywhere, and certainly not those who perished at Auschwitz, deserve such a fate whether as objects of punishment or as sacrificial offerings, then faith in the God of Sinai fails of all credibility. Having endured Auschwitz, the vast majority of Jews find themselves confronted by an impossible religious dilemma. They can neither reject the God of the Fathers nor can they accept even the remotest hint that the victims of the *Shoah* somehow were rightly killed.

Elie Wiesel's ambivalence expresses the ambivalence of the Jewish world and carries with it the authority of his roots in the world of traditional Judaism and his distinctive role of survivor-witness. It is not only Wiesel but every religious Jew who can neither finally say yes or no to the God of Sinai. That is why Emil Fackenheim's 614th commandment enjoining Jews not to deny or despair of God lest Hitler be given "yet other posthumous victories" has had so powerful an effect on Jewish thought concerning the Holocaust. In the face of the most demonic assault in all of history against Judaism, there are few Jews who are prepared to say that the religion for which they and their ancestors have suffered so much was built upon a foundation wholly lacking in credibility.

That, however, is precisely the theological message of Primo Levi. No one who reads Levi's professions of unbelief can doubt his honesty or his lucidity. Moreover, the message of unbelief is expressed implicitly in almost every word he ever wrote about his experience. Although Levi wrote as a Jewish witness to the greatest catastrophe ever endured by Jews, it is Wiesel rather than Levi who will be the preeminent Jewish witness to the *Shoah*. There are hints of consolation in the corpus of Wiesel's writing; Levi remained inconsolable to the very end.

On April 11, 1987 two days before Passover, Primo Levi either fell or threw himself to his death down the stairwell of the apartment house in Turin in which he had lived his entire adult life. Some of those closest to him have been unable to believe that Levi could have committed suicide. Rita Levi Montalcini, his friend for forty years, protested that such an act was impossible because it would have contradicted the message of courage to be found in all of his books.[35] Risa Sodi, who knew Levi and interviewed him shortly before he died, argues that he did in fact commit suicide and that the key to his action is to be found in his last book, *The Drowned and the Saved*. Sodi writes concerning the book, "Scrupulously honest, it is written with singular equanimity. But it also betrays the slow-burning rage of a man who sees detachment in the world's reaction to the Holocaust, who sees justice unfulfilled."[36] Sodi's opinion is shared by critic Clive James who cites the fact that in *The Drowned and the Saved*, Levi quotes his friend Jean Amery, who was tortured by the Gestapo and committed suicide decades later, "Anyone who has been tortured remains tortured . . . never again will be able to be at ease in the world, the abomination of annihilation is never extinguished. Faith in humanity, already cracked by the first slap in the face, then demolished by torture is never acquired again."

James argues that Levi's vocation as witness both kept him sane and continually threatened to undo him. He lived by a continuous act of will. All that it took to unhinge that will to survive was a fit of depression induced by recent surgery. He had never absorbed the pain and had never found consolation for a gratuitous violence that could never be forgotten. James finds part of Levi's greatness as a writer in the fact that he warns us "against drawing up a phony balance sheet."[37]

James's analysis is not inconsistent with Sodi's. Beneath the equanimity of Levi's cool style, the demand for justice and the rage at justice unfulfilled is inescapable. To the extent that Levi remained a believer, it was in the possibility that the witness who gave, as did he, honest testimony renders the only justice possible to the victims. His suicide leaves us with the agonizing question of whether he finally despaired of even that belief.

NOTES

1. Even in his native land, Levi was never awarded the *Portico d'Ottavia* Literary Prize awarded bi-annually for the best work published in Italy expressing the "Hebraic spirit." This is especially puzzling to this writer, the 1977 recipient of the prize. If any writer deserved the prize, it was Levi.

2. Primo Levi, *The Drowned and the Saved*, trans. Raymond Rosenthal (London: Sphere Books, 1988), p. 118.

3. Elie Wiesel, *Night*, trans. Stella Rodway (New York: Avon Books, 1970), pp. 12–13.

4. See Richard L. Rubenstein and John K. Roth, *Approaches to Auschwitz: The Holocaust and Its Legacy* (Atlanta: John Knox Press, 1987), p. 285.

5. For an informed exploration of the theological significance of Elie Wiesel, see Michael Berenbaum, *Elie Wiesel: The Vision of the Void* (Middletown, CT: Wesleyan University Press, 1979). See also John K. Roth, *A Consuming Fire: Encounters with Elie Wiesel and the Holocaust* (Atlanta: John K. Roth, 1979). For an interesting Christian interpretation of Wiesel, see Graham B. Walker, Jr., *Elie Wiesel: A Challenge to Theology* (Jefferson, NC: McFarland and Co., 1988).

6. Primo Levi, "Beyond Survival," *Prooftexts*, Vol. 4, 1984, p. 19.

7. Clive James, "Last Will and Testament," *The New Yorker*, May 23, 1988, p. 89. This is a review essay of Levi's last book, *The Drowned and the Saved*.

8. Primo Levi, *The Periodic Table*, trans. Raymond Rosenthal (London: Sphere Books, 1986), p. 3.

9. Primo Levi, *The Periodic Table*, p. 4.

10. Primo Levi, "Beyond Survival," pp. 9–10.

11. Primo Levi, *The Periodic Table*, p. 36.

12. Primo Levi, "Beyond Survival," p. 12.

13. Primo Levi, *The Periodic Table*, p. 40.

14. Primo Levi, *The Periodic Table*, p. 41.

15. Primo Levi, *The Periodic Table*, p. 42.

16. Ferinando Camon, *Conversations with Primo Levi*, trans. John Shepley (Marlboro, VT: The Marlboro Press, 1989), p. 13.

17. Primo Levi, *The Periodic Table*, pp. 130–131.

18. Primo Levi, *The Periodic Table*, p. 48.

19. Primo Levi, *Survival in Auschwitz: The Nazi Assault on Humanity*, trans. Stuart Woolf (New York: Collier Books, 1978), p. 9.

20. Primo Levi, *The Periodic Table*, trans. Raymond Rosenthal (London: Sphere, 1986), p. 134. See also Levi's Letter to the Editor of *Commentary*, February 1986, pp. 6–7.

21. See Richard L. Rubenstein, "The Health Professions and Corporate Enterprise at Auschwitz," in *The Cunning of History* (New York: Harper and Row, 1975), pp. 48–67.

22. Primo Levi, *Survival in Auschwitz*, p. 23.

23. Primo Levi, *Survival in Auschwitz*, p. 82.
24. Primo Levi, *The Drowned and the Saved*, p. 118.
25. Primo Levi, *The Drowned and the Saved*, pp. 31–32.
26. Primo Levi, *The Drowned and the Saved*, p. 35.
27. Primo Levi, *The Drowned and the Saved*, p. 37.
28. Primo Levi, *The Drowned and the Saved*, p. 43.
29. Primo Levi, *Survival in Auschwitz*, p. 79.
30. Primo Levi, *Survival in Auschwitz*, p. 111.
31. Primo Levi, loc. cit.
32. Primo Levi, *Survival in Auschwitz*, p. 118.
33. Primo Levi, *The Periodic Table*, p. 52.
34. Ferinando Camon, *Conversations with Primo Levi*, pp. 67–68.
35. Rita Levi Montalcini, "Non si è suicidato," *Panorama*, May 3, 1987, p. 62. I am indebted for this reference to Risa Sodi, "The Memory of Justice: Primo Levi and Auschwitz," *Holocaust and Genocide Studies*, Vol. 4, No. 1, p. 90, 1989.
36. Sodi, loc. cit.
37. Clive James, op. cit., p. 91.

12. Leivick's Quest

Emanuel S. Goldsmith

Had the Prophets of Israel been exclusively poets or wise men, foretellers of the future or "forth-tellers" expressing the divine will, our interest in them today would be solely literary, historical or theological. The existential hold of the Prophets on our hearts, minds and consciences is the result of their unparalleled insight, courage and vision, and the deeply moral and rational content of their utterances. In modern Jewish letters, only two writers may be said to have been similarly touched by the divine fire to such a degree as to have been almost entirely consumed by it. Only of Ḥayyim Naḥman Bialik and H. Leivick, among Jewish writers in the twentieth century, can it be said that their writings, both poetry and prose, convey such conviction and authority as to border on the realm of "meta-literature." While this assertion may appear exaggerated, it was tacitly shared by hundreds of thousands of Hebrew and Yiddish readers. Despite the fact that more has been written about Bialik and Leivick than about any other twentieth-century Hebrew and Yiddish authors, critics are still unable to satisfactorily account for the spiritual, psychological and literary appeal they continue to have for their readers.

Translations from the Yiddish and Hebrew in this essay are by Emanuel S. Goldsmith.

Bialik's modern hymns of praise to the world of traditional Judaism, which were simultaneously songs of farewell to a vanishing way of life, eased the passage of masses of Eastern European Jews into the modern world. His castigations of frightened pogrom victims became calls to arms and self-defense. His erotic poems liberated many from the taboos and restrictions of a puritanical tradition. His concern for the welfare of his brothers in Zion strengthened the desire of many to leave the Diaspora for the distant Land of Promise. His profound love of the Jewish heritage fortified the Hebrew renaissance of modern times.

In similar fashion, Leivick's Messianic poems and dramas restored confidence in the essential relevance and significance of the Jewish heritage in the modern world. They enabled Jews to come to terms with a revolution against tyranny in which they had put so much hope but which in the end rejected them and turned against itself. His ability to find comfort in suffering and hope in despair helped them to live through unspeakable tragedy. His vision of triumph over tribulation and meaning despite absurdity helped many to rebuild lives broken and aspirations shattered following the Holocaust. His championing of Yiddish in a period of decline fired the determination of lovers of the language to continue their struggle for its preservation and advancement.

Leivick's impact on Yiddish readers is often compared to that of Y. L. Peretz, one of the founding fathers of modern Yiddish literature. Both emphasized ethical and spiritual values and universalized particularistic elements of the Jewish heritage. Both sought direction for the future in the past and were ardent defenders of Yiddish who wrote essays and dramas as well as poetry. Leivick, however, achieved an influence on Yiddish readers from the 1920s on, which far exceeded that ever attained by Peretz. While Peretz's significance was sometimes contested by the Yiddish literati (especially in America), Leivick won almost unanimous respect and admiration with his first book of poems in 1918 and especially after the publication of *The Golem* in 1921.

Leivick was born in 1888 and raised in Igumen, an isolated White

Russian shtetl in which legends of the prophet Elijah, Messianic hopes and tales of the thirty-six hidden saints upon whom the world rests, still flourished. He grew up in abject poverty—his mother baking bread and bagels which she sold in the marketplace, and his father teaching local girls to read and write Yiddish. The oldest of nine children, Leivick witnessed the psychological torment of his angry, frustrated father. When he was six years old, he saw his four-year-old sister, who was blinded and burned when her dress caught fire from the oven, writhe in pain for an entire year before she expired.

> We lower the silence into the grave
> As suddenly the storm subsides
> Revealing—contorted and frightened—
> My sister's shining, golden locks.
>
> Like wanderers we return home
> To the mourning little house of clay
> Bearing bits of earth from the touch of the grave
> And an empty tray beneath our arm.
>
> Mother and father remove their shoes
> To mourn in stockinged feet. I do the same.
> As I sit I dream my stockings are blond—
> Woven from the gold of my sister's locks.
>
> *Mayn Shvester*

Even in his studies at school, young Leivick seemed to be drawn to suffering. His first childhood vision was that of the ram trapped in the thicket by its horns and destined to be slaughtered in Isaac's stead. If Isaac's neck managed to escape the knife, did another neck have to take its place? asked Leivick. Could not the altar remain vacant? In his nightmares he saw the mutilated horns of the ram and its round, fiery eyes yearning to cry out but unable to do so.

The horns fall to earth like cut-off branches,
The ram's head suddenly turns gray as if it were human.
The eyes want to scream but are silent,
Faithful to Isaac's silence which entered them.

Mayn Ershte Yinglshe Zeung

In his first book of poems Leivick was to recall that already as a child he felt that he was in possession of a great secret which had to be concealed from others. Observing how people suffer in silence, he absorbed their silence and imagined that when he grew up something great and wonderful would emerge from suffering.

I will be the first to see the great and wondrous,
No longer hide it from anyone.
I will go from door to door, knock on every window pane
To announce the bright morning.
I know not who chose me from among all,
Estranging and alienating me in shame.
With head hung low, I accepted my fate,
Purifying my youth in anticipation.

Yinglvayz

A brilliant yeshiva student, Leivick soon discovered Hebrew Haskalah literature and early Zionist writings. He was especially taken with Jewish history and in particular with books about the Spanish Inquisition. Expelled from the yeshiva when he was caught reading the first modern Hebrew novel, Abraham Mapu's *Love of Zion*, he eventually abandoned the piety of his father and of the yeshiva, and joined the Jewish Labor Bund so that he might contribute to the realization of the age-old dream of redemption. Arrested for revolutionary activity during the revolution of 1905 and refusing the assistance of a defense attorney, he was sentenced to four years of imprisonment to be followed by permanent exile in Siberia.[1] The words the young revolutionary spoke to his accusers are familiar to every reader of Yiddish literature. "I do not wish to defend myself. I do not want to deny anything. I am a member of the Jewish revolutionary party, the Bund. I do everything I can to overthrow the self-appointed Czarist regime of bloody hangmen together with you."[2]

Leivick later looked on his years in prison and in Siberia as providing his fundamental training in compassion and human values. Here he was witness to frightful pain, suffering and degradation, but here too he saw magnificent displays of compassion and empathy. "I saw hangings in the prison courtyard. . . . I stood on the abyss of human suffering, but I saw the victim's ecstasy as well as pain. . . . In suffering I also felt exaltation."[3]

Leivick's suffering did not cease when he escaped to America in 1913. For most of his life he earned his livelihood as a paperhanger in New York.

> We went to look for work
> Holding each other's hands.
> It was still dark. The city slept.
> Street lamps burned.
>
> We searched everywhere,
> Knocked on so many doors.
> Others arrived before us
> And took the work themselves.
>
> We returned home
> Ashamed to enter the house.
> So we wandered through the street
> Holding each other's hands.
>
> *Arbet Zukhn*

Leivick contracted tuberculosis and spent several years in sanatoria in Denver, Colorado, and Liberty, New York. The experience in Denver provided the basis for "The Ballad of the Denver Sanatorium," one of his most haunting longer poems.

Leivick won international claim when his drama, *The Golem*, was produced on stages around the world and when, in Hebrew translation, it became part of the standard repertoire of the Habima Theater in Palestine. In *The Golem*, Leivick successfully clothed a realistic analysis of contemporary events (the Russian revolution of 1917) in the garments of medieval Jewish legend—a formula to which he returned in several later dramas. His *Rags*, a play about Jewish immigrant life in America, was also a major success when it was produced by Maurice Schwartz in the Yiddish Art Theater in New York.

In the 1920s and early 1930s, Leivick's position in the world of Yiddish letters brought him invitations to address audiences the world over. His trips to Poland, the Soviet Union, Palestine and South America were important events in the cultural history of their Jewish communities.

While highly critical of the Soviet regime, Leivick was sympathetic to the objectives of communism and contributed to Yiddish communist newspapers and magazines in the United States. He sundered his ties with the communists, however, when they supported the Arab cause during the Palestine riots of 1929. Following the signing of the Stalin-Hitler pact of 1939, he repudiated his ties with all Yiddish organizations and publications in any way sympathetic to the left. He helped establish new Yiddish cultural publications such as *Yiddish*, *Vokh* and *Zamlbikher*, and organizations such as the Yiddish Literary Society and the Congress for Jewish Culture. From 1930 on, he became a regular contribution to *Der Tog*, a pro-Zionist daily in which he published both articles and poems.

With the rise of Nazism, many of the nightmares and prophecies of horror contained in Leivick's writing through the years seemed to be coming true. Yiddish readers could not help but regard him as a modern-day Jeremiah who had foretold the destruction and was now bewailing it. During the Holocaust, he became the seismograph of world Jewry and his reactions to what was taking place were expressed in hundreds of articles and poems. The verses in *I Was Not in Treblinka* (1945) and the plays *Miracle in the Ghetto* (1944), *The Rabbi of Rothenberg* (1945) and *The Wedding in Fernwald* (1947) are among the most important literary works to emerge from those terrible years. Leivick's experiences during a tour of the displaced persons camps on behalf of the World Jewish Congress after the war are contained in his book, *With the Surviving Remnant* (1947).

The address "The Individual Jew," which Leivick delivered at the Ideological Conference in Jerusalem in 1957, was a major attempt to heal the rifts between Israel and the Diaspora and between Hebraists and Yiddishists following the Holocaust and the establishment of Israel. "Here, on the soil of Jerusalem, I can say again that *galut* was bad, ugly and we must be redeemed from it, but the Jew in *galut* was beautiful. It is our pride to be the heirs of such beauty." He proclaimed that an Israeli Jew who denies his relationship with every Jew outside Israel and feels that *galut* Jewry is in any sense less worthy than he, has lost the essence of his Jewish image. It was not true that with Yiddish the Jew of the *galut* marched only to the gas chamber. "With Yiddish the Jew of the *galut* also ascended many a national height. . . . The Yiddish language has developed a great national literature which is incomparable in its vitality, in its encouragement of Jewish survival, and in its bemoaning of the destruction of our people in the Hitler era, in shattering expressions of lamentation."[4]

In his last dramatic poem, *In the Days of Job* (1953), and in his final volumes of verse, *A Leaf on an Apple Tree* (1955), and *Songs to the Eternal* (1959), Leivick reached new heights of literary attainment and artistic insight. They are justly regarded as the crowning achievements of his literary career. The paralytic stroke which he suffered in 1958 and which rendered him mute and immobile until his death in 1962, appeared once again to many of his readers to be an uncanny fulfillment of premonitions that had been expressed in his poems through the years.

In Leivick's earliest poems, a melancholy evocation of lyrical beauty blossomed in Yiddish amid the shroud white of the Siberian landscape. The rhythm of his first poems was that of the heavy dragging of clanging chains plowing through the Siberian wastelands, and of the whir of whips cutting stripes into flogged humanity.[5] Two symbols dominate these poems: white snow and chains. The connection between purity and pain, thus established in Leivick's earliest work, is reminiscent of the biblical and Talmudic doctrine of suffering as atonement.

> Somewhere far, somewhere far
> Lies the forbidden land.
> The hills there are silvery-blue,
> No one has yet trodden them.
> Somewhere deep, somewhere deep
> Kneaded into the earth
> Treasures await us,
> Buried treasures wait.
> Somewhere far, somewhere far
> A prisoner lies alone.
> O'er his head dies the light
> Of the setting sun.
> Someone wanders about
> Deep in the blanketing snow
> Unable to find the path
> To the forbidden land.
>
> *Ergets Vayt*

The appreciation of beauty and the awareness of mystery, which came to the fore in Leivick's later writings, are already evident in this poem. Here, too, are the sensitivity to suffering and disappointment, to hopelessness and pain, which are at once profoundly Jewish and deeply human and universal.

Although many readers and critics were at first repelled by Leivick's obsession with suffering which seemed to verge on the aberrational, they knew that it was very much in keeping with Jewish religious tradition. Jewish law prescribes the reading of the biblical story of the binding of Isaac both as part of daily worship and as the scriptural reading for the second day of Rosh Hashanah. Moreover, the tale of the martyrdom of the Ten Rabbis of the Hadrianic era is part of the Yom Kippur liturgy because martyrdom is both a religious value and a means of atonement. By poetically objectifying his flogged body and trampled soul, and by sublimating his guilt feelings into a symbol of human conscience, Leivick corroborated the Jewish concept of martyrdom. With its concomitant elements of conscience and asceticism, martyrdom in Judaism is more than a compensation for powerlessness. It is an affirmative and optimistic approach to life because it encourages both a reconciliation with reality and a hope in the development of a higher, more sensitive and more courageous type of human being.[6] *Kiddush hashem* or martyrdom took on a new meaning during the persecutions of modern times which culminated in the Holocaust. Such motifs, which dominated many of Leivick's poems of the 1920s, appeared prophetic when viewed from the perspective of the 1930s and 1940s.

Despite his conviction that what the victims of unspeakable terror experienced during their last moments could never be told, and that poets could only leave marks on unknown graves, Leivick produced a number of significant poems on the Holocaust.

> The heart of a seven year-old Jewish lad
> Lies gasping on a golden violin,
> And the heart of a seven year-old girl
> Dies on the violin case,
>   And hordes of people go past
>   And never even notice.

A Zibn-Yorik Yidele

When Leivick proclaimed in a poem that he personally preferred the martyrdom of the Ten Rabbis to the Maccabees, his voice reverberated with Jewish pride and authenticity. But his poems of the Holocaust, while identifying with the victims and expressing his guilt for not having shared the fate of the martyrs, also sounded notes of defiance and revenge.

Arise, Jews, don't succumb to despair!
Thus proclaimed the Jews of Warsaw
In their transcendent revolt.
They proclaimed,
They inscribed the words,
They hung the placard
In homes, in courtyards,
In houses of study—
To the Ten Commandments an Eleventh they added:
Arise, Jews, don't succumb to despair!
What does the word "arise" signify here?
The word "arise" here stands for *forever*.
Not once forever
But seven times seven forever.

They also had rifles,
These Jews of Warsaw,
And bullets, grenades,
These Jews of Warsaw.
They fired
And struck their target,
These Jews of Warsaw.
And blessed be
Every Jewish bullet
That pierced
The heart of a Nazi.
But doubly blessed be—
Forever blessed be—
The placard of six short words.
To the Ten Commandments an Eleventh they added:
Arise, Jews, don't succumb to despair!

The rifles had bullets
That soon were depleted.
Alas, depleted.
The Nazis, the Germans, had more.
Alas, had more.
They had bombs,

They had cannon,
They had airplanes.
The Germans silenced everything
Except the six short words—
To the Ten Commandments the Eleventh they added:
Arise, Jews, don't succumb to despair!

What does the word "arise" signify here?
The word "arise" here stands for *forever*.
Not once forever
But seven times seven forever.

Gvald, Yidn, Zayt Zikh Nit Meyaesh

After the Holocaust, the poet bade the prophet Isaiah to reappear and fulfill his vision of the end of days.

Dream your dream again, great prophet,
Appear again amid the crumbling walls,
Pay no heed that he who calls is weary—
He's crying for the lad who lies here burned.

A wolf will live together with a lamb,
The lad will lead them by the hand.
But now, O prophet, comfort the mother
Who cries and mourns her lad who lies here burned.

The mother climbs out of the bunker
With cradling arms turned to you.
O prophet, bring the end of days,
Restore to life the lad who lies here burned.

Un A Yingele Vet Zey Firn

Leivick's poetry shows the influences of medieval Jewish ethics, mysticism and asceticism. These concerns were very much alive in the Jewish community of the Russia of his youth. Echoes of the mystical parables of the Hasidic master, Rabbi Nahman of Bratzlav, of the ethical concerns of the Mussar or ethical movement of Rabbi Israel

Salanter, and of the historical and nationalist concerns of the Yiddish poet and revolutionary, Abraham Walt Lyessin (1872–1938), are very much in evidence in Leivick's work. There is also an affinity between Leivick's preoccupation with suffering and the pathos and moral seriousness of the great Russian writers of the nineteenth century. Leivick successfully linked the ambiance of the Russian writers with the Yiddish literary tradition. In his own person, "he succeeded in forging a rich Jewish artistic personality which, however influenced at first by the Slavic mood, nevertheless managed to relate that influence to the more profound dream world of his Jewish childhood."[7] In the United States, Leivick deepened his concern for the suffering and downtrodden but also learned to control his pathos and exploit the power of silence in his poetry. He sought, as he put it in a poem, to "tear seven hides from words and peel their skins until the kernels deep inside were revealed in their pristine splendor" (*Vort un Zakhn*).

In the 1920s, Leivick was associated with *Di Yunge*—the "young rebels" of American Yiddish literature who sought to divest Yiddish writing of ideological overweight and bring literary refinement and new aesthetic standards to the Yiddish word. Leivick was attracted to the *Yunge* because he felt that the seriousness with which they approached their work made Yiddish writing an almost religious experience. For Leivick, literature had to have profound spiritual significance since he viewed it as an extension of the traditional Jewish quest for the holy. He looked askance at the attempt of some of the young rebels to totally dissociate themselves from the concerns of society and form an isolated, aesthetic island in the sea of Jewish life. In one of his longer poems, "A Letter from America to a Distant Friend" (1927), he confessed that while the Yiddish poets had indeed dreamed of a holy life in America, "in order to live a holy life, apparently life needs more than singing words." Where many of the *Yunge* were satisfied with the pursuit of art for art's sake, Leivick was concerned with morality and with the meaning and destiny of life for both the individual and society.

The existential engagement of Leivick's work repelled many of the *Yunge* who were preoccupied with finding homespun Yiddish words and images to make their poems more supple. They would have none of what they regarded as Leivick's sanctimoniousness and self-righteousness. They also failed to appreciate his linguistic innovativeness. "In their attempt to find poetic terms and images for things in their familiar environment and in normal human experience, the *Yunge* failed to take note of Leivick's great achievement in finding terms for things which lacked words in Yiddish until then."[8]

Leivick's relationship with words was unique in the annals of world literature. He expected words to behave morally. "He strongly demanded of the word that it 'adjust' its private life to the role it plays publicly in the poem. This conception of the word as a living soul with consciousness and responsibility, of which moral demands could be made, is one of Leivick's infrequent concurrences with Yiddish folklore."[9] During his last trip to Israel, in 1957, Leivick wrote a poem in which he opened the cages in which he kept his words so that they might wander freely through the hills of Jerusalem.

> On your soil, O Jerusalem,
> I love to be silent.
> For my words I open
> All their cages.
>
> I let them out
> With complete freedom
> And thank and praise them
> For their exceptional loyalty.
>
> I liberate them and say:
> Over the mountains all about,
> Over the hills of Jerusalem,
> Fly freely, my precious ones.
> Choose the most sacred places—
> For they are all yours,
> And rest, yes rest on them.
> Leave me in seclusion
> With my dream
> Of having just one minute
> Of complete peace with myself.

On your soil, O Jerusalem,
Silence goldens by day
And turns blue at night.
Suddenly I say to myself:
Is this where Isaiah stood?
Is this the very place?

The faithful moment of the night
Responds: yes, yes.

In astonishment I call to my words:
Return from your places.
Return, return
My precious ones.
Help me give silent voice to the joy
Of standing on the soil on which Isaiah stood.

Af Dayn Erd, Yerusholayim

Leivick differed from the *Yunge* also because of the mystical bent of much of his writing. He always had a deep concern with what he termed the "other side of things." He was preoccupied with the meaning and destiny of reality and often transported himself poetically into the past or the future.

I see now that everything happening today
Is less than the dust of the road.
The poet's demon wails within me
And I fall to the other side of things.

Af Yener Zayt fun Zakhn

Leivick's lyrical poems are reminiscent of the so-called reflective poetry (*shirey higayon*) of the Hebrew literature of the Haskalah. They combine "emotional expression and personal impression with a reflective reaction which is sometimes exegetical and revelatory." The reflection, which sometimes appears tangential or insignificant, is in fact the point of the poem because Leivick was never an indifferent spectator of life, observing and satisfying himself merely with the formulation of the visible. To Leivick living meant experiencing affectively and cognitively, and experience always involved the quest for meaning. Leivick never sought to mask experience or delude himself by posing solutions to the difficult problems of human experience. Instead, he was "the great protester, the stubborn questioner tearing veils from the face of reality. . . . Since he did not pretend that he knew the answers or had ready-made solutions, he sometimes sought escape from reality in the abstract, the ideal, the desirable." [10]

Two of Leivick's younger colleagues in American Yiddish poetry, both founders of the *Inzikhist* or introspective school, were among those who sought to assess Leivick's unique contribution to Yiddish poetry. According to Jacob Glatstein, Leivick's significance lay in his mastery of "the short line as well as the startling aftercry which always wraps his line in an afterglow. . . . The simple statement and the accompanying echo that turns simplicity into celebration." [11] "In almost every one of Leivick's poems," according to Aaron Glanz-Leyeless, "there is a line or two which flashes through the mind . . . which startles the reader and makes him want to read the poem again and again. . . . Leivick writes about himself but in him I also see myself and he is actually also writing about me." [12]

Throughout his literary career, Leivick grappled with one of the great ideas of Jewish history and produced a trilogy of plays (*Chains of the Messiah, The Golem* and *The Comedy of Redemption*), the poetic drama *The Wedding in Fernwald*, and a number of shorter poems on the Messianic theme. Taken together, these works comprise a major poetic history of the Messianic idea, a record of the growth of the hope and the longing in the heart of the author and his contemporaries, and a framework in which the Messiah symbol might become relevant in our time.

In a foreward to the Hebrew translation of the redemption trilogy, Leivick wrote that "especially now, after years of catastrophe and destruction in our lives, events which were followed by the miracle of the birth of the State of Israel—only now does it seem to me that we stand anew before the first sensing of Messiah's existence, before the feeling that he is with us, but we still do not see his full countenance, his revealed likeness. We are in the minutes of the Beginning, and feel his existence in the tremor of the heart, as on the day in which there arose in us the legend of his birth."[13]

The dominant motif of Leivick's Messianic plays and poems is the sense of responsibility for all that suffers. In addition, he emphasizes that the redemption cannot be forced. Until the spirit necessary for deliverance emerges, until moral responsibility and conscience prevail on earth, redeemers will be "only a pretext, only a joke for the last fool on the street."[14] Like the Messiah of whom Isaiah spoke, who would act with justice to the hopeless and decide fairly for the humble (Isa. 11:4), Leivick's Messiah is motivated by a horrifying sense of responsibility for those that suffer and those who are wronged. Leivick's message is that people must be made aware that Messiah can be found in their own midst. Like the pioneers of Israel, "with white fingers he frees the dust and stone" (*Der Goyel in Negev*). "What is sorrow?" asked Leivick. "Sorrow is responsibility for everything, for everyone, for all times."[15] Only when all people share in the moral conscience and responsibility which is the essence of Messiah will their encounter with him really take place.

> Tanks come, airplanes come, but Messiah does not come on them.
> Messiah does not come nor will he come on an airplane,
> Messiah does not come nor will he come on a tank,
> Brothers, utter forth these words with joy
> And so that you may unite with those of our people,
> With those of us—weak, shunned, cheated,
> Who in their very last moment of loneliness
> Did not cease to comfort themselves and say:
> Though he tarry we will not stop waiting for him.
> Thus it follows, brothers,
> That Messiah will come in no way but that in which
> All our old visionaries dreamed of him,
> That Messiah will not show himself except as a pauper
> Who will come on a very small and simple donkey
> In the midst and in the deepness of our night.

The whole world is drunk in a sea of blood today
Only because it permitted itself one drop.
The heaviest death cloud hovers over the little house.
It is the little door that really mourns
And not the gate of fortresses and towers.
It is the little broken window that cries out to God
And not the big mouth of bells and trumpets.
For God Himself is not in fortresses
But in a little grain of sand dust that the wind lifts
And carries, leading it to a leaf on a tree
And putting it to sleep on thin, soft hairs.
So stay away from dark despair, brothers,
And guard the smallest bit of breath in the last no man's land,
And guard the wonder of the dust that the wind lifts,
And guard the fluttering of the weakest sprouting blade of grass
That waits so patiently to be touched by Messiah's foot,
That waits and senses with you, brothers,
That Messiah will appear only as a pauper
Who will come very quietly in the depth of our night.

Tanken Kumen, Nor Moshiakh Kumt Nit

In *The Wedding in Fernwald*, Messiah refuses to resume his task in the land of the living after the horrors of the Holocaust. But when he visits the displaced persons and witnesses the zeal with which they rebuild their lives, he comes to realize that he must accept his responsibility to remain with the Jews who have survived the destruction. Like the people of Israel, Messiah too must agree to live. "Just as long ago, after he had been in Egypt, the Jew accepted the Torah, so must he now, after Dachau, accept life. For as the Torah is holy, so the life of a Jew is holy—and perhaps even holier."[16]

Leivick's love for the Jewish people and his identification with the Jews of all ages found expression in hundreds of poems, plays, essays, addresses and articles. "To belong to the Jewish people is a great privilege and a great responsibility," states Leivick's Rabbi of Rothenberg. "And, sometimes, the greater the responsibility, the greater the privilege."[17] In *The Wedding in Fernwald*, Messiah goes to the crematoria together with the victims. When a sick and half-blind Jew falls to the ground, Messiah lifts him on his shoulders, carries him, and goes with him and the others to the oven in Dachau. When asked what he accomplishes, if of his own will he goes to the gas chamber, Messiah replies: "It is not I who accomplish. It is the love of Israel that accomplishes. Today I can do nothing but carry out the will to love the Jewish people which goes to the gas chamber."[18] In "The Ballad of the Desert," Leivick links the generation of the Exodus with the generation of the Holocaust. Leivick, his parents, his elementary school teacher, and Moses and Aaron are the heroes of this poetic fantasy which views Jewish history as an ever-recurring cycle in which God is forever rediscovered in the pain of the bush's flames which burn and burn but are never extinguished.

> Jews march through the desert
> In dream and reality
> For three thousand years.
> Jews leave Egypt
> And so do I—I march
> In line with the tribes.
> I'm not seven years old yet.
> My teacher Shimen-Leyb
> Raises his long hand
> And shows me that it's all recorded
> In Numbers or Deuteronomy.
> Now I have additional proof
> That no one else can have:
> Row on row of graves
> I dug myself
> With my little hand
> On the march to Canaan
> Through the desert.

Di Balade fun Midber

As a major spokesman of Yiddish culture in the twentieth century, Leivick reacted in poetry and prose to the bitter fate of the Yiddish language and its cultural representatives as a result of the European Holocaust, Soviet persecution, Israeli antipathy, and American-Jewish callousness.

> When I think about us, Yiddish poets,
> Such sadness envelopes me.
> I want to shout and plead with myself
> But just then my words turn mute.

Yidishe Poetn

> In disgrace my spirit mourns
> In a night of dreams:
> A friend angrily rips
> My poems to shreds
> And hurls the word "Jargon" at me.
> For him my poems are tainted.
> He predicts my death
> In New York, Tel Aviv and Haifa.
> I speak to him, recall
> Our fathers, ancestors.
> But he insists it's still "Jargon."
> "The angel of death owns you now.
> Go to your eternal rest.
> Yiddish is dead."
> He promises me the funeral
> Of a celebrated victim.
> How happy I am! I burst with joy!
> I am a rich poet indeed!
> In Moscow I hang from a rope,
> In New York and Tel Aviv on a friend's sense of justice.

In Farshemung

In his play *The Poet Has Gone Blind* (1934), about the Yiddish poet Morris Rosenfeld (1862–1923), Leivick dealt with the abandonment of Yiddish in America. The poem "Ecstatically, In Trance Supreme!" treats the same theme.

A fellow poet spoke to me and said:
Let us all compose the last poem.
We'll place it in a coffin and carry it
Through streets in which the American Jew resides.
With blue cloth we'll cover it
Or perhaps wrap it in simple white,
In the white of the pages of all our books
Which lie in cellars—food for mice,
And in the red of the pages of our purged poets
Who wither in dungeons or by the North Sea,
Or who may be dead to the glory of killers,
Spoil for every Cain who feigns innocence.
And anyone who has ever written a one-line poem
Will raise the bedecked coffin in his hand
And, parading through our broadest avenues,
March to the shore of the land.
At the head with pen in hand will march the youngest,
With a great to-do he'll smatter his pen to bits,
He'll throw it to the ground and we'll all follow
In this march from East Broadway to the Brooklyn Bridge.
From the Bridge to Brownsville and Flatbush and Brighton,
To Coney Island and Seagate and to the Atlantic Ocean,
And to the waves, to far, far off distances,
In the stormy whirlpool—we'll throw our last rhyme.
Then we'll all stand by the shore of the Atlantic
And watch the waves tower in foam
In anger or praise for poets who, by themselves,
Gave the fluttering of their dream away to the abyss.
And afterwards?—afterwards, faithful to the dream
We'll part and search out the broken point of a pen
And write a new song, a lamentation on the funeral,
And we'll write it ecstatically, in trance supreme!

Hislahavesdik, Mit Hekhstn Bren!

A constantly recurring word in Leivick's poetry through the years
has been the word *eybik*—eternal. It occurs in his reminiscences of
his childhood, in the title of one of his most famous poems, and again

in the title of his final volume of verse: *Lider Tsum Eybikn*—Songs to the Eternal (1959). The word links the poet to the Divine Presence and simultaneously conveys intimations of personal and collective immortality.

> Father leads me by the hand to the synagogue
> The day is bright and sunny.
> The day is—holy day.
>
> My hand—in father's right hand.
> My hand—a little hand
> In father's—a big, warm hand,
> Secure in the holiness of rest,
> Guarded and protected by God, praised be He.
> The day is—Passover.
> We cross the wide, empty market place.
> Father walks and I jump behind him.
> His narrow shoulders rise to the sky,
> His red beard smiles to the sun.
> Father walks and I dance behind him.
> My small shadow dances into his,
> My small shadow barely reaches his knees.
> Today father is as mild as the holy day.
>
> All the shops in town are closed,
> But the market place itself is wide open
> On all four sides.
> All the little houses stand erect and bright,
> Blessed with the gracious gift of rest,
> As secure in the hand of God, praised be He,
> As my hand in the hand of father.
>
> I was five years old then,
> And father's age was—eternity.
>
> *Yontev*

The world grabs me with hands that pierce.
It carries me to the pyre, to the auto-da-fé.
I burn and burn but am not consumed
I rise again and march away.
I sow my poems as one sows seeds,
They sprout and grow like stalks and weeds,
A plow am I and turn the soil,
I rise again and march away.

Eybik

The sense of immortality and the closeness to God is powerfully conveyed in "Stars."

I lift my eyes to a heaven of stars
And behold as the stars whisper secrets to stars,
And behold as a star draws so nigh to a star.

I'm small but still smaller are stars,
I barely can see them. I search in the stars for the star
Who may be my own guardian and guide among stars.
My father once said: Everyone has a star,
A guardian in heaven. You too have a star.

He also once said: Every Jew is a star
For God promised Abram—As stars
Will your folk be and countless, God's stars.

As a child and a grownup, in the course of the stars,
My paths and my circles were drawn by my star.
Before I was born—my dream among stars
And after I leave—my truth 'mid the stars.

As evening begins, with emergence of stars,
I'm illumined with peace by the light of my star.
At midnight, when sorrow envelops the stars,
I know that my fate is decreed in the stars.
And then, before dawn, with the parting of stars,
There rains upon me an explosion of stars

That hurls me aside until my own star
Covers me with itself and a Voice calls: Your star
Implores kindness for you from the Master of Stars.

I lie 'neath the cover and hear my own star
Conveying my name to the Master of Stars.

Shtern

Although Leivick's poetry is more concerned with human morality and destiny than with God, the sense of God's presence has an important place in his poems. Leivick often compared Yiddish poetry to traditional Jewish prayer. "It seems to me," he said, "that Yiddish poetry today is undoubtedly still an emanation of our entire millennial mentality and essentially a religious experience. . . . I often feel when I write a poem as if I were praying. I feel the poem itself as a prayer. . . . These are moments when your entire approach to yourself, to your quest to convey your own life and the most secret aspect of yourself, seeks to be revealed and heard. At such moments you sense a religious exaltation like that of a Jew in prayer."[19]

Leivick's work was essentially an affirmation of the sacredness of human life and the durability of the human spirit.

Life today is not sacred.
Indeed, it's trampled underfoot.
Whoever can steps on it
With feet, with rifle or spear.
And yet, oh heart, don't lose hope.
May the faith flourish in my poem
That those who are truly noble
Kneel before every human limb.

Di Balade fun Denver Sanatoriyum

For death is life and earth is fire,
Flesh is tempestuous and flows like light.
Everything in the world wants to be beloved and precious,
Everything in the world wants to be kissed like a face.

A Briv fun Amerike tsu a Vaytn Fraynd

Leivick's poetry appeals to the modern temper because it affirms meaning despite chaos and hope despite tragedy. In *In the Days of Job* he explored the cosmic dimension of human relationships and pondered the need for empathy with the sufferings of other species.[20] He always knew how to evoke sparks of compassion and humanity in his readers. Despite his preoccupation with pain and sorrow, his quest for the meaning of suffering was aglow with assurance and hope. He universalized his own odyssey and his people's history in order to renew the prophetic vision of brotherhood and redemption for all humanity. In the valley of death he reaffirmed the transcendent dimension of suffering and the sacredness of life by "weaving God's sorrow into himself and carrying the song of God's words everywhere" (*Shtil Vi Du*).

> The joke of the jester will not part us
> Nor the deceit of the false fool.
> Brothers in suffering, we will walk
> The path of comradeship through new sorrow.
>
> I shall not deny, my friend,
> That loneliness grows along with joy.
> On my heart I feel the blight
> Of disintegrated words.
>
> Is this to be my fate forever?
> No. Something better lies in store.
> I shall yet live as a child, be happy—
> That is why I'm on this earth.
>
> Don't stop, don't look behind you.
> The stonethrower's hand will tire . . .
> Behind us—a dying winter.
> Before us—a rising land.
>
> *Gleybik*

Leivick's distinctive path in Yiddish poetry wends its way from suffering to sublimation through identification with the destiny of one's people, humanity and the cosmos. In Leivick's poetic *oeuvre* there is a wonderful confluence of the spiritual and aesthetic quests which fascinates the reader with its uniqueness, persuasiveness and authenticity.

NOTES

1. Leivick's memoirs of his years in imprisonment and in Siberia are contained in his *Af Tsarisher Katorge*, Tel Aviv, 1959.
2. Quoted in J. Pat, *Shmuesn mit Yidishe Shrayber*, New York, 1954, p. 147.
3. Ibid., p. 147f.
4. H. Leivick, "The Individual Jew," translated by Emanuel S. Goldsmith, *Reconstructionist*, Vol. 23, No. 17 (December 27, 1957), pp. 7–12.
5. Cf. M. Gross-Zimerman, *Intimer Videranand*, Tel Aviv, 1964, p. 138.
6. Cf. S. Bickel, *Detaln un Sakhaklen*, New York, 1943, p. 93.
7. J. Glatstein, *Af Greyte Temes*, Tel Aviv, 1967, p. 85.
8. A. Tabachnik, *Dikhter un Dikhtung*, New York, 1965, p. 280.
9. S. Bickel, op. cit., p. 101.
10. K. A. Bertini, "Aharit-Davar," in H. Leivick, *Al Tehomot Holekh Veshar*, Tel Aviv, 1977, p. 88.
11. J. Glatstein, *In Tokh Genumen*, New York, 1947, p. 73.
12. A. Glanz-Leyeless, *Velt un Vort*, New York, 1958, p. 66.
13. H. Leivick, *Hezyoney Geulah*, Jerusalem, 1956, p. ix.
14. H. Leivick, *Ale Verk*, New York, 1940, vol. 2, p. 156.
15. Ibid., p. 261f.
16. H. Leivick, *Di Khasene in Fernvald*, New York, 1949, p. 147.
17. H. Leivick, *Maharam fun Rutenberg*, New York, 1945, p. 85.
18. *Di Khasene in Fernvald*, p. 89.
19. H. Leivick, *Eseyen un Redes*, New York, 1963, p. 47.
20. Cf. S. Niger, *Yidishe Shrayber in Tsvantsikstn Yorhundert*, New York, 1972, p. 195.

13. Amichai's Struggle with Faith

Rivka Maoz

In 1982 Yehuda Amichai was awarded the prestigious Israel Prize for his life-long contribution to Hebrew literature. The Board of Judges praised his writing particularly for "having expressed a generation which, after participating in all of Israel's wars, suddenly found itself confronted with the deep disillusionment of a society emptied of its values."

The poet himself summed up his experience and that of his generation in a speech he called "Generations in the Land" that he delivered at the 23rd Israeli Writers' Convention in April, 1968:

> The credo, the "I believe," of my generation is "I do not believe. . . ."
> The generations prior to 1948 had many "I believes." The generation of
> the fifties had only "I do not believe." It is a generation of doubts and
> contradictions, uncertainties and suspicions, in both words and deeds.
> Three times I have heard the cry "Get thee out of thy land!" The first
> time I left the warm, protected land of my childhood. The second time I
> left the secure region of faith in God and in the order of his world. The

221

third time, I had to abandon the belief in man, in his ability to make a
better world, and in progress and the security of human ventures. What
is left is nothing but the struggle with the "I do not believe" of our
times. When men believed in the moon and the stars and the trees and
then stopped believing in them, at least they were left with the moon
and the stars and the trees, for they still existed. But what is left to us?[1]

It is clear that although he declared his credo as "I do not believe,"
Amichai is far from being cynical and nihilistic. Rather he mourns the
loss of belief in man and God, longing for the Paradise from which he
and his generation have been expelled. No doubt, this ambivalent
attitude towards faith and values, an attitude shared by many Israelis,
is one of the main reasons why Amichai's poetry proved so popular.
Indeed, although Amichai's writing is largely autobiographical in the
sense that it serves as a mental and emotional diary which records the
poet's personal life and reactions, it also presents the essence of Israeli
experience.

   Amichai's biography, as revealed by him in numerous interviews
and in his poetry, tells of a happy childhood in pre-war Germany
where he was born to a very Orthodox but unscholarly family in 1924.
Both of his grandfathers were farmers in small rural communities in
Bavaria:

> Grandfather, Grandfather who converted heavy-eyed cows
> In his barn underneath the kitchen and rose at four in the morning.
>
> Grandfather, grandfather, chief rabbi of my life,
> Sell my pains the way you used to sell
> Hametz on Passover eve. . . .
>
>   *"A Luxury"*[2]

Amichai's father moved to the town of Würzburg where he became an
itinerant haberdashery peddler. The poet considers the fact that his
forebears were simple village Jews as an advantage. To his mind, both
the major part of German Orthodox Jewry that was centered in

Frankfurt, and those Eastern European Jews who studied in the *yeshivot*, were restricted by what he calls "the chains of scholarly Judaism."[3] His family observed every single *mitzvah*, seeing themselves as German Jews, while living among the Gentiles. Both Gentiles and Jews were conscious of the latter being different, but as Amichai sees it, they respected each other and the Jews led a double life—that of the Jewish community and that of the German community—without feeling divided. On the contrary, Amichai proclaims his family to have been "wholesome people."[4]

His father fought in the German army in the First World War, but sent his son to an Orthodox Jewish kindergarten in which the children learned to read the Hebrew prayers. Later on the young Yehuda attended a religious Jewish primary school and at his father's request was also tutored in *Gemara* and *Shulḥan 'Arukh*. Würzburg was a communal center for Jews in Southern Germany, with its own hospital, old-age home and Teachers' College. However, even before the rise of the Nazis, Yehuda had been conscious of anti-Semitism, which he views as a natural product of Catholic dogma.[5] Amichai's father, although a Zionist, had never been active in any Zionist party, but with the rise of Nazi anti-Semitism he decided to emigrate to Palestine. Amichai still recalls the cry: "Dirty Jew, go to Palestine," which to his mind was eventually transformed into the anti-Israel cry: "Dirty Jew, go from Palestine."[6]

> The family arrived in Haifa in 1936, during the Arab riots:
> You came via Haifa. The harbor was new, the child was new.
> You lay on your belly, not to kiss the Holy Land
> But because of the riots of 1936.
>
> *"The Travels of the Last Benjamin of Tudela"*[7]

After a year in Petach-Tikva, they moved to Jerusalem where Amichai attended the religious high school *Maaleh*. Although he completed his studies there, Amichai abandoned formal religious practice at the age of fifteen, as did other pupils of *Maaleh*, who became prominent writers and members of the academic world.

And my childhood, of blessed memory. I filled my quota
Of rebelliousness, I did my duty as a disobedient son,
I made my contribution to the war of the generations and to the wildness
Of adolescence.

"Travels of the Last Benjamin of Tudela"[8]

> On a Sabbath eve, at dusk on a summer day
> When I was a child,
> When the odors of food and prayer drifted up from all the houses
> And the wings of the Sabbath angels rustled in the air,
> I began to lie to my father
> "I went to another synagogue."
>
> I don't know if he believed me or not
> But the lie was very sweet in my mouth.

"A Song of Lies on Sabbath Eve"[9]

Apart from the obvious explanation of rebellion against religion as the act of an adolescent, Amichai also provides other reasons for his abandoning institutionalized religion. He perceives the various practical *mitzvot* as rituals which served to distinguish the Jews from the Gentiles among whom they lived in the Diaspora. Once in Eretz Israel, he feels this function is no longer needed and subsequently the *mitzvot* have lost their importance.[10] This approach to *mitzvot* is shared by many secular Zionists, who maintain that the Jewishness of the Israeli is sufficiently provided for by the fact that he lives in Israel.[11]

According to Amichai, observing the *mitzvot* in Eretz Yisrael, like for instance, wearing the *Tallit Katan*—the small fringed shawl worn under a male's clothes—seems out of place and causes much discomfort. It is associated by him with the typical knee-length shorts— "Zalman pants"—the much-mocked "trade mark" of new immigrants, and of German immigrants in particular.

You ate and were filled, you came
In your twelfth year, in the thirties
Of the world, with short pants that reached down to your knees,
Tassels dangling from your undershawl
Sticky between your legs in the sweltering land.

"Travels of the Last Benjamin of Tudela"[12]

The new socio-political context also renders observing the *mitzvot* out of place and obsolete: the Socialist-Zionist movement, that dominated the scene in Eretz Israel, was atheistic and negated the traditional Jewish way of life associated with the Diaspora. Although never a member of any party (for a short time he belonged to the Zionist religious youth movement *Bnei Akiva*, Amichai sympathized, at least temporarily, with the left-wing Zionists. He even wrote an obituary poem on the occasion of Stalin's death, which was published in *Al ha-Mishmar*, the organ of *haShomer haTzair*. Amichai views the writing of that poem as succumbing to the vogue current in a society that sought gods to worship.[13]

Apart from the above weighty reasons for ceasing to observe *mitzvot*, Amichai adds a more prosaic one: the sheer boredom of performing the technicalities of religious ritual, of repeating time and again the same prayer text, of bothering with the intricate laws of *kashrut*.

What did I learn from my father? To cry fully and laugh out loud
And to pray three times a day.
And what did I learn from my mother? To close my mouth and my collar,
My closet, my dream, my suitcase, to put everything
Back in its place and to pray
Three times a day.

Now I've recovered from that lesson. . . .

"You Can Rely on Him"[14]

Amichai felt that institutionalized religion is not only restrictive, but has also succeeded in diminishing the spiritual experience of God, turning him into a tedious pedantic bureaucrat who is forever engaged in the petty matters of laws such as the exact amount of hours a person should wait after eating dairy food before eating meat, and vice versa.[15]

> We begged you, Lord, to divide right from wrong
> And instead you divided the waters above the firmament
> From those beneath it. We begged
> For the knowledge of good and evil, and you gave us
> All kinds of rules like the rules of soccer.

"The Course of a Life"[16]

In his occasional descriptions of the performance of *mitzvot*, Amichai renders them odd, contrived, verging on the grotesque:

> And on Sabbath eve they sewed my handkerchief
> To the corner of my pants pocket so that I wouldn't sin by carrying it
> On the Sabbath. And on holy days *Kohanim* blessed me
> From inside the white caves of their prayer-shawls, with fingers
> Twisted like epileptics. I looked at them
> And God didn't thunder: and since then his thunder has grown
> More and more remote and become a huge
> Silence.

"Travels of the Last Benjamin of Tudela"[17]

Referring to the *mitzvah* of *Biur Hametz* (removing all leavened bread in preparation for the Passover festival) Amichai points out the uselessness and artificiality of this ritual:

> The last evening I told you
> The parable of my father, who
> On Pesach Eve meticulously cut
> Bread in precise squares and placed
> Them on the windowsill, so
> That he can find them with

His heavy eyes in the light
Of a candle dancing *mitzvah*-dances
So that his blessing will not be
In vain.

That is the way to live:
To be our own stage managers
Cheating stage managers
Believing fully, almost,
So that we will not be
In vain.

"My Father on Pesach Eve"[18]

In spite of all these rational explanations and Amichai's seemingly firm conviction of the rectitude of his deeds, nevertheless his poetry and fiction betray an acute feeling of guilt which assumes such gigantic proportions that the poet feels that he has murdered his father by rejecting his world. So, for example, the death of the father caused by his son's abandoning him, is closely associated with the son's abandonment of religious practice in the story "My Father's Deaths." After we are told by the first-person narrator that he no longer puts phylacteries on his arm and forehead, he tells how he failed to save his dying father:

Once I was walking along the ancient Appian Way in Rome. I was carrying my father on my shoulders. Suddenly his head sagged and I was afraid he was going to die. I laid him down at the side of the road and put a stone under his head, and went to call a taxi.[19]

However, the son never returns with the much-needed help. Instead, the story ends with a growing distance between the dying father and his son: "I turned around again and saw him, a very distant object, through the ancient arches of San Sebastian Gate."[20]

> Your life and your death father
> Weigh upon my shoulders.
> My little wife will
> Bring us water.
>
> Let's drink, father
> To my flowers, to the ideology
> That you hoped for me
> And don't hope anymore.
>
> *"Your Life and Death, Father."*[21]

His father's death is a knife of guilt raised above the son's head:

> My father blessed me and his hands trembled
> (The attitude of adults to children is one of trembling).
>
> In his eyes—
> All my future sins were reflected.
> We were playing the binding of Abraham and Isaac.
>
> His early death has been the knife
> Raised above me. Always hovering.
>
> *"Yom Kippur. Evening. My Father."*[22]

There is no human judge who can try the erring son for his betrayal of his father's commandments:

> Father, now I love to wash and brush my hair,
> But apart from that I have not changed.
>
> ———
>
> ———
>
> There is no police I can go to
> To confess that I am a murderer.
>
> When I come home, I will lie on my back,
> My arms spread as if crucified.
>
> *"My Father's Memorial Day"*[23]

When as an adolescent he trespassed the commandments of religion, Amichai felt he had to account to his father for his misbehavior:

> Angels looked like Torah scrolls in velvet dresses and petticoats
> Of white silk, with crowns and silver bells, angels
> Fluttered around me and sniffed at my heart and cried ah!
> Ah!
> To one another with adult smiles: "I'll tell your father."
>
> *"Travels of the Last Benjamin of Tudela"*[24]

Even when mature, the poet still feels guilty for having failed his parents:

> The old parents visit their aging son.
> Had he fallen in one of the wars
> He would have spared them and himself
> Much shame and sorrow.
>
> *"The Old Parents"*[25]

The feeling of shame and guilt is accompanied by a deep conviction that he is imperfect, fragmented, as compared with his father's spiritual wholeness:

> In the sands of prayer my father saw angels' traces.
> He bequeathed me a route but I answered him with many ways.
> That's why his face was bright and mine scorched.
> Like an old office calendar, I'm covered with dates.
>
> *"In a Right Angle; A Cycle of Quatrains, 1"*[26]

Measured against the world of his father, which is imbued with a totality of faith, firm belief in God and religious tradition, the secular world of the poet emerges as confused and full of uncertainties—as poignantly described in his story "My Father's Death":

God who is very high up, filled my father to the brim.

I was filled with other things and not always from high towers. Sometimes the pressure was weak and I was only filled with dreams and ideas . . . No one knows where Moses was buried, but we know all about his life. Nowadays everything is the other way around. We know only where the burial places are. Where we live is unfixed and unknown. We roam about, we change, we shift. Only our burial place is known.[27]

Although Amichai's poems and stories deal with the very personal experience of father-son relationship, they nevertheless involve much broader issues, as Robert Friend notes: "Yet there was another 'father' to whom he (Amichai) was proving unfaithful: the Jewish people, which had kept itself alive through the centuries by its faith."[28]

At the time of consummately passionate love-making the voice of his forefathers interferes to rebuke him:

> Who are you?
> A small Jewish boy from the Diaspora
> Scullcap on head. From there. From that time.
>
> At night we're together without
> Heavy memories, without sticky feelings. Only
> Tensing the muscles and then letting go.
>
> Far from here, on another continent of time,
> The dead rabbis of my childhood are clearly seen,
> Holding the gravestones
> High above their heads.
> Their soul is bound
> In my life's knot
>
> My God, my God
> Why have you not forsaken me!?
>
> *"Shirei Akhziv"*[29]

No fewer than six leading literary critics quote the previous passage from "My Father's Deaths" as telling testimony of the contemporary rootless and faithless young Israelis. The critics view Amichai's writing as a confession of a generation that is aware of its malady and envies the secure spiritual and moral world of traditional Judaism.[30]

Amichai's initial loss of faith acquired a further major reinforcement with the poet's traumatic experience as a young soldier in the War of Independence. In many ways this war was the most important event shaping the consciousness of the Israelis; it was far more important than the Holocaust that occurred so far away and had such vast numbers of victims—six million—that at first it seemed unreal and was incomprehensible. Amichai's poetry was triggered by the War of Independence. Indeed, the judges who awarded him the Shlonsky Prize in 1957 for his first book of poems: *Now and In Other Days* (1955), rightly observed that although Amichai was speaking in an individual voice, because of the themes and feelings described, he was actually expressing an experience shared by an entire generation: "The period portrayed in this book is signified by a personal, poetic biography which uses the war experience as the main thrust, as a point of departure and as constant refrain . . . It is a personal blending which reveals the face of a generation destined to confront both greatness and terror."

In the beginning of 1948 Amichai joined the 7th Regiment of the *Palmach* which participated in bitter fighting against the Egyptian army in the Negev. Twenty years later he recalled:

During the War of Independence there were many months of heavy fighting of battles for every inch of land. Thus experiences matured slowly and in later years were expressed in a wide range of literature. The Six-Day War was like a very sharp knife while the War of Independence was a dull, blunt blade which hacked and left scars—deep and ugly—on the landscape and on the man . . . Twenty years ago the 7th Regiment of the *Palmach* marched to the Negev. Most of the soldiers were so young that Colonel Marcus thought they were scouts out on a jaunt. Near Be'er Tuvia, the men of the *Givati* Brigade passed us, returning from an unsuccessful attack on the Iraq-Sudan fortress. In the gray light of dawn I saw their young faces; the tatters and the staring eyes. A few days later we also returned from an unsuccessful attack on the same fortress during the same hours, after a day of horror.[31]

In an interview thirty years later Amichai again returns to the shocking experience of that fighting in the Negev:

> The most terrible battle was in Ashdod. Militarily, this was evaluated as the decisive battle on the Southern Front, and possibly of the whole war. This was a battle that saved Tel Aviv from being taken by the Egyptians. Personally, however, I underwent a traumatic experience there. For miles in the sands I carried a wounded friend on my back and only when I arrived did I discover that he was dead.[32]

About the time he gave the above interview he also wrote the moving poem "Since Then" in which he declares that he died in the pale, terrible sands of Ashdod in 1948—together with the friend whom he carried on his back, a sad burden imposed on him by heaven:

> I carried my comrade on my back.
> Since then I always feel his dead body
> Like weighted heaven upon me,
> Since then he feels my arched back under him,
> Like an arched segment of the earth's crust.
> For I fell in the terrible sands of Ashdod,
> Not only he.[33]

Characteristically, the title of Amichai's first book of poetry derives from a poem that declares God pitiless—using the battle in the Negev sands as ample demonstration of man's cruel fate:

> God has pity on kindergarten children.
> He has less pity on school children
> And on grownups he has no pity at all,
> He leaves them alone,
> And sometimes they must crawl on all fours
> In the burning sand
> To reach the first-aid station
> Covered with blood.
>
> *"God has Pity on Kindergarten Children"*[34]

Human death in war as the most indisputable proof of God's lack of mercy is stressed again in Amichai's book, *In the Distance of Two Hopes* (1958), especially in the well-known poem: "O, Lord Full of Mercy," the first stanza of which reads:

> O, Lord full of mercy!
> If the Lord were not so full of mercy
> There would be mercy in the world
> And not only in him.
> I who picked flowers on the mountains
> And looked into all the valleys,
> I who brought corpses from the hills,
> I can say that the world is devoid of mercy.[35]

The tender age of the dead soldiers is stressed again and again in Amichai's poems, a fact which makes God's behavior seem even more cruel:

> A young soldier lies in the springtime, cut off from his name,
> His body is budding and flowering. From artery and vein
> His blood babbles on, uncomprehending and small.
> God boils the flesh of the lamb in his mother's pain.

> *"In a Right Angel: A Cycle of Quatrains"*[36]

The poet's sarcasm grows even more bitter:

> The Lord is a man of war,
> His Name is the Lord of Hosts,
> The soldier is a man of youth,
> His name is engraved on a disc.

> He who created man
> And filled him full of holes[37]

> Will do the same to soldiers
> Afterwards, in war.

> *"A Memory in Abu Tor"*[38]

The shocking experience of the battle near Yad Mordechai in the Negev, in the War of Independence, where Amichai lost his best friend and commander, Dikky, forms the central part of his long moving poem "Lamentations for the War Dead" published on the anniversary of the establishment of the State. In that poem God is described as a cruel deity "the glutton of hearts." He is old and powerless, and much like Bialik's God in "The City of Slaughter" written after the Kishinev pogrom of 1904. But unlike God in Bialik's poem, Amichai's God enjoys the suffering of the world;

> O sweet world, soaked like bread
> In sweet milk for the terrible
> Toothless God.[39]

This poem also laments soldiers who died in other wars, particularly a young soldier, who only yesterday was a toddler fed by his father:

> As a child he would mash his potatoes
> To a gold mush.
> Afterwards they die.

A special poem in the same book is dedicated to the dead of the Yom Kippur War, again stressing their young age:

> A soldier is filling bags with the soft sand
> He used to play in.

The poem concludes with the wild, irrational, pathetic, hopeless hope:

> And because of the war
> I repeat, for the sake of a last, simple sweetness:
> The sun goes around the earth, yes,
> The earth is flat as a lost drifting board, yes,
> There is God in heaven. Yes.

"Shirei Eretz Zion, Yerushalayim"[40]

Again, in his subsequent book, *Time* (1977), Amichai describes the disastrous effects of a bomb, concluding with a prophetlike protest:

> And I won't even mention the crying of orphans
> That reaches up to the throne of God and
> Beyond, making
> A circle with no end and no God.

"20"[41]

God is not only guilty of letting people die in war-time. Reading the biblical phrase "Lord of Hosts" literally, Amichai describes God as a military general who is forever waging war against the Jewish people:

> What's Jewish time? God's experimental places
> Where he tests new ideas and new weaponry
> A training-ground for his angels and demons.
> A red flag warns: Firing range!
>
> What's the Jewish people? The quota that can be killed in training,
> That's the Jewish people,
> Which has not yet grown up, like a child that still uses the
> Baby talk of its first years,
> And still can't say
> God's real name but says Elokim, Hashem, Adonai,
> Dada, Gaga, Yaya, for ever and ever, sweet distortions.

"For Ever and Ever Sweet Distortions"[42]

Amichai's word play on the phrase "Lord of Hosts" is just one example of his extensive usage of religious sources such as the Bible, the liturgy and the Midrash. So, for instance, the title and the refrain of his famous poem "And This Is Your Praise" (*Ve-Hi Tehillatekha*) derives from a prayer in the Yom Kippur *mussaf* service. The original prayer tells that the angels and all the marvels of the universe fear and praise God, but He desires also the praise of simple, ordinary, weak and even wicked people. In his poem "And This Is Your Praise," Amichai

provides the desired prayer; his poem reads as a modern prayer of a
tired, disenchanted, weak, suffering man, who strives for divine grace.
Ironically, however, unlike in the Yom Kippur prayers, Amichai's God
is incapable of fulfilling human expectations for a better world, no
matter how hard he tries. God is either indifferent, cruel, or an
impotent well-wisher, but nevertheless Amichai has not yet given up:

> With my great silence and my small cry
> I plough mingled seed.
> I've been through water and fire
> I've been in Jerusalem and in Rome. Maybe I'll get to Mecca.
> But this time God is hiding
> And man shouts: "Where art thou?"
> And this is your praise.
>
> God lies on his back under the universe,
> Always fixing, something always goes wrong.
> I wanted to see him whole, but I see
> Only the soles of his shoes, and I weep.
> And this is his praise.[43]

The search for God persists in spite of doubt and ironical awareness;

> A man told me that he's going to Sinai
> Because he wants to be alone with his God.
> I warned him.
>
> *"Relativity"*[44]

Talking about what he calls "condition humaine" in Natan Alter-
man's personal poetry, the literary critic Barukh Kurzweil detects
what he sees as a general tendency shared by modern Hebrew writers
and by modern man in general. They seek in Eros a substitute for the
religion they have lost. However, according to Kurzweil's diagnosis,
this attempt invariably fails, as Eros proves to be an inadequate,
temporary solution.[45]

Amichai, who more than any other modern Hebrew writer has

singled out love as the only possible way for coping with the terrors
and uncertainties of human existence, is the first to acknowledge that
the Eros solution is only temporary:

> You helped me to live for a couple of months
> Without needing religion
> Or a point of view.

"Gifts of Love"[46]

Caught in a state of anguish and disillusionment, Amichai, the modern Israeli Jew, longs for hope and consolation, for a solid source of
certainties and belief, for *The Hour of Grace*, wishing that the original
call: "Dust thou art and unto dust shalt thou return" would become:
From Man Thou Art and *Unto Man Shalt Thou Return* (the titles of
his last two books). His long quarrel with God—in the best biblical
tradition of Job and the prophets—acquires a new dimension: that of
the praying man in the Psalms who seeks God's support. In his last
book Amichai includes a prayerlike poem, the title and refrain of
which are: "God, I Am in Great Trouble."[47]

NOTES

1. "Dorot ba'Aretz," *La-Merhav*, May 3, 1968.
2. *'Akhshav baRa'ash*, Tel Aviv, Schocken Books, 1968, p. 41.
3. An interview by Dan Omer: "In This Scorching Land Words Should
   Provide Shade," *Proza*, Tel Aviv, 1978, No. 25. p. 4.
4. Ibid.
5. An interview by Sarit Shay, "Likhtov Shir Ze Kmo La'alot Gerah," *Ha-
   'Olam haZe*, March 28, 1983, p. 12.
6. In a radio interview after the Yom Kippur War.
7. *'Akhshav baRa'ash*, p. 101.
8. Ibid., pp. 118f.
9. *Shalvah Gedolah, Sheelot uTeshuvot*, Tel Aviv, Schocken Books, 1980,
   p. 69.
10. A private interview by the author of this paper, October 1989.

11. See for instance, A. B. Yehoshua, *Between Right and Right*, Garden City, Doubleday, 1981.
12. *'Akhshav baRa'ash*, p. 95.
13. "In This Scorching Land," pp. 6f.
14. *Shalvah Gedolah*, p. 19.
15. Numerous talks of the poet with students at the Rothberg School for Overseas Students during the last twenty years.
16. *MeAdam Ata veEl Adam Tashuv*, Tel Aviv, Schocken Books, 1985, p. 68.
17. *'Akhshav baRa'ash*, p. 100.
18. Ibid., pp. 45f.
19. *BaRuah haNoraah haZot*, Tel Aviv, Schocken Books, 1961, p. 141.
20. Ibid.
21. *Shirim 1948–1962*, Tel Aviv, Schocken Books, 1963, p. 28.
22. *'Akhshav baRa'ash*, pp. 39f.
23. Ibid., p. 70.
24. Ibid., p. 101.
25. *Sh'at haHesed*, Tel Aviv, Schocken Books, 1982.
26. *Shirim*, p. 120.
27. *BaRuah haNoraah haZot*, p. 140.
28. S. Burnshaw, T. Carmi, E. Spicehandler, eds. *The Modern Hebrew Poem Itself*, New York, Schocken Books, 1965, p. 167.
29. *'Akhshav baRa'ash*, pp. 199f.
30. Avraham Blat, "Sippure haToda'ah haPenimit," *HaZofeh*, March 31, 1961; Adir Cohen, *"BaRuah haNoraah haZot,"* *HaBoker*, November 24, 1961; Dor Moshe, "Proza sheHi Piyut: Sippurav shel Yehuda Amichai—'BaRuah haNoraah haZot' ", *Maariv*, November 24, 1961; Baruch Kurzweil, "Sippure Yehuda Amichai," *Davar*, April 21, 1961; Eli Schweid, "Osher shel Dalut: al 'BaRuah haNoraah haZot' le—Y. Amichai," *LaMerhav*, March 10, 1961; Gershon Shaked, " 'BaRuah *haNoraah haZot*' shel Yehuda Amichai," *Ha-Arez*, April 6, 1961.
31. "Dorot baArez."
32. "In This Scorching Land," p. 6.
33. *Shalvah Gedolah*, pp. 9ff.
34. *Shirim*, p. 15.
35. Ibid., p. 69.
36. Ibid., pp. 129f.

37. The Hebrew refers to a prayer said after defecating, thanking God for having created a man with orifices.

38. *Shalvah Gedolah*, p. 80.

39. *Meahore Kol Ze Mistater Osher Gadol*, Tel Aviv, Schocken Books, 1974, p. 91.

40. Ibid., p. 8.

41. *Time*, 20.

42. *Shalvah Gedolah*, p. 57.

43. *Shirim*, p. 71.

44. *Shalvah Gedolah*, p. 88.

45. *Bein Hazon leVein haAbsurdi*, Tel Aviv, Schocken Books, 1973, pp. 213ff.

46. *VeLo 'Al Menat Lizkor*, Tel Aviv, Schocken Books, 1975, p. 128.

47. *MeAdam Ata veEl Adam Tashuv*, Tel Aviv, Schocken Books, pp. 26f.

Biographical Notes

Aḥad Ha-am (1856–1927), pen-name of Asher Ginsberg. Leading Hebrew essayist, editor, and thinker; architect of cultural Zionism. In English: *Nationalism and the Jewish Ethic*; *Selected Essays*; *Essays, Letters, Memoirs*.

Yehuda Amichai (born 1924). Hebrew poet, novelist and playwright. In English: *Selected Poems, Poems of Jerusalem, Love Poems, Amen*, etc.

Leo Baeck (1873–1956). German rabbi and theologian; deported to Theresienstadt concentration camp in 1943, he settled in London following the war. His works include *The Essence of Judaism, Judaism and Christianity, This People Israel.*

Martin Buber (1878–1965). Religious thinker, biblical scholar and Zionist leader. Renowned for his "philosophy of dialogue" and writings on Hasidism. His numerous works include *I and Thou, Hasidism and Modern Man, On Judaism, On the Bible.*

Abraham Joshua Heschel (1907–1972). Theologian, Professor of Jewish Ethics and Mysticism at the Jewish Theological Seminary in New York. Author of *Man is Not Alone, Man's Quest for God, God in Search of Man, A Passion for Truth*, etc.

Mordecai M. Kaplan (1881–1983). Rabbi, theologian, founder of Reconstructionist Judaism. Dean of the Teachers' Institute and Professor of Homiletics in the Rabbinical School of the Jewish

Theological Seminary. Author of *Judaism as a Civilization, The Future of the American Jew, Judaism Without Supernaturalism, The Religion of Ethical Nationhood,* etc.

Abraham Isaac Kook (1865–1935). Zionist leader, theologian and mystic. Chief Rabbi of Palestine from 1921. In English: *Orot, The Lights of Penitence, The Essential Writings of Abraham Isaac Kook.*

H. Leivick (1888–1962), pen-name of Leivick Halper. Yiddish poet, playwright, essayist. Major figure of twentieth-century Yiddish culture; renowned for his messianic dramas, *The Golem* and *The Comedy of Redemption.*

Primo Levi (1919–1987). Italian writer and chemist. Captured by the Nazis in 1943 and eventually sent to Auschwitz. After being liberated, he wrote many books and essays on the Holocaust. In English: *Survival in Auschwitz, The Periodic Table, The Drowned and the Saved, If not Now, When?,* etc.

Asher Zelig Margaliot (1900–1969). Rabbi and mystic. Leader of the ultra-orthodox anti-Zionist group in Jerusalem. Author of thirty books on Jewish ethics, ritual and mysticism.

Franz Rosenzweig (1886–1929). German Jewish existentialist philosopher, Bible translator and educator. In English: *The Star of Redemption, On Jewish Learning, Understanding the Sick and the Healthy.*

Joseph B. Soloveitchik (1903–1993). Rabbi, philosopher and authority on Jewish law. Professor of Talmud at the Rabbi Isaac Elchanan Theological Seminary of Yeshiva University in New York. Foremost exponent of Orthodox Judaism in America. His works include *The Lonely Man of Faith, Halakhic Man, The Halakhic Mind, On Repentance.*